THE MARSHALL CAVENDISH ILLUSTRATED

Encyclopedia of Gardening

EDITOR: Peter Hunt

AMERICAN EDITOR: Edwin F. Steffek

ART CONSULTANT: Al Rockall

ART EDITOR: Brian Liddle

VOLUME 9

MARSHALL CAVENDISH CORPORATION / NEW YORK

CONTENTS

THE MARSHALL CAVENDISH ILLUSTRATED

Encyclopedia of Gardening

PHOTOGRAPHS IN THIS VOLUME BY: Bernard Alfieri; H. R. Allen; D. C. Arminson; P. Becker; Kenneth Beckett; Carlo Bevilacqua; Tony Birks; D. V. Blogg; J. Blossom (NHPA); Pamela Booth; British Travel Association; J. K. Burras; Norman Chaffer; P. R. Chapman; Michael Chiswick; Kenneth Collier; R. J. Corbin; C. J. Dawkins; A. de Rahm; Douglas Dickens; Gordon Douglas; J. E. Downward; Valerie Finnis; C. and R. Foord (NHPA); The Garden Machine Centre, Sunningdale (photo John Hovell); Paul Genereux; Ambrose Greenway; A. P. Hamilton; Iris Hardwick; A. G. L. Hellyer; Ingrid Holford; Peter Hunt; A. J. Huxley; G. E. Hyde; Jacobsen MFG. Co., Wisconsin; Leslie Johns; Reginald Kaye; D. J. Kesby; John Markham; Maxicrop Ltd.; Elsa M. Megson; Robert G. Milne; H. Alan Morrison; Frank Naylor; Maurice Nimmo; Keith Paisley; Ronald Parrett; Reg Perry; Picturepoint; Ray Procter; Reprinted by permission of the Committee of Management of the Chelsea Physic Garden (photo Mansell); G. A. Robinson; Gerald Rodway; E. R. Rotherham; J. T. Salmon; Kay N. Sanecki; E. S. Satchell; Scotts, Marysville, Ohio; Donald Smith; Harry Smith; Tourist Photo Library; Anthony Turner; C. Williams; Dennis Woodland.

ARTWORK: George Kingbourn; Joy Simpson; Cynthia Newsome-Taylor; Eric Jewell Assocs.

Lindelofia (lin-de-lof-e-a)

Commemorating Friedrich von Lindelof, a German patron of botany *(Boraginaceae)*. A small genus of hardy perennials of the borage family, mostly from central Asia, of which one species only is commonly grown. This is *L. longifolia*, (syn. *L. spectabilis*) which grows to 1½ feet, and has purple flowers in July. It is commonly known as the Himalayan lungwort.

Cultivation The plant will grow well in ordinary soil, provided it is well-drained, and it does best in a sunny position. It can be planted in the autumn or spring. Occasional feeding during its flowering period is appreciated, and a mulch with organic matter in spring will be beneficial also. The dead flowering stems should be removed in September. The plant can be propagated by dividing the roots in spring or by seed sown in sandy soil out of doors during the spring, transplanting the seedlings in late summer to the positions where they are to flower the following year.

Linden—see Tilia

Lindera (lin-der-a)

Commemorating Johann Linder, a Swedish botanist, 1678–1723 *(Lauraceae)*. A genus of trees and bushes, slightly tender and hardy, both deciduous and evergreen, from eastern Asia and North America. They can be extremely aromatic, and at one time the genus was called *Benzoin*. They were first brought to England in the seventeenth century.

Species cultivated *L. benzoin* (D), spice bush, 15–20 feet, deciduous, yellow flowers, spring, red berries and yellow leaves in the autumn, North America. *L. megaphylla* (E), 15–20 feet, yellow flowers, spring, China. *L. praecox* (D), 8 feet, yellow, March, yellow fruit, Japan.

Cultivation To obtain the best results linderas should be grown in moist, lime-free soil. An open and sunny position is the most suitable. *L. praecox* is rather tender and should preferably be given the shelter of a warm spot. Plant during the autumn or in spring, and prune immediately after flowering. To propagate, use cuttings of shoots 6–8 inches long, put in sandy soil in a shaded and sheltered position out of doors in October or November, or layer in spring.

Lindmania

The name commemorates Carl Axel Magnus Lindmann (1856–1928), a Swedish botanist who collected in South America *(Bromeliaceae)*. This is one of the less common genera of the tropical South American bromeliads. A number of new species have been relatively recently described from Venezuela. They have the usual rosette form, and, as with other bromeliads, the flowering scape forms the terminal growth of the rosette. After flowering, new plants develop from

Accurate marking cannot be achieved unless the line is used correctly. One end is made firm and the line stretched.

buds on the stem beneath the old rosette of leaves. The only species likely to be found in cultivation is the Peruvian *L. penduliflora*, 4–6 inches, a small plant, the largest leaves are about 12 inches long. It bears a slender, 12-inch flowering scape; the small flowers, white with green sepals form a lax panicle.

Cultivation The plants require a warm moist greenhouse with a minimum temperature of 60°F (16°C) in winter. As with most bromeliads, water is stored in the central 'vase' formed by the leaves and the plants are capable of withstanding dryish conditions at the roots. Care must be taken in winter since the plants can be easily overwatered. The medium must be freely draining i.e. 1 part of moss, 2 parts of peat, 1 part of sand. Propagation is usually by seed, or by division of the offsets. The seed is sown when ripe, on to the top of a peaty or mossy compost. When the seedlings are large enough they are pricked out into a pan and grown on until they are ready for potting individually.

Linear

A term usually used to describe leaves which are long and narrow, the sides parallel or nearly parallel, as in the blades of grasses.

Lines

There are several different types of garden line available including the home-made ones which consist of a length of string or thin, covered electrical cable, fastened to two pieces of wood. As the line is an essential piece of garden equipment, a good one should be purchased. The type which consists of a metal reel on which the line can be wound or unwound, is ideal. The other end of the line is attached to a strong metal pin. There are other designs which can be wound up on a drum like a measuring tape.

In the new garden or where a garden is being reclaimed, the garden line is

The small bell-shaped pink flowers of Linnaea borealis, a North American plant which commemorates Carl Linnaeus.

essential during the marking out and measuring of beds, paths, greenhouse or shed sites. In fact, where the garden is a large one, it may well be necessary to employ more than one line, especially where big areas are to be marked out, such as the lawn.

Neatness in the garden is important not only because it makes the layout more attractive, but it also facilitates routine cultivation. Straight rows also provide adequate planting distances for plants, which in turn should encourage better growth. The garden line has an important role in routine work such as planting out. It is especially important to use a line when the various vegetables are sown or planted.

Accurate marking cannot be achieved unless the line is used correctly. It must always be pulled as taut as possible so that, during planting, nicking out of the soil or the drawing out of a drill, the line cannot be slackened or disturbed. When the line is placed in position close by the marker pegs, due allowance must be made so that, plants for example, can be planted in line with the edge of the markers.

Ling—see Calluna vulgaris and Trapa bicornuta

Linnaea (lin-ne-a)
Commemorating Carolus Linnaeus,

1707–78, the Swedish botanist, since *L. borealis* was one of his favourite plants *(Caprifoliaceae)*. A small genus (according to some authorities, one species only), of hardy evergreen trailing plants suitable for growing in a shady, moist place on the rock garden. *Linnaea borealis* is found to be fully circumpolar; also one of the rarest native plants. The tiny, bell-like, pale-pink, fragrant flowers occur in pairs, hence the common name, twin-flower; they appear between May and September. *L. borealis*, var. *americana*, from North America, is somewhat more vigorous than the European type and is a better plant.

Cultivation The soil should be a medium made up of acid upland peat (no lime) and should not be allowed to dry out, especially in the growing season, from March to October. In addition to outdoor cultivation, these plants may also be grown in hanging baskets in a cold greenhouse. Propagation is by division, by layering the trailing shoots, or by cuttings, which may take a long time to root.

Linnaeus, Carolus
Linnaeus (Carl von Linné) was one of

the greatest naturalists in history and a botanist of considerable importance to gardeners. He was born in 1707, the son of a penurious pastor in the south of Sweden. He was intended for the church, but at school was considered so dull that he was nearly apprenticed as a tailor or a shoemaker. The family doctor, however, realised that the boy was a remarkable naturalist, and helped him to get to the University of Lund. He moved the following year to the University of Uppsala, where he distinguished himself. Natural history in any form was not then considered of scholastic consequence and Linnaeus had a hard life, particularly as he was not easy to get on with and had a much wider knowledge than his supposed superiors. (He had to leave Hamburg University, so great was the feeling against him after he had demonstrated that the seven-headed hydra was no more than a legend). He travelled widely and amassed a vast knowledge based on observation and fact rather than on book-learning. At last he was appointed to a professorship at Uppsala University, and his merits were internationally appreciated. In 1737 he published *Genera Plantarum*, the starting point of modern systematic botany, followed by his *Species Plantarum* in 1753.

Very briefly, what he did was to go through his massive collection of descriptions and group them together, according to similarities. The final major division was a genus (plural, genera) which was in turn divided into species. Thus a plant had two names, the generic and its specific epithet. For example, the wych elm now belongs to the genus *Ulmus* (the Latin name for an elm) and is the species *glabra,* meaning smooth (a reference to its comparatively smooth bark). Early botanists had called it *Ulmus folio latissimo scabro!* Unfortunately, modern botanists and horticulturists have, at least from the point of view of the practical gardener, brought about systems which are illogical and confusing. Linnaeus died in 1778.

Linospadix (lie-no-spay-dix)
From the Greek *linos,* linear and *spadix,* referring to the slender spadix *(Palmae).* A small genus of palms from New Guinea and Australia, occasionally seen in botanic gardens in this country. They are the smallest of the Old World palms. The genus was at one time more commonly known under its synonym *Bacularia.*

Species cultivated *L. minor,* several trunks, 2–5 feet in height, $\frac{1}{2}$ inch in diameter, leaves $3\frac{1}{2}$ feet long, leaflets 6–10 inches long, toothed at apex, fruit bright red, New South Wales and coastal Queensland. *L. monostachya,* walking stick palm, several trunks 6 to 12 feet in height and 1 inch in diameter, leaves pinnate, 2–4 feet long, leaflets up to 12 inches long, flower stems longer than

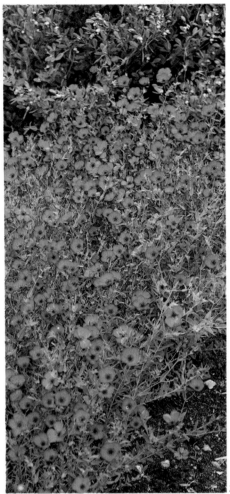

the leaves, flowers cream, fruits ½ inch long, red, New South Wales and coastal Queensland.

Cultivation These palms require shady conditions as, in nature, they grow under the forest canopy. They make attractive clumps in the warmhouse, either grown in beds of well-drained soil, or in pots, in a mixture of 2 parts of loam, 1 part of peat, and 1 part of sand. Daily syringeing with water is beneficial during warm weather. The older trunks can be removed as younger ones grow to replace them. Propagate by seed or dividing clumps. South Florida outdoors.

Linum (li-num)

From the old Greek name, *linon*, used by Theophrastus *(Linaceae)*. Flax. This important genus contains, besides the economically valuable annual which supplies flax and linseed oil, a number of very decorative garden plants. The flower colour which seems characteristic of the genus is a fine pale blue but there are a number of shrubs with yellow blossoms, and a lovely scarlet annual. The genus is widely distributed in the temperate regions of the world.

Species cultivated Perennial: *L. alpinum*, 6 inches, blue, July–August, Alps. *L. campanulatum*, 1 foot, yellow, June–August, south Europe. *L. capitatum*, 9 inches, yellow, June–August, south Europe, Asia Minor. *L. flavum*, 1–1½ feet,

The Flaxes provide a number of very decorative garden plants, in addition to the economically valuable supplies of flax and linseed oil.
1 The yellow-flowered Linum 'Gemmell's Hybrid' a very floriferous plant.
2 The annual Flax, Linum rubrum grandiflorum, has deep rose-red flowers.
3 In summer, Linum salsoloides has dainty thin-textured flowers of white tinged with pinkish-mauve.
4 Linum narbonense is a favourite garden plant, a native of Europe.

---

yellow, June–August, Germany, Russia. *L. hirsutum*, 15 inches, blue with white eye, summer, south Europe, Asia Minor. *L. monogynum*, 2 feet, white, June–July, New Zealand. *L. narbonense*, 2 feet, blue, May–July, south Europe. *L. perenne*, 1½ feet, blue, June–July, Europe. *L. salsoloides*, 9 inches, pink, June–July, south Europe.

Annual: *L. grandiflorum*, 6–12 inches, rose, summer, North Africa; vars. *coccineum*, rose-crimson; *rubrum*, brighter than type; 'Venice Red' is a large-flowered cultivar with carmine-scarlet flowers. *L. usitatissimum*, common flax, 1½ feet, blue, June–July, Europe. Historically this is the world's most famous fibre plant; it was known to the Egyptians. Shrubby: *L. arboreum*, 1 foot, yellow, May–June, Crete.

Cultivation The flaxes are not fussy about soil provided it is well-drained and

the South and in other warm regions i[t] will grow outdoors with ease, it i[s] generally grown in a large pot which i[s] set out for the summer and returne[d] under glass for the winter. It is wort[h] noting that when, at the end of th[e] autumn, this plant sheds its leaves the[y] may be collected and will retain thei[r] sweet lemon fragrance for a considerabl[e] time. A standard loam, sand and leaf mould mixture is suitable for pot culti[-] vation. Severe pruning in February wil[l] result in the production of a fine crop o[f] scented leaves. Water freely in spring and summer, but keep on the dry side when the plant is dormant in winter.

Liquidambar (lik-quid-am-bar)
From the Latin *liquidus*, liquid, and *ambar*, the Arabic word for amber, referring to the fragrant resin obtained

1 **Lippia citriodora**, the Lemon Verbena, the leaves of which are strongly fragrant of lemon.
2 **Liparis atropurpurea**, from Ceylon, has a spike of purple flowers in June. The leaves are remarkably smooth.
3 The Sweet Gum Tree, **Liquidambar styraciflua** has corky bark, and is grown for its striking autumn leaf-colour.

will do very well on an alkaline medium. The annuals need the standard treatment for this group. Sometimes *L. grandiflorum* is sown in pots in July to decorate the greenhouse in the autumn, but whether grown outside or in, it is one of the best annuals for display. Most of the perennials and shrubby species will be happy and certainly look well on the rock garden in full sun. *L. arboreum* is not entirely hardy. Propagate by seed sown in April outdoors, or by firm cuttings taken in summer and kept close until rooted.

Lion's Ear—see Leonotis leonurus

Liparia (li-par-e-a)
From the Greek *liparos* meaning oily or shiny, referring to the shiny leaves *(Leguminosae)*. A genus of 4 species of erect, very leafy, evergreen shrubs with yellow flowers in terminal heads, natives of the Cape of Good Hope.
Species cultivated *L. parva*, 1–2 feet, flowers $1\frac{1}{2}$ inches across, March and April. *L. sphaerica*, mountain dahlia, spreading habit, 2–6 feet tall, orange flowers in dense nodding heads 3–4 inches in diameter.
Cultivation These are plants for the cool greenhouse needing a mixture of fibrous loam and good quality peat with added sand. Watering must always be done with very great care. Propagation is by cuttings of young shoots, inserted in sand in a propagating case. *L. sphaerica* is especially recommended, but it is rare in the wild as well as in cultivation.

Liparis (li-par-is)
From the Greek *liparos*, smooth, or oily,

in reference to the main characteristic of the leaves *(Orchidaceae)*. A large, widely distributed genus of both terrestrial and epiphytic orchids of variable habit and height. The tall spikes carry many small, usually closely set flowers.
Species cultivated *L. atropurpurea*, purple, June, Ceylon. *L. elata*, greenish-purple, yellowish, or whitish, summer, West Indies, Brazil. *L. fulgens*, deep red, summer, Philippines. *L. lacerata*, pink and red, fringed, summer, Borneo, Malaya. *L. reflexa*, yellowish-green to orange, scented, autumn, Australia. *L. tricallosa*, 2 feet, greenish-yellow to purple, summer, Borneo.
Cultivation Provide these orchids with a mixture of osmunda fibre and sphagnum moss with a little loam fibre and coarse sand. Maintain a winter temperature of 60°F (16°C), higher in summer. Propagation is by division.

Lippia (lip-ee-a)
Commemorating Auguste Lippi, born 1678, an Italian naturalist and botanist *(Verbenaceae)*. A genus of shrubs and herbaceous perennials from North and South America and Africa, once known as *Aloysia*. The only species in common cultivation is *L. citriodora* (syns. *Aloysia citriodora*, *Verbena triphylla*), the lemon verbena or lemon-scented verbena. This deciduous shrub from Chile grows 6–10 feet tall and in late summer bears spikes of pale purple flowers. It is not, however, grown for these but for the delicious lemon scent of its foliage when bruised. The essential oil of verbena is distilled from the leaves.
Cultivation The lemon-scented verbena is, unfortunately, tender and though in

3

from *L. orientalis (Hamamelidaceae)*. A small genus of hardy deciduous trees with fragrant, maple-like leaves and inconspicuous flowers.

Species cultivated *L. orientalis,* Oriental sweet gum, in the South a hardy, slow-growing but tall tree, west to east China and Formosa. *L. styraciflua,* sweet gum, hardy pyramidal tree to 90 feet, with corky bark, grown for its bright red, crimson, and orange autumn leaf colours, eastern United States to Gulf and Mexico.

Cultivation Moist, well-drained fertile soil is required. Plant in October or November or in early spring and prune to shape when necessary in November. Propagation is by imported seed which may not germinate until the second year, or by layers which root quickly and may be separated from the parent in late autumn after rooting.

Liquid Feeding—see Feeding

Liquorice Plant—see Glycyrrhiza glabra

Liriodendron (lir-e-o-dendron) From the Greek *leirion,* lily, and *dendron,*

tree, in reference to the very ornamental and unusual flowers *(Magnoliaceae)*. A genus of 2 species, large deciduous hardy trees with leaves distinctively square-cut at the ends and bearing greenish-yellow, tulip-shaped flowers at the ends of shoots, from about the fifteenth year onwards.

Species cultivated *L. chinense,* Chinese tulip tree, rare tree similar to but smaller than the next species, Central China. *L, tulipifera,* tulip tree, large tree to 200 feet, yellow, large scented flowers in summer, leaves bright clear yellow in autumn, east US to Florida, Mississippi; vars. *aureo-marginatum,* leaves edged with yellow; *fastigiatum,* tall-growing, erect form.

Cultivation The tulip trees require moist but well-drained fertile soil, in a sheltered but sunny situation. Plant only early spring, then difficult, and prune to keep the trees tidy in November

1 The Tulip Tree, Liriodendron tulipifera is a large tree, the foliage of which turns a clear yellow in autumn. The leaves are distinctive in shape.
2 The sweetly-scented flowers of Liriodendron tulipifera have earned the tree its English name, Tulip Tree.

1 Liriope muscari, a tuberous-rooted plant with grass-like leaves and deep purple flowers in autumn.
2 Lissochilus roseus, a plant introduced from Sierra Leone in 1841, has deep rose and brown flowers with broad upright stiff leaves.

or December. Propagate by seed sown in moist sandy loam in autumn in a little heat. Only collected seed is obtainable, and this is often of low fertility. The trunks of young trees should be protected from rabbits and hares.

Liriope (li-ri-o-pe)
Commemorating the nymph Liriope *(Liliaceae)*. Turf lily. A genus of 2 species (according to some authorities one only), interesting but not showy, small, grassy-leaved, evergreen herbs, natives of China and Japan, related to *Ophiopogon*. They are stemless, and the leaves and spikes of flowers spring straight from a rootstock. The small, rather rounded blossoms are borne in spikes and are followed by blue-black berries, thus giving a long period of interest.
Species cultivated *L. muscari* (syn. *L. graminifolia densiflora*), 1½ feet, thick tubers and strong tufts of leaves, flowers deep purple, autumn. *L. spicata*, creeping, distinctly grassy foliage, lilac flowers, sometimes white, autumn.
Cultivation When grown in the open these make good edging plants in most parts of the US; they are tolerant of some shade, and do best in a sandy loam. Plant in spring. Propagation is by division of the roots in March, or seed may be sown in sandy loam. Plants may also be grown in the cool greenhouse or conservatory, in pots of a well-drained mix.

Lissanthe (liss-an-thee)
From the Greek *lissos*, smooth, and *anthos*, a flower *(Epacridaceae)*. A genus of 4 species confined to Australia and Tasmania, pretty, erect, evergreen shrubs with white or pink narrow tubular flowers borne in small spikes or racemes, the leaves small and stiff.
Species cultivated *L. sapida*, an erect shrub, 2–3 feet, with spreading branches and stiff, sharply-pointed leaves and loose racemes of white flowers in May, followed by red fruits. *L. strigosa*, erect shrub about 2 feet high, with leaves tapering into a sharp point and white or pale pink flowers crowded in short racemes, followed by pink or white fruits.
Cultivation Well-grown specimens make good shrubs suitable for the cool greenhouse, and should be potted in a mixture of good fibrous bracken peat and sharp sand in well-drained pots. Watering must be done carefully at all times. Propagation is by cuttings. The plants should be treated in the same way as *Epacris*.

Lissochilus (liss-o-kye-lus)
From the Greek *lissos*, smooth, and *cheilos*, lip, in reference to the labellum *(Orchidaceae)*. A genus of terrestrial orchids, mainly from Africa, with tuberous roots or rhizomatous pseudobulbs which grow on the soil surface or just below it. Long upright spikes are produced from the base of pseudobulbs and carry many large showy flowers.
Species cultivated *L. arenarius*, 2–3 feet, green, mauve-purple and yellow, summer, tropical Africa. *L. bellus*, 2–2½ feet, greenish-yellow and red, spring,

Malawi. *L. giganteus*, very tall, up to 16 feet, rose-purple, lip bright purple, autumn, Congo. *L. horsfallii*, 4–6 feet, purple and rose, autumn, W. Africa. *L. krebsii*, 4 feet, yellow and reddish-brown, lip with purple blotches, summer, Natal. *L. roseus*, 3–5 feet, brown and deep rose, summer, Sierra Leone. *L. speciosus*, up to 7 feet, yellow, purple and whitish, fragrant, summer, S. Africa.

Cultivation A mixture of 3 parts of loam fibre and 1 part of leafmould, sand, and sphagnum moss, is required and plants should preferably be grown in large well-drained pans. These plants like a very warm moist atmosphere, 65–80°F (18–27°C) when in growth, and abundant water and light shade. In autumn they should be fully exposed to the light, and in winter a complete rest, with no water, at 60°F (16°C) is required. Propagation is by division of large plants in spring.

Litchi (lee-chee- or lie-chee)
The native Chinese name *(Sapindaceae)*. A genus of 2 species of which one only is in cultivation. This is *L. chinensis* (syns. *Nephelium litchi, Scytalia chinensis*), an evergreen tree, to 40 feet in China. Grows outdoors in south parts of Fla. and Calif. Not hardy but stands some frost if well-established. Leathery shining pinnate leaves are handsome. The whitish flowers are borne in terminal panicles up to 1 foot long. But the tree is not grown for its flowers but for its edible fruits. The thin egg-shell-like outer skin of the fruit is of a glowing red colour, which later turns a dull brown, and is covered with small rough tubercles. Within the succulent, fleshy, edible aril is a single large seed. The fruits, which have something of the flavour of a muscat grape, as well as a pleasant fragrance, are shelled and eaten fresh, or they may be dried, or preserved in syrup.

Cultivation Deep well-drained loam is required by the litchi, and abundant water during the growing season. It may be propagated from seed which germinates readily, but air-layering is a much quicker method where a tree is available upon which to practise this operation.

Lithocarpus (lith-o-carp-us)
From the Greek *lithos*, a stone and *karpos*, fruit, a reference to the hard, acorn-like fruit *(Fagaceae)*. A genus of about 100 species of evergreen trees, mostly natives of Asia and western N. America. All are very similar to oaks and formerly classified as *Quercus*, the principal difference being that in *Lithocarpus* the pollen-bearing catkins are more or less erect. Few are hardy except in the South and California.

Species cultivated *L. cleistocarpa*, to 50 feet in nature, makes a small tree in Britain, but is very slow growing elsewhere, leaves up to 1 foot long, China. *L. densiflora*, the tan-bark oak,

1 Lithocarpus edulis, an evergreen tree from Japan has glabrous shoots and leaves. Hardy in the South and California. Lithops, Stone Plants or Pebble Plants, succulents from South Africa. 2 Lithops erniana has white daisy-like flowers and 3 L. kuibesebsis yellow flowers.

70–90 feet, the hardiest, with striking white undersides to the leaves, California and Oregon. *L. edulis*, 30 feet, usually only a shrub but hardy in mild districts, Japan. *L. glabra*, 30 feet, laurel-like leaves, with acorns in triplets, one only developing, in Cornwall reaching tree size, Japan. *L. henryi*, 50 feet,

resembling *L. cleistocarpa*, but very tender, China.
Cultivation These trees will grow in ordinary soil in warm, sheltered situations. Propagation is by means of the acorns when produced in the US, otherwise imported, which must be sown without delay.

Lithops (lith-ops)
From the Greek *lithos*, a stone, and *ops*, appearance, in reference to the resemblance of these plants to stones *(Aizoaceae)*. Pebble plants, living stones. The lithops are succulent greenhouse plants from South Africa, never more than an

inch high, but making large groups with age. They consist of a pair of leaves joined half way up or completely, leaving only a small slit on the surface. The top is almost flat and many species having markings similar to some bird's eggs. Flowers are either white or yellow, the yellow varieties flower in July and August, the white from September to November.

Species cultivated *L. aucampiae,* a fine plant with large bodies, almost brick red, Transvaal. *L. bella,* well-marked plant body white flowers, south-west Africa. *L. bromfieldii,* rather brown with many markings, Cape Province. *L. christinae,* grey-blue body, south-west Africa. *L. de boeri,* well mottled face to bodies. *L. dorotheae,* very handsome with distinct markings, Bushmanland. *L. fulleri,* grey with brown markings, Little Namaqualand. *L. leslei,* green face with reddish spots, Transvaal. It is worth noting that many species are thought by some specialists to be varieties only.

Cultivation A very porous mixture is required; a porous cactus-succulent mix with ¼ part added of roughage, consisting of coarse sharp sand, or grit, broken brick and granulated charcoal, is suitable. Repotting is required every three years, in May or June, or when the

1 **Lithops leslei, one of the stone-like plants, has a flat upper surface netted with brown and green.**
2 **Lithospermum diffusum has numerous deep blue flowers in summer.**
3 **Lithospermum oleifolium, not often grown, is an attractive rock garden plant, with deep blue flowers.**

plant reaches the side of the pot. A winter minimum temperature of 40°F (4°C) is required; in summer the normal seasonal temperature within the greenhouse suits them. They do not need shade. Do not water in the early part of the year. New plants form inside the old pair of leaves, these leaves being absorbed until only a paperlike skin is left to protect the new plant, and no water must be given until the old leaves have dried up. Then water carefully up to November, and give very little in December. No exact time can be given for starting watering after the resting period, as the species differ considerably as to when water is needed.

Propagate by seed, which need only be sown on the top of the medium. A porous cactus-succulent mix, sifted through a perforated zinc sieve can be used. Place the coarsest particles over the crocks, then cover with unsifted compost, and

finish the top inch with the finest particles from sifting. Sow in March in a temperature of 70–80°F (21–27°C) and shade from sun, but give light until the seedlings appear. Propagate also by division, by cutting off individual heads with a small piece of stem attached.

Lithospermum (ˈith-o-sper-mum)

From the Greek *lithos,* a stone, and *sperma,* a seed, in reference to the extreme hardness of the seed (*Boraginaceae*). Gromwell. A genus of about 40 species of biennials, herbaceous perennials and sub-shrubs, grown for their flowers, which are predominantly bright blue. Those in cultivation are mostly trailing evergreen sub-shrubs or perennials from the Mediterranean region, and are generally grown among other plants on a sunny rock garden, though *L. diffusum* and its garden forms are somewhat invasive, and *L. purpureocaeruleum,* a rare native plant is even more so. Some species are now included in *Moltkia.*

Species cultivated *L. canescens,* puccoon, red root, 1 foot, yellow, July, Ontario to Texas. *L. diffusum* (syn. *L. prostratum*), 6 inches, blue, summer, southern Europe; cultivars are 'Grace Ward', 3 inches, bright blue, late spring;

eavenly Blue', smaller flowers. *L. oerfloeri,* 1 foot, erect, deep purple, May nd June. *L. gastoni,* 1 foot, blue, ummer, western Pyrenees. *L. oleifolium,* inches, prostrate shrub, violet to blue, ummer, rare, Pyrenees. *L. purpureo-eruleum,* 1 foot, creeping habit, purple, ummer, Europe. *L. rosmarinifolium,* 1½ et, bright azure blue, February, Italy, oes best in the alpine house.

ultivation A well-drained coarse soil is uitable for these plants, and they do est in alkaline soils, except for *L. iffusum,* which requires a lime-free acid ne. Keep the soil just moist in winter. ut back *L. diffusum* after flowering. ropagate by means of green cuttings in une, or seed may be sown. *L. diffusum*

is grown most easily from cuttings of the preceding year's shoots, rooted in fine peat and sand, and kept cool and shaded for a few weeks.

Littonia (lit-o-nee-a)

Commemorating Dr S. Litton, a former Professor of Botany in Dublin *(Liliaceae).* A genus of 2 species of climbing plants, unlike any other plant with the exception of the nearly related *Gloriosa.* The colour of the somewhat bell-shaped, pendent flowers is orange. The only species cultivated, *L. modesta,* from South Africa, is a tender herbaceous perennial with storage roots. As with the gloriosa the leaves have the central vein prolonged into a tendril, by means

of which the ascending plant is able to secure itself to plants or other objects. The plant, which requires greenhouse treatment, attains a height of 2–6 feet and flowers in early summer.

Cultivation During the growing period a temperature of 60–70°F (16–21°C) is required, but in winter the storage roots will, when dry, endure a much lower temperature. The soil should consist of equal parts of peat, leaf-soil, loam and sand. Give plenty of water in summer, but much less in winter. Some support is needed upon which this climber can secure itself, in a position which is exposed to full sun. Plants are readily raised from seed or may be increased by division of the fleshy roots in March.

Litsea (lit-se-a)

From the Japanese name *(Lauraceae).* Though there are 150 species in this tropical genus, mostly from the Far East and Australia, they are generally deciduous or evergreen forest trees, or shrubs unsuitable for cultivation in most of the US, except in greenhouses, although they succeed out of doors in California.

Species cultivated *L. geniculata* (D), 6 feet, shrub, tiny yellow flowers in umbels, May, south-west United States of America, warm greenhouse. *L. glauca* (E), to 30 feet, shrub or small tree, white summer, Japan, cool greenhouse. *L. japonica* (E), 3–5 feet, shrub, white, September–January, Japan, warm greenhouse.

Cultivation These shrubs are not particular about soil, although they do best if it is well-drained, but need generous watering when in full growth. Though they may be planted in large pots or tubs, they are better suited to the greenhouse border. Winter temperature for *L. glauca* should not be less than 40°F (4°C) and for the other two species mentioned it should be at least 50°F (10°C). Prune only to tidy straggling shoots. Propagation is by seed, when available, sown in heat in spring, or by cuttings taken at almost any time, rooted in sandy compost in a propagating frame with bottom heat.

Little cherry—see Virus diseases

Little Quaking Grass—see Briza minor

Live Oak—see Quercus virginiana

Liver of sulphur—see Sulphide of potassium

Livingstone Daisy—see Mesembryanthemum

Living Stones—see Lithops, Pleiospilos

Littonia modesta is a tender herbaceous perennial from South Africa.

Livistona (liv-iss-toe-na)
Commemorating Patrick Murray, Baron of Livingstone the founder of the Edinburgh Botanic Gardens *(Palmae)*. A genus of some 30 species of palms with stout rigid trunks, ranging from east tropical Asia, Malaya, New Guinea and Australia. They have a terminal crown of fan-shaped leaves, divided into numerous segments, which are split at the ends, and frequently have threads hanging. The petiole is spiny near the base. The trunks are often clothed with the remains of dead leaf-sheaths. The flower stalks are long, the flowers greenish, and the fruits black, blue, yellow or brown. The leaves of some species are used for roofing and making hats. The fibre from the leaf bases is used for making ropes. The central growing point of *L. australis,* the cabbage palm, is eaten raw or cooked by the aborigines of Australia.

Species cultivated *L. australis,* cabbage palm, trunk 40 to 80 feet, leaves 3 to 4 feet in diameter, leaflets drooping at tips, fruit round, $\frac{1}{2}$ to $\frac{3}{4}$ inches in diameter, reddish-brown, Australia. *L. chinesis,* Chinese fan palm, trunk 20 to 30 feet, leaves 6 feet in diameter, leaflets drooping at tips, fruit $\frac{3}{4}$ inch long, greeny-blue to black, Central China. *L. humilis,* trunk 4 to 16 feet, leaves 3 feet in diameter, deep green, Australia. *L. rotundifolia,* trunk up to 50 feet, prominently ringed, leaves 3 to 5 feet in diameter nearly round, flowers yellow, fruits round, $\frac{3}{4}$ inch in diameter, brownish-black, Malaya.

Cultivation *L. rotundifolia* needs to be grown in a warm house *L. humilis, L. australis* and *L. chinensis* require sufficient heat to keep the frost out. *L. chinensis* will grow out of doors in California and south Florida. Any well-drained soil is suitable if the palms are grown in the greenhouse border, or for pot culture, use a mixture of 2 parts of loam, 1 part of peat and 1 part of sand. An occasional syringeing over of the foliage with water during warm weather will be beneficial. Propagation is by seeds, sown $\frac{1}{2}$ inch deep in light, rich soil, in February or March, in a temperature of 80–90°F (27–32°C).

Lloydia (loy-dee-a)
Commemorating Edward Lloyd, 1660–1709, a Welsh botanist *(Liliaceae)*. A small genus of bulbous plants, natives of the Northern Hemisphere, of which one species only, *L. serotina,* is likely to be found in cultivation. This, known as the mountain spider-wort, grows to about 6 inches high and is a rare European plant, found in North Wales, mainly in Snowdonia. It has grass-like leaves and, in June, bears small white or yellow flowers, reddish striped on the inside.

Cultivation This is not an easy plant, though it may be grown in sandy loam in a well-drained, cool situation on the rock garden. Plant the narrow bulbs in

An Australian Palm, Livistona australis.

September or October, 3–4 inches deep, lifting and replanting only when the plants begin to look unhealthy. Propagation is by offsets removed at planting time.

Loam
This term is used to describe a type of soil, determined by its texture when compared with other types. The main constituents of most soils are sand, silt and clay. At one extreme are the very sandy types; at the other, those with a high clay content. Soils classed as loam can vary between sandy loams and clay loams, loam itself being intermediate in texture between these, containing sand, silt and clay in roughly equal proportions.

An average sample of soil classed as loam contains: coarse sand (2–0.2 mm.), 20 per cent; fine sand (0·2–0·02 mm.), 30 per cent; silt (0·02–0·002 mm.), 25 per cent; and clay (0·002 mm.), 25 per cent. For comparison, the analysis of sandy loam is: coarse sand, 25 per cent; fine sand, 40 per cent; silt, 20 per cent; clay, 15 per cent; that of clay loam: coarse sand, 10 per cent; fine sand, 30 per cent; silt, 20 per cent; and clay, 40 per cent.

Loams are among the most fertile soils for gardening purposes, being moisture and nutrient retentive. Almost all crops can be grown well on them. They can become sticky if worked when too wet but otherwise are easily managed.

The term loam is mostly encountered by gardeners in connection with the content of made-up potting mixtures.

1 In the preparation of loam for potting mixtures the top spit of pasture land is used and turves lifted with as much fibrous material as possible in them. Sulphate of ammonia is sprinkled over the surface to help break down the turf.
2 A second layer of turves is put on and can again be covered with sulphate of ammonia.
3 The process is repeated for the heap.

The bulky ingredients of the prepared potting mixtures, for instance, are loam, peat and sand. Loam here describes the portion of soil content apart from the other two almost inert materials.

Ideally, loam is taken from the top spit of pasture land and will contain enough sand for good drainage, plus enough clay to retain moisture. The object of taking it from pasture land is to obtain a high proportion of fibrous roots which will help to keep the compost open as it breaks down.

Recommendations for the preparation of potting mixtures often state the maximum particle size of the loam, obtained by passing it through a suitable sieve. As much fibrous material as possible should be retained, however, for the purpose stated.

If top-spit loam is obtainable, it should be allowed to break down by stacking the turves grass side down. Loam stacks should be left for at least a year before use to ensure that the grass is properly decayed. If desired, the loam will remain in good condition for some years. Stacks should be made either with a ridged top to prevent rain penetration, or have some other covering, such as plastic sheeting provided.

It is a good plan to make loam stacks every couple of years to ensure a continuous supply of compost material. Partial sterilisation is of course a usual safeguard against the presence of latent soil troubles.

Loasa (lo-a-sa)

A native South American name (*Loasaceae*). A genus of half hardy annual or biennial plants, related to *Blumenbachia,* all climbing or scrambling in habit, armed with stinging hairs. Unlike the stinging nettle, they compensate by having flowers of complex and beautiful shape. They are natives of tropical America and are well worth cultivation, particularly as they do not flower until mid-September. The species most likely to be found in cultivation is *L. vulcanica* from Ecuador, which grows 3 feet tall and has lobed leaves, the lobes cut, and white, red and yellow flowers in late summer and autumn. Treat as annual.

Cultivation Out of doors, a position against a sunny wall in ordinary soil is suitable. In the greenhouse the plant requires a well-drained mixture, and should be watered freely during the summer. An occasional application of liquid fertiliser is beneficial when the plants are flowering. Propagate by seed sown in a well-drained seed mix in a temperature of 65°F (18°C) in March. Transplant to 3-inch pots when 1 inch high, and then plant out in June, or pot on when 6 inches high, and provide some support.

Lobb Brothers

William Lobb (1809–1863) and Thomas Lobb (died 1894) were brothers born in Cornwall, both of whom were plant hunters for the famous Victorian firm of nurserymen, James Veitch and Sons, of Exeter and Chelsea. Curiously enough their paths never crossed and while William was noted for his introductions of trees and shrubs, Thomas collected, in vastly different conditions, for orchids.

William was the first to travel abroad when he was sent to South America in 1840, particularly to send back seed of the monkey puzzle tree (*Araucaria araucana)* to become such a popular feature of Victorian lawns. It is to William we should all be grateful for his introduction of those magnificently coloured and exciting flowering trees and shrubs from Chile, the fire bush (*Embothrium coccineum), Desfontainea spinosa, Escallonia macrantha, Lapageria rosea* and that most popular of the berberis, *B. darwinii.*

Later, in 1849, he followed in the footsteps of David Douglas on the Pacific seaboard of North America to find, and send back in quantity, cones and seeds of the many outstanding conifers Douglas had first introduced. Among those Lobb sent home are *Pinus radiata, ponderosa, sabiniana, coulteri, muricata* and *tuberculata, Abies nobilis,*

1 Loasa vulcanica, from Ecuador, is a very useful annual plant because it flowers late in the season.
2 This Orchid, Vanda caerulea was introduced from Burma by Thomas Lobb, together with many other Orchids.
3 The Pitcher Plant from Malaya, Nepenthes sanguinea, also found by Lobb.

Three of the plants introduced by William Lobb from his various trips.
4 Pinus ponderosa from American West.
5 The popular Berberis darwinii which came from Chile about 1840, and which is attractive in both flower and fruit.
6 Sequoia gigantea (in the centre of this group) was introduced in 1853.

6 *grandis*, and *magnifica* and *Sequoia sempervirens*. In 1853 in the Sierra Nevada he found the first seeds and cones of the great redwood, *Sequoia gigantea (S. wellingtonia)*, ever to be received in cultivation. After a short spell at home he returned to California in 1854 and until 1863 continued to send collections of seeds home. In that year he was seized with paralysis in both legs and died in San Francisco.

Thomas Lobb, from 1843, for 20 years plant hunted for Messrs Veitch in Java, Assam, Mulmein, Lower Burma, Malaya and Borneo.

From 1848 onwards, in India and Burma, Lobb collected and introduced many new orchids including *Vanda caerulea, Pleione lagenaria, Aerides multiflora lobbii, A. m. veitchii*, various dendrobiums and *Cypripedium villosum*.

From North Borneo and Sarawak and the islands he discovered and introduced the Javanico-Jasminiflorum hybrid rhododendrons, the originals being *R. javanico, lobbii, jasminiflorum* and *brookeanum*. From the same region he introduced some of the first nepenthes (pitcher plants) to be grown in British hot houses, including *N. rafflesiana, veitchii, sanguinea* and *ampullaria* as well as many other orchids, including vandas, calanthes, coelogynes and, from Manila, phalaenopsis.

James Veitch said of Thomas Lobb: British gardens were enriched with more beautiful plants of Indo-Malayan origin (by Lobb) than by any other single collector of his own or any other time.

Thomas Lobb died in Devoran, Cornwall, in 1894 at an advanced age, having had to retire after losing a leg through exposure on his long and arduous jungle treks.

The genus *Lobbia* of the order *Aristolochiaceae* was founded by Planchon on

1 Lobelia cardinalis, the Cardinal
Flower, is a perennial which reaches
3 feet and produces deep red flowers.
2 The tall-growing Lobelia tupa, has red
flowers in autumn and is a useful
addition to the herbaceous border.
3 The small-flowered annual Lobelias
are useful for hanging baskets.
4 One of the many bedding Lobelias,
'Emperor William'.

a specimen collected by Thomas in
Singapore called *Lobbia dependens,* the
generic name being given to commemorate the outstanding work of the
two brothers.

Lobelia (lobe-ee-lee-a)

Commemorating Matthias de L'Obel,
1538–1616, a Fleming, botanist and
physician to James I *(Campanulaceae).*
A genus of some 200 species of annuals,
herbaceous perennials or sub-shrubs,
widely distributed over temperate and
tropical regions. Some should be regarded as half hardy, although many
herbaceous perennials will survive out
of doors with ease in most parts of
the country. *L. cardinalis,* bright red,
native from New Brunswick to Florida
to Texas, may well be grown in the
garden. Where difficulty is experienced
in wintering it, carry it over in a
cold frame. Almost as showy is blue
L. syphilitica, native from Maine to
Louisiana. The red flowered lobelias
have the added charm of dark purple-
bronze leaves.

Species cultivated *L. cardinalis,* cardinal
flower, perennial, 3 feet, scarlet, late
summer, North America; var. *alba,*
white; 'Queen Victoria' is a cultivar
with bronze foliage, deep scarlet flowers.
L. erinus, annual, 6 inches, blue, summer, South Africa; cultivars include
'Blue Gown', dwarf, sky blue; 'Blue
Stone', clear blue without eye; 'Crystal
Palace', bronze foliage, intense blue

flowers: 'Emperor William', compact,
bright blue, very good for bedding;
'Prima Donna', wine; 'Rosamund', deep
carmine-red with white eye. This is the
lobelia much used for summer bedding.
L. fulgens, perennial, 3 feet, scarlet,
May–September, Mexico. *L.* × *gerardii,*
perennial, 3–4 feet, pink to violet-purple,
July, hybrid. *L. syphilitica,* perennial, 2
feet, blue, autumn, Eastern United
States, fully hardy. *L. tenuior,* annual,
1 foot, blue, September, Western
Australia, the lobelia of trailing habit,
used for hanging baskets. *L. tupa,*
perennial, 6–8 feet, reddish-scarlet,
autumn.

Cultivation The scarlet-flowered *L. cardinalis* and *L. c. alba* when planted in
the border need frequent watering since
in their native habitat they are stream-
side plants. They are otherwise not
difficult plants to raise except that
they are not always long-lived perennials. Propagation of these is by
seeds, sown in sandy mixture in autumn
in a cold frame, or in a temperature of
55°F (13°C) in March, or by cuttings

rooted in a warm propagating frame.
Plants may also be divided in March.
The bedding lobelias with blue flowers
may be grown from seed sown in February in the greenhouse, in the orthodox
half hardy annual method, but in September these plants may be lifted and
stored in the greenhouse to provide
cuttings for rooting in a heated propagating frame in March.

Lobivia (lob-iv-e-a)

The name is an anagram of Bolivia
where the plants are found *(Cactaceae).*
A genus of greenhouse succulents,
mostly dwarf and cylindrical with large
and colourful flowers for the size of the
plant.

Species cultivated *L. aurea,* globular to
columnar ridged stems, yellow flowers.
L. backebergii, a handsome plant with
carmine flowers. *L. famatimensis,* yellow
to red; vars. *albiflora,* white or pale
yellow; *aurantiaca,* golden-orange; *hae-
matantha,* blood-red; *rosiflora,* pink. *L.
hertrichiana,* small globular bodies, few
spines, bright red flowers, produced

offsets very freely. *L. jajoiana*, very handsome, dark red flowers with black centre.

Cultivation Use a well-drained potting mixture with ⅙ part extra of sand, grit and broken brick. Plants should be re-potted every two years and given a very sunny position. Water between March and September, but keep very dry in winter. The summer temperature can be between 65°F (18°C) and 85°F (30°C); winter temperature should not drop below 40°F (4°C). Propagate by seed sown in well-drained seed mix, just covered, and kept close in a temperature of 70°F (25°C). Plants may also be propagated from offsets rooted in coarse sand.

Loblolly Pine—see Pinus taeda

Lobostemon (lo-bo-stay-mon)
From the Greek *lobos*, a lobe and *stemon*, a stamen, referring to the position of the stamens opposite the lobes of the corolla *(Boraginaceae)*. A genus of small summer-flowering herbs, sub-shrubs or shrubs, natives of South Africa, related to *Echium*, with stalkless leaves and pale yellow or white to bluish flowers in terminal inflorescences.

Species cultivated *L. argenteus*, bristly, branched shrub up to 3 feet tall, flowers blue, in spikes, June. *L. fruticosus*, to 3 feet, soft-wooded branching shrub with pink to blue flowers in spike-like inflorescences, May. *L. trigonus*, shrub, to 12 inches tall, with rough hairy leaves

Typical Lobivias, Cactus plants from Bolivia, with cylindrical ribbed growth, and comparatively large flowers.
1 Lobivia carmianantha.
2 Lobivia sublimiflora.
3 Lobostemon fruticosus, a summer-flowering shrub from South Africa, has soft growth and pink to blue flowers.

South America. The stems are densely clothed with small stiff leaves giving a plaited appearance. The smallish flowers are attractive and in many species are bright yellow; they are of complex structure and have large bracts and appear mainly at the top of the stem.

Species cultivated *L. acuta,* 6 inches, bright yellow and red, June, Trinidad. *L. lunifera,* 4–15 inches, creamy-yellow, summer, Brazil. *L. robusta* (syn. *L. oerstedii*), 2 feet, bright yellow, various seasons, Guatemala. *L. verrucosa,* 1 foot, bright yellow and red, autumn, Guatemala.

Cultivation These orchids prefer a mixture of equal parts of osmunda fibre and sphagnum moss. The smaller growing ones are grown, ideally, in pans, the larger ones in pots, but in both cases, drainage must be good. Keep the atmosphere humid to produce the longest stems, and give less water in winter, but do not withhold it altogether as these orchids do not have a definite resting period. The winter temperature should be about 60°F (16°C) and about 70°F (21°C) and upwards in summer. Propagate by division of plants when large enough, while repotting in the spring.

Locust Tree—see Robinia pseudoacacia and Ceratonia

Loganberry

The loganberry is, perhaps, the supreme bramble type of berry, as it is ideal for stewing, jam- and jelly-making, bottling, canning, juice extraction and wine-making. The berries can also be eaten as dessert when fully ripe, but may be too tart for some palates.

Opinions are divided as to whether the loganberry is a red-fruiting form of the common Californian blackberry, *Rubus ursinus vitifolius,* or a seedling from a cross between the 'Red Antwerp' raspberry and the American blackberry 'Aughinburgh'. The plant appeared in 1881 in the garden of Judge J. H. Logan of Santa Cruz, California, for whom it is named. They can be grown but are not always dependable in the Northeast.

The loganberry produces vigorous, prickly canes carrying 3- to 5-lobed leaves. As flowering is late, the plants may be grown in low-lying situations; spring frosts rarely damage the blossom, though severe winters may affect the canes. Loganberries are self-compatible and yield heavy crops of blunt, firm, very juicy, deep red berries of a rich flavour, from August to September. The yield may be sustained for 15 years or more. The berries do not plug, so are picked complete with core. Picking is best done when the berries are quite dry.

Heavy, rather than limey and light and dry, soils are preferred—limey soils induce iron and manganese deficiencies. Well-drained loams and brick earths are ideal. Loganberries love rich soil and respond to generous manuring. Nitrogen

and stems, and pink flower buds which open a clear blue.

Cultivation These are plants for the cool greenhouse, which should be grown in a sandy medium. Propagation is by cuttings, but rooted plants are obtained much quicker by layering. Herbaceous species may be easily raised from seed.

Lobster Cactus—see Zygocactus truncatus

Lobster Claw—see Clianthus

Lobularia (lob-u-lar-i-a)

From the Greek *lobulus,* a little lobe, a diminutive of *lobos,* the lower part of the ear, possibly referring to the forked hairs on the leaves *(Cruciferae).* A small genus of plants closely related to *Alyssum.* There are four species, natives of the Mediterranean region, but only one of any garden value. This is *L. maritima* (syn. *Alyssum maritimum*), 9–10 inches tall, the well-known sweet alyssum or sweet Alison. Though it is really a perennial it is treated as a hardy annual and flowers in early summer. It is a popular edging plant grown for the sake

Lobularia maritima, Sweet Alyssum, is the only species of any garden value. It has white flowers and is usually treated as an annual and used as edging.

of its sweetly-scented white flower.

Some varieties and cultivars are: *minimum,* very small-growing, white; *nanum* ('Little Dorrit'), compact, short-growing, white; 'Lilac Queen', pale lilac; 'Pink Heather', compact; 'Rosie O'Day', deep rose; 'Violet Queen', bright violet, very floriferous; *procumbens*,'Snow Cloth', compact mass of pure white flowers; 'Royal Carpet', very dwarf, dark purple.

Cultivation There is no difficulty in growing this fragrant plant, which can be put in open borders or rock gardens. Seeds are sown in spring or autumn where the plants are to grow, and plants will survive through a mild winter. It will reproduce itself quite readily from self-sown seeds.

Lockhartia (lok-hart-e-a)

Named in honour of David Lockhart of Trinidad, died 1846, who introduced *L. elegans (Orchidaceae).* A genus of curious tufted epiphytic orchids mainly from

1 is the most important plant food requirement. Mulch annually with farmyard manure in late autumn or feed with 2 ounces of fish manure and 1 ounce of sulphate of potash per square yard.

A sunny and open but sheltered site is best with protection in the Northeast. The rows should run north-south.

Propagation can be by tip-layering between June and mid-August. The tips of young canes are pegged down 2–3 inches deep (or weighted with a flat stone), into small pots filled with a rooting mixture and sunk in the ground. The young plants are severed from the parent canes when well-rooted the following April–May. Alternatively, leaf bud cuttings are rooted 2 inches apart in a bed of sandy soil in a closed and shaded garden frame in July or August. Each cutting consists of a leaf and bud with a 1-inch length of cane bark devoid of pith. Roots are produced in three to four weeks; the young plants are hardened off a month later and transplanted the following spring.

Rooted tips or cuttings are planted 6–10 feet apart in March and April against fences, north or east walls, and up arches. Post and wire supports with wires at 2, 4 and 6 feet from soil level are used on open sites. Shorten the young plants to 9 inches after planting, to encourage the production of strong new shoots on which fruit will be borne the

1 The Loganberry is a vigorous plant, producing long whippy runners and big juicy berries with a distinctive flavour.
2 The long runners can be laced over horizontal wires for support.
3 Loganberries can be propagated by tip-layering. Here the bud has started.

1 Lomatia longifolia, from New South Wales is grown for its foliage and reaches about 10 feet.
2 The Alpine Azalea, Loiseleuria procumbens in its natural habitat. It is a hardy flowering evergreen shrub.

following year. To reduce disease infection from the older canes, the young canes may be trained fan-wise on the opposite side from the old canes. The two ages of cane occupy alternate sides annually. Ten to 12 fruiting canes are retained per plant. Fruiting is on one-year-old canes which are cut down to ground level in October after fruit harvest.

Pests and diseases are the same as those which attack raspberries (see Pests and diseases, Raspberries).

Two good varieties are the following: 'LY 59', which is a virus-free clone available since the late 1950s. It is free from the debilitating viruses which reduce the crop of infected loganberries. It is the heaviest cropper—it may yield 17½ pounds of fruit per bush; 'American Thornless', a prickle-free mutation found in 1933. It is a pleasure to prune it. Slightly less vigorous than the common loganberry, it is an ideal variety for the smaller garden and may yield up to 15 pounds of fruit per bush (see also *Rubus loganobaccus*).

Loiseleuria (loys-el-eur-e-a)
Commemorating J. L. A. Loiseleur-Deslongchamps, 1774–1849, a French botanist *(Ericaceae)*. This genus contains only the species known as *L. procum-*

bens (syns. *Azalea procumbens, Chamaecistus procumbens)*, the alpine azalea. It is a hardy flowering evergreen shrub, and comes from sub-arctic regions. Both flowers and leaves are small and the plant itself scrambles happily among granite rocks, rising a few inches only from the ground. It is rare in the United States. Although circumpolar, it is confined to some mountain tops. It needs moisture and full sun to induce the production of its white or pink flowers in July and August.
Cultivation Loiseleuria needs sandy peat, and though it is generally grown on a rock garden (granite rock), it is also a suitable plant for alpine house cultivation. Propagation is by taking cuttings or making layers from late July to September.

Lomaria—see Blechnum

Lomaridium—see Blechnum

Lomatia (lo-ma-te-a)
From the Greek *loma*, a border, in reference to the winged edge of the seeds *(Proteaceae)*. This genus contains a few greenhouse trees and shrubs cultivated for the sake of their foliage, which is generally leathery and feathery (pinnate). They are exclusively native plants of the Southern Hemisphere. Though the genus has ten species they have not all been considered worthy of cultivation, and none of them has outstanding beauty of flower or fruit.
Species cultivated *L. ferruginea*, 10 feet,

shoots covered with rust-coloured felt, pinnate foliage, small red and yellow flowers, July, Chile. *L. longifolia*, 10 feet, New South Wales. *L. obliqua*, 20 feet, Chile. *L. silaifolia*, 3 feet, New South Wales. *L. tinctoria*, 3 feet, Tasmania.
Cultivation Greenhouse treatment is usual, as are full light conditions. The potting mixture should consist of loam, peat and sand in equal parts. Water only moderately in winter, but more generously during the more rapid period of growth from April to September. The winter temperature should not be below 45°F (7°C). Increase by cuttings under a hand light or in a propagating frame with a temperature of 60–70°F (16–21°C). Outdoors in warm regions.

Lombardy Poplar—see Populus italica

Lomatophyllum (lo-ma-toff-ill-um)
From the Greek *lomatos*, a border, *phyllon*, a leaf, referring to the horny-edged leaves *(Liliaceae)*. A small genus of succulent plants, resembling and related to *Aloe*. One species, *L. borbonicum*, from Mauritius, is cultivated. This has a thick stem, 6–8 feet tall, bearing fleshy leaves up to 3 feet long, green edged with red and with horny teeth along the margins. It bears spikes of small flowers, yellow inside, reddish-brown on the outsides.
Cultivation This plant needs the protection of a sunny greenhouse in which a minimum winter temperature of 45–50°F (7–10°C) can be maintained, rising in

summer with normal sun heat to 65°F (18°C), although the pots may be stood out of doors in a sunny, sheltered spot during the summer months. A suitable mixture consists of 2 parts of loam, 1 part peat, 1 part sharp coarse grit or sand and a little slow-acting complete food per bushel. Large pots or tubs are necessary for mature plants. Water when the soil is dry, between April and September, but give the plants a rest, keeping the soil almost dry, during the winter. Propagation is by seed sown in spring in a temperature of 70°F (21°C) or by offsets removed when the plants are repotted in spring.

Lonas (lo-nas)

Derivation uncertain (Compositae). There is but one species in the genus, *L. annua,* African daisy, an uncommon and hardy annual, a branching plant, 1 foot tall. The clustered flowers, produced from July to October, resemble those of an ageratum but they are golden-yellow. An added attraction of this Mediterranean plant is that the flowers may be treated as everlasting to combine with other dried material to use as winter decoration.

Cultivation The plant will grow in any kind of soil, but needs a sunny aspect. Propagate by seed sown out of doors in

1 Lonas annua, is an African Daisy with clustered flowers of golden yellow, which are papery and can be used as 'everlasting flowers'.

2 Melbourne Hall, Derbyshire, where the garden was designed by George London.

April, where the plants are to flower.

London, George and Wise, Henry

Little is known of the origins of George London (d. 1713) other than that he learned to garden in the French style of the great Le Notre. He was gardener to Henry Compton, Bishop of London from 1675 to 1713, who at Fulham Palace had a remarkable garden including many plants recently introduced, particularly from North America. London also took a daring and active part in the escape of Princess—later Queen—Anne.

In 1681, in collaboration with other prominent gardeners, he opened a nursery business at Brompton in London. This was on a large scale and was clearly organised to compete with the Dutch who dominated the nursery trade. Within a few years, the business had become the property of two partners only, London and Henry Wise (1653–1738) who virtually monopolised the designing, supplying of plants to, and sometimes the maintenance of the great gardens of the nobility.

London travelled the country to meet and plan with his clients, while for long Wise remained chiefly in London in charge of the business side and the nursery, which had become one of the

biggest in Europe. The numerous gardens for which they were responsible ranged from Chatsworth to Hampton Court at the time of Wren's additions.

After London's death, Wise carried on, becoming gardener to Queen Anne. He was particularly associated, too, with the vast gardens at Blenheim Palace, where he was one of the few employed in that great undertaking who never quarrelled with the trying Duchess of Marlborough.

The landscape fashion that was soon to follow on Wise's death tragically swept away almost all trace of the magnificent gardens inspired by the French style that the partners created. By far the best surviving example is at Melbourne Hall in Derbyshire. There are some remains at Chatsworth, also in Derbyshire, and at Hampton Court, while remaining features of Wrest Park in Bedfordshire are in the same manner, but probably not by the partners.

London Pride—see Saxifraga umbrosa

Long Moss—see Tillandsia usneoides

Long-leaf Pine—see Pinus palustris

Long-leaved Indian Pine—see Pinus roxburghii

Lonicera (lon-is-er-a)
From the name of a German botanist, Adam Lonicer, 1528–86 (*Caprifoliaceae*). Honeysuckle. This genus of nearly 200 species, is of great garden importance, and has shrubby and climbing deciduous and evergreen species. Many of them have extremely sweetly scented flowers. Most species and hybrids are hardy, and two are among the finest of Britain's hedgerow plants, filling the summer evening air with their fragrance. The species are widely spread over the Northern Hemisphere.

Species cultivated Climbing: *L. alseus-moides* (E), leaves narrow, flowers yellow and purple, July to October, fruits blue-black, China. *L. × americana* (D), 25–30 feet, flowers fragrant white, ageing to yellow, flushed purple outside, June and July, hybrid. *L. × brownii* (SE), scarlet trumpet honeysuckle, 10–15 feet, flowers orange-scarlet, May to August, hybrid; vars. *fuchsioides*, similar, *plantierensis*, flowers coral-red and orange. *L. caprifolium* (D), 20 feet, yellowish, fragrant, June and July, Europe; var. *pauciflora*, flowers flushed purple on the outside. *L. ciliata* (D), yellow tinged purple, Quebec, Northeast to Minnesota. *L. dioica* (D), yellow and pink, June and July, east N. Amer. *L. etrusca* (D), 20–30 feet, creamy-yellow and purple, fragrant, July to August, Mediterranean region. *L. flava* (D), 10 feet, yellow, fragrant, June, N.C. west to Okla. *L. giraldii* (E), vigorous, purple-red flowers, whole plant rather hairy, summer-

flowering, China. *L. glauca* (*L. dioica*), yellow, summer, east N. America. *L. × heckrottii* (D), rather a shrubby climber, deep yellow and pink, fragrant, summer, hybrid. *L. henryi* (E), 20–30 feet, glossy dark green leaves, flowers small, red and yellow, June and July, fruits black, China. *L. hildebrandiana* (D), giant honeysuckle, 60–80 feet, flowers fragrant, creamy-yellow, ageing to orange, 4 inches or more long, June to August, Burma, China, Siam, hardy only in the mildest regions, otherwise needs cool greenhouse treatment. *L. implexa* (SE), 8–10 feet, yellow flushed pink, June to

August, Mediterranean, not fully hardy. *L. japonica* (E), 20 feet, red and white, very fragrant, June and July, Japan, Korea, China; vars. *aureo-reticulate* veins at leaves bright yellow, seldom flowers; *halliana,* white and yellow, very fragrant, all summer; *flexuosa* (*repens*) leaf veins purplish, red and white flowers. *L. periclymenum* (D), woodbine

1 One of the deciduous Honeysuckles, Lonicera hildebrandiana grows up to 80 feet and has large fragrant flowers, creamy yellow, fading to orange.
2 Lonicera × tellmanniana a vigorous hybrid Honeysuckle, likes the shade.

1 Lonicera periclymenum, the Common Honeysuckle or Woodbine, grows wild in Britain and has strongly fragrant flowers. 2 Lonicera scrambles naturally and is used here to cover a pillar.

10–20 feet, yellow-white to purple, fragrant, June to August, Europe, North Africa, Asia Minor; vars. *belgica*, early Dutch honeysuckle, deep purple-red to yellow, May and June; *serotina*, late Dutch honeysuckle, red-purple, July to October. *L. sempervirens* (E), trumpet honeysuckle, 15 feet, yellow and scarlet, June to August, Conn. to Fla. to Texas. Evergreen in South, semi in North. *L. similis delavayi* (E or SE), white, ageing to yellow, August, China. *L. splendida* (E), 15–20 feet, leaves bluish-green, flowers cream, reddish outside, June to August, Spain. *L.* x *tellmanniana* (D), 15–20 feet, leaves large, flowers coppery-yellow, June and July, hybrid, prefers shade. *L. tragophylla* (D), 15 feet, showy orange-yellow flowers, June, China, prefers shade.

Shrubby: *L. alpigena* (D), 6 feet, yellow and red, April and May, Central Europe. *L. angustifolia* (D), 9–10 feet, pink and white, fragrant, April, Himalaya. *L. chaetocarpa* (D), 6 feet,

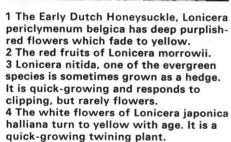

1 The Early Dutch Honeysuckle, Lonicera periclymenum belgica has deep purplish-red flowers which fade to yellow.
2 The red fruits of Lonicera morrowii.
3 Lonicera nitida, one of the evergreen species is sometimes grown as a hedge. It is quick-growing and responds to clipping, but rarely flowers.
4 The white flowers of Lonicera japonica halliana turn to yellow with age. It is a quick-growing twining plant.

primrose-yellow, May, China. *L. chrysantha* (D), 12 feet, pale yellow colour, flowers appear in May and June. Native to northeast Asia. *L. caerulea* (D), grows to a height of about 3–5 feet, yellow-white flowers, blue fruit, April and May, Northern Hemisphere. *L. fragrantissima* (SE), 6–8 feet, creamy-white, very fragrant, December to March, China. *L. hispida* (D), 3–5 feet, yellowish-white, May and June, Turkistan. *L. involucrata* (D), 4 feet, yellow, red bracts, June, Quebec to Alaska to Mexico. *L. korolkowii* (D), 12 feet, leaves greyish-blue, flowers rosy-pink, June, fruits red, Turkistan; var. *zabelii*, flowers deeper in colour. *L. ledebourii* (D), 9 feet, orange, June, California. *L. maackii* (D), 10–15 feet, white to yellow, fragrant, May and June, fruits red, Manchuria, Korea; var. *podocarpa*, a better form, branches more horizontal, freely-fruiting, China. *L. morrowii* (D), 8 feet, creamy-white to yellow, June, Japan. *L. myrtillus* (D), 3 feet, creamy-white, fragrant, May, fruits orange-red, Himalaya. *L. nitida* (E), 6–10 feet, densely leafed with very small leaves, much used for hedging, rarely flowers, China. *L. pileata* (E), 3–5 feet, small, yellowish-white fragrant flowers, May, fruits violet-purplish, China, sometimes used for planting under trees or on banks, but does not flower reliably. *L. × purpusii* (D), 6–8 feet, cream, fragrant, winter, hybrid. *L. pyrenaica* (D), 3 feet, slow-growing, cream and pink, May and June, Pyrenees, Balearic Isles. *L. quinquelocularis* (D), 8–10 feet, flowers white, ageing to yellow, June, fruits translucent white, Himalaya. *L. rupicola* (D), 3–4 feet, flowers fragrant, pink, May and June, Himalaya. *L. spinosa albertii* (syn. *L. albertii*) (D), prostrate, flowers fragrant, pinkish-lilac, May, Turkistan. *L. standishii* (SE), 6–8 feet, creamy-white, very fragrant, November to March, China. *L. syringantha* (D), 6–8 feet, rosy-lilac, very fragrant, May and June, China. *L. tartarica* (D), Tartarian honey-

1 Lonicera periclymenum has formed a quick-growing screen supported by a light trellis by this door.
2 The ripening fruits of Lonicera periclymenum in late summer.
3 Lonicera × americana, a strong-growing hybrid with long yellow and pink flowers in June and July.
4 Lonicera sempervirens, the Trumpet Honeysuckle is an evergreen, or semi-deciduous species for mild districts.

suckle, 8–10 feet, flowers pink, May and June, fruits red, Russia, Turkistan; vars. *alba,* white; *sibirica,* flowers rosy-red. *L. thibetica* (D), 4–6 feet, leaves white below, flowers fragrant, lilac-pink, May and June, fruits red, Tibet, western China. *L. trichosantha* (D), 5–6 feet, flowers pale to deep yellow, June, fruits red, China. *L. × vilmorinii* (D), 6–9 feet, flowers yellow, summer, fruits pink, hybrid. *L. xylosteum* (D), fly honeysuckle, 10 feet, yellowish white, May–June, Europe.

Cultivation Generous treatment of these climbers and shrubs produces good results. On the whole they are not very fastidious about soil, although they do better in one which is on the moist side. The shrubby species do best in full sun, the climbing kinds like shade at the roots, but should be so planted that the top can reach full light. Plant in October or March; any pruning which is required to restrict size should be done in early spring. Support in the form of fences, arbours or walls is needed by the climbers, and since they climb by twining, the wall or fence should have some wire or trellis to which they can cling. Species used for hedges, as *L. nitida,* should be planted when not more than 18 inches high at 18 inches apart, in October or April. Cut back to 9 inches high after planting to make sure that the base is well furnished with shoots. Thereafter trim as required in the

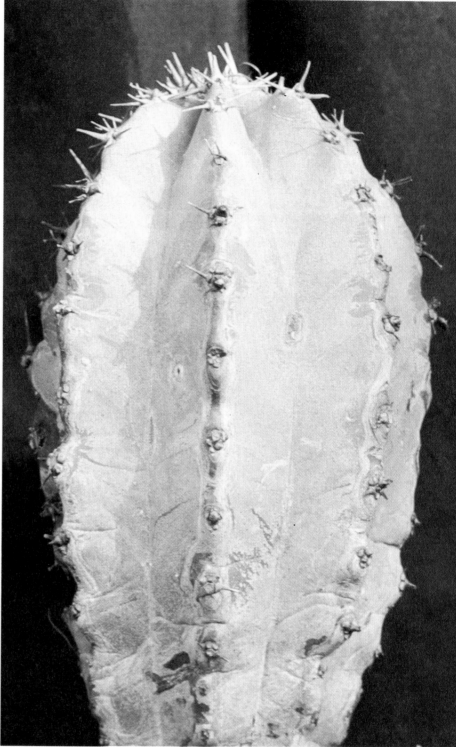

1 Lopezia lineata, a cool greenhouse plant with pinkish red flowers, comes from Central America.
2 A tall cactus from Arizona, Lophocereus schottii, has stout strong spines and green and pink flowers which open at night.

growing season until the height wanted is obtained (see also Hedges, Screens and Shelterbelts). Propagate loniceras from cuttings of firm young shoots in July or August placed in sandy soil in a shaded frame, or by layering, August to November. Seed, when available, can be sown in well-drained soil in a temperature of 55–60°F (13–16°C) in February–March.

Loofah Gourd—see Luffa

Loosestrife—see Lysimachia

Loosestrife, Purple—see Lythrum salicaria

Lopezia (lo-pe-zee-a)
Commemorating Thomas Lopez, a Spanish botanist of the sixteenth century who wrote on the flora of America *(Onagraceae).* Though there are between 15 and 20 species in . this Central American genus of shrubs, herbaceous, and annual plants, three only are to be found in gardens. The small flowers, of complex structure, usually in bright colours, are produced in decorative racemes. Grown in greenhouses or out of doors in the warmest states.

Species cultivated *L. albiflora,* 2 feet, perennial, white flowers, late summer–autumn, may be grown in a pot in the greenhouse. *L. coronata,* 1 foot, half hardy annual, red flowers, August. *L. lineata,* 3 feet, sub-shrub, red flowers, late summer, tender.
Cultivation *L. albiflora* can be grown from seed in pots of well-drained potting mix in the cool greenhouse, and needs full sun. *L. coronata* may be given half hardy annual treatment. Sow seed in March under glass, and plant out at the end · of May. *L. lineata* may be grown in the cool greenhouse in the

same way as *L. albiflora* but it can be propagated by cuttings of firm wood.

Lophocereus (loff-o-seer-ee-us)
From the Greek *lophos,* a crest, and *cereus,* referring to the bristly top of the flowering stem *(Cactaceae).* There is one species only in this genus, *L. schottii* from Arizona, a tall cactus with thick stems with short, strong spines. A few offsets are produced at the base of the plant. Flowering areoles develop long bristles at right angles to the stem. The flowers are pale green outside, pink inside, and open at night. A monstrous

rm of this plant is also cultivated. This as irregular ribs and no spines. The lant has a knobbly appearance.

ultivation The medium should consist f good cactus mix with ⅛ part added of oarse sand, grit or broken brick. Vinter temperature should be a minimum of 45°F (7°C). In summer normal reenhouse temperatures suffice. It may e grown in either shade or full sun. ropagation is mainly by seed sown in ell-drained seed mix and kept moist nd shaded at 70°F (21°C) until seedlings ppear when more light can be given. ffsets on the tops of tall plants can be emoved and rooted in a mixture of oarse sand and peat after allowing the ut surface to dry for two days.

ophomyrtus (loff-o-mir-tus)

rom the Greek *lophos*, a crest, and *Myrtus*, to which the genus is related *(Myrtaceae)*. A New Zealand genus of mall evergreen trees which will grow in moist shady conditions; in cultivation in Vorth they are grown in cool, frost-free reenhouses, outdoors where warm. They evelop a broadly columnar habit.

pecies cultivated *L. bullata*, 10–25 feet, eaves copper-coloured blistered, 1–2 nches long, the most attractive feature f this plant, flowers white, myrtle-like; hough attractive in themselves, they are hardly noticeable against the foliage. *L. obcordata*, 5–15 feet, the leaves are much smaller than the last species and they also lack the copper colour, flowers white, small. *L.* × *ralphii*, 7–15 feet, a naturally occurring hybrid between the above two species, intermediate in form between them.

Cultivation Though relatively slow growing lophomyrtus are generally easy to grow either in a soil bed or as pot plants. Only enough heat is required in winter to keep out the frosts. The soil should be well-drained and slightly acid, such as a mixture of lime-free loam, peat, leafmould and sand. Semi-ripe cuttings can be rooted, with some care, using a mist unit, or closed frame. The initial potting and establishment must be done carefully so as to avoid any root damage. Older plants produce berries containing several seeds which can be sown when ripe.

Lophophora (loff-off-or-a)

From the Greek *lophos*, a crest, and *phoreo*, I bear, referring to the hairs borne on the areoles *(Cactaceae)*. A small genus of greenhouse cacti from Central America, previously known as *Anaholium* and once placed under *Echinocactus*. The drug called mescal or peyotl is extracted from them and was used by the ancient Mexicans in religious rites. It is supposed to give the eaters hallucinations when they hear sweet music and have pleasant dreams. Recent research has shown it to be a powerful emetic. The plants have a strong root-stock, no main ridges and no spines. Areoles are present with tufts of wool.

Species cultivated *L. lewinii*, larger-growing version of the following species, small pink flowers, summer. *L. williamsii*, plump, almost round stem, no spines, pink flowers, summer. There is a cristate form of this in cultivation. *L. zeigleri*, a single head, pale yellow flowers.

Cultivation Lophophoras will grow well in a well-drained potting mixture with ⅙ part added of sharp sand, grit and broken brick. They require re-potting every three or four years, and the sunniest position in the greenhouse. Do not water between October and March, and in the remaining time, only when the soil has dried out. Temperature in the winter should be 40°F (4°C) minimum, but the normal seasonal summer temperature will be satisfactory. Plants

The plump, almost round stem of the cactus Lophophora williamsii, which sometimes bears pink flowers.

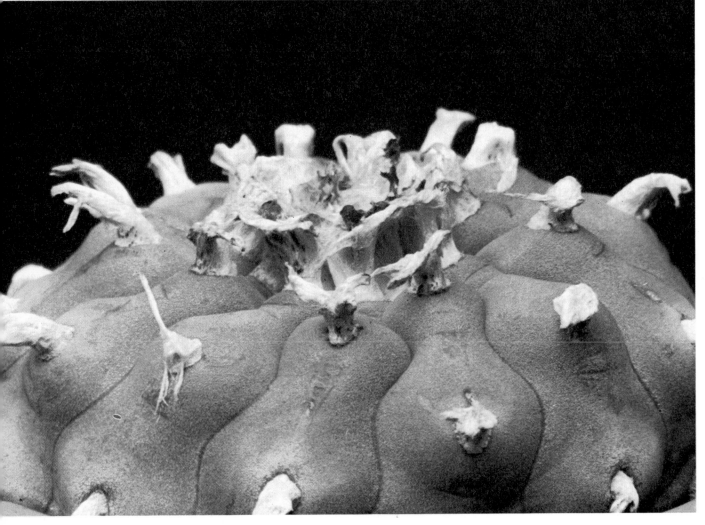

tend to shrink and become very soft in winter, but quickly firm up when watered. Propagate from seed sown in well-drained seed mixture and lightly covered. Keep shaded and moist at a temperature of 75°F (24°C). The plants make offsets when older, but these are difficult to remove for cuttings.

Lopping
A term used to describe a severe pruning operation in which large branches of a tree are removed. The operation should not be undertaken lightly since it usually adversely alters the balance and symmetry of a tree. With conifers, lopping can be disastrous as they do not generally have the ability to produce new growth, which is a property of the broad-leaved trees. The operation known as pollarding and coppicing are really special kinds of lopping. When lopping is essential it should not be undertaken at the time when the sap is rising, and with deciduous trees should be completed while they are leafless. The wounds should be painted with a fungicidal paint, such as Arbrex, to prevent infection and decay.

Loquat—see Eriobotrya japonica

Lord Anson's Pea—see Lathyrus magellanicus

Lords and Ladies—see Arum maculatum

Loropetalum (lor-o-pet-al-um)
From the Greek *loron*, a thong, and *petalon*, a petal, in reference to the thong-shaped petals *(Hamamelidaceae)*. A genus of a single species, *L. sinense*, a valuable, though tender, Chinese evergreen shrub, 12 feet tall, which produces its clusters of white flowers in February, when they are very welcome. The flower clusters somewhat resemble those of the witch hazel *(Hamamelis)* though the fact that the flowers are white and the leaves evergreen, sufficiently distinguishes this shrub from *Hamamelis* species.

Though *L. sinense* is tender and can be grown outdoors only in warm areas, it grows farther north with protection. Elsewhere it needs cold greenhouse treatment. It needs sun, but should not be forced. From June to October the potted shrub may be placed out of doors to ripen the new growth fully. Prune only to maintain shape. Propagation is by cuttings placed in sandy soil in a frame from July to October, or by seeds sown in similar soil at any time.

Lotus (lo-tus)
From the Greek *lotos*, an ancient Greek name for certain plants in this family *(Leguminosae)*. A genus of 60 species of low-growing herbs and sub-shrubs, with pea-like flowers, from the temperate regions of the world, including Britain, but absent from the Americas. This

genus should not be confused with the sacred lotus belonging to the genus *Nelumbo*.

Species cultivated *L. angustissimus*, prostrate, flowers yellow tipped red, May and June, southern Europe, rock garden. *L. australis*, to 2 feet, white or reddish-purple, July, Australia. *L. bertholetii*, coral gem, 2 feet, scarlet, alpine house, Teneriffe. *L. corniculatus*, bird's foot trefoil, creeping, yellow marked with red, Northern Hemisphere including Britain. *L. gebelia*, creeping, red, fading to pink, June and July, greenhouse, Asia Minor. *L. jacobaeus*, 1–3 feet, dark purple and yellow, summer, greenhouse, Cape Verde Island. *L. uliginosus*, 3–4 inches, yellow, summer, Europe, Asia, North Africa, moist places.

Cultivation Most species are fully hardy

1 Loropetalum sinense, a tender evergreen shrub, related to the witch hazel (Hamamelis), flowers in February.
2 Lopping is a drastic pruning operation. Here a large branch has been lopped from a pear tree. The cut surface has been painted to prevent decay.

in mild areas and are mostly used on dry places in the rock garden, where they will grow with abandon. The exception is *L. uliginosus* which is a plant for the pond side or a bog garden. Of the tender species, *L. bertholetii* is the species most commonly grown. It needs a sandy, open mixture that is not too rich, in full sun and with plenty of ventilation; avoid stagnant winter conditions. These tender species can be grown out of doors during the summer months and housed in winter, although they are often used to furnish an alpine house during the summer. Propagation is by division of the clumps or by cuttings taken of the young growths during spring. The seeds often have a hard coat and benefit from scarification before sowing (see also Nymphaea and Nelumbo).

Lotus Tree—see Diospyros lotus

Loudon, John Claudius and Jane
Born at Cambuslang, Lanarkshire, John Claudius Loudon (1783–1843) soon showed signs of remarkable energy and intelligence, and moved to Edinburgh so that he might have a better education. At fourteen years of age he was apprenticed to a firm of nurserymen. In the evenings, he studied and taught himself French and Italian, making translations of works in these languages for a publisher. He also studied botany.

In 1803 he came to London, and was stricken with illness which dogged him all his life. During convalescence, he took up farming and with his highly efficient methods soon made a fortune. At the same time he wrote books and journalism. Investing his fortune, he travelled widely in Europe during the last stages of the Napoleonic wars. On

1 Tetragonolobus maritimus.
2 Lotus criticus has small yellow flowers and sparse blue-green leaves.

his return, he found his fortune had gone, and for the rest of his life suffered financial troubles.

He produced in 1822 his *Encyclopaedia of Gardening,* which went through several editions, and in 1826 launched the first British gardening periodical, *The Gardener's Magazine*. In these, he pioneered a scientific approach, pleading, too, for increased education and better social conditions for working gardeners.

In 1828 he reviewed an early example of science fiction, *The Mummy*. It impressed him as a forecast of the twenty-second century, and he arranged a meeting with the author. To his surprise, it proved to be a young woman, Jane Webb (1807–58), whom he married. From then on, they worked in close collaboration, Mrs Loudon pioneering gardening for women.

In 1838 he published his 8-volume *Arboretum et Fruticetum Britannicum,* still the greatest and most detailed study of trees and shrubs hardy in Britain that has been published.

After his death, his widow carried on with his work. Their garden in Porchester Terrace, Bayswater, was famous for the remarkable collection of plants they grew in it. A preservation order was placed upon the house in 1968.

Lousewort—see Pedicularis

Love Apple—see Tomato

Love Grass—see Eragrostis

Love Tree—see Cercis siliquastrum

Lovage
This is a valuable tall perennial herb, known botanically as *Ligusticum officinale (Umbelliferae)*. The decorative compound leaves have a delicate savoury taste somewhere between that of parsley and celery. Its flavour is so good that it is surprising that it is not more used in salads and as a garnish. In a herb garden its height of 7 feet gives it distinction, and, as it is capable of spreading considerably, it should be widely spaced in the bed, and may be combined with other large herbs such as fennel and angelica.
Cultivation Lovage is propagated from seed, or the roots may be divided in the autumn, and the divisions spaced 1 foot apart. It will grow in any ordinary garden soil.

Love-in-a-mist—see Nigella damascena

Love-lies-bleeding—see Amaranthus caudatus

Low-bush Blueberry—see Vaccinium angustifolium

Lucerne—see Medicago sativa

Lucombe Oak—see Quercus x hispanica lucombeana

Luculia (lu-ku-lee-a)

Probably from *Luculi Swa,* the native Nepalese name *(Rubiaceae).* A small genus of beautiful, tall half-hardy evergreen shrubs from temperate east Asia. The foliage is good and the plants bear clusters of pink or white very sweetly-scented flowers. Tender.

Species cultivated *L. gratissima,* 14 feet, rose-pink, autumn-winter flowering, Himalaya. *L. pinceana,* 6–10 feet, white changing to creamy-pink, May–September, Himalaya.

Cultivation These shrubs should be planted in a border in the warm greenhouse in April, or they may be grown in very large pots or tubs. Good drainage is important. Water well during the summer, especially outdoors. Keep soil barely moist from December until April. In summer the foliage should be sprayed twice daily, as this treatment helps to combat attacks of red spider mite. Prune hard back in December after the flowers have died, to encourage strong new growths on which next season's flowers will appear. Propagation is by seed, seedlings can take two to three years to flower, or by cuttings of half-ripe shoots rooted in a propagating frame with bottom heat.

Lucuma (lu-su-ma)

The Peruvian name for *L. obovata (Sapotaceae).* A genus of trees and shrubs, most of them natives of tropical America, some grown in their native countries for their edible fruits. They need warmhouse treatment. Can be grown outdoors in south Florida.

Species cultivated *L. mammosa* (E), marmalade fruit, mamey sapote, sapote, to 100 feet in nature, leaves light green, leathery, to 10 inches long, flowers white, in small clusters, fruits rounded or egg-shaped, to 7 inches long, reddish-brown, edible, South America. *L. nervosa* (E), egg fruit, to 25 feet in nature, leaves bright green, to 8 inches long, flowers greenish-white, fruits rounded or egg-shaped, to 4 inches long, orange-yellow, edible, South America.

Cultivation Grow these plants in large containers in the warmhouse, in a mixture of 2 parts of sandy loam and 1 part of peat. Maintain a minimum winter temperature of 55–60°F (13–16°C), rising in summer to 65–70°F (18–21°C). Plants will need ample water in spring and summer, less in winter, though the soil should never be allowed to dry out. Propagation is by seeds, sown in heat in spring, or by short cuttings, made from well-ripened growths and rooted in a propagating frame with bottom heat.

Ludwigia (lud-wig-ee-a)

Commemorating the eighteenth-century German botanist, C. G. Ludwig, *(Onagraceae).* A genus of about 30 species of aquatic or water-side plants, mainly from warm and temperate regions of

1 A tender evergreen shrub, Luculia pinceana, grows up to 10 feet and has creamy white flowers fading to pink, in succession from May to September.
2 The plant from which loofahs are obtained, Luffa cylindrica.

South America. The name is sometimes spelt Ludvigia. One species only, *L. natans,* is in common cultivation. It is a creeping aquatic with small leaves, dark green on the upper surface, purplish below. It has small, yellow, insignificant flowers.

Cultivation This may be planted at any time in an aquarium as a submerged aquatic, or in spring, out of doors by the edges of pools. Propagation is by cuttings or division at any time, or by seeds sown in March in pans of loam covered with water.

Luffa (lu-fa)

From *louff,* the Arabic name of *L. cylindrica (Cucurbitaceae).* A small genus of tender annuals, climbing by means of tendrils, widely spread throughout the warmer parts of the world. The only species likely to be found in cultivation is *L. cylindrica,* the dishcloth gourd, loofah, suakwa or vegetable sponge, which grows to 10 feet or more. It has yellow flowers in summer, but is grown for its club-shaped fruits, up to 1 foot long, which are edible when young, but, when mature and when the soft matter has rotted away, form the fibrous bathroom loofahs of commerce.

Cultivation Seeds are raised in spring in a temperature of 70°F (21°C). Pot up and carry indoors until it is warm enough to set outdoors. They can also be planted directly in the garden provided that the season is both warm enough and long enough. Moisture must be generously supplied throughout the growing season, and some syringeing is essential.

unaria (loon-air-e-a)
rom the Latin *luna,* the moon, referring
the round and silvery seed cases
Cruciferae). Honesty, moonwort or
oneywort. A genus of 2 species, of
hich *L. annua,* a hardy biennial, has,
nce it was introduced from Europe
bout 400 years ago, managed to escape
om gardens and establish itself here
nd there in the wild. It has two features
hich have ensured its popularity; the
right purple or mauve flowers and the
nsuing flattened pod, called a siliqua.
his siliqua has a central transparent
artition, the replum, upon which the
attened seeds are placed. When the two
uter valves fall away or are rubbed
way the replum is revealed as a moon-
haped pearly translucent object of some
eauty. In this state it is much used in
rrangements of dried flowers, seed-pods
nd other plant material.

pecies cultivated *L. annua* (syn. *L.
iennis*), 2½ feet, biennial, white, purple
r pink flowers, May–July; var. *varie-
ata,* cream variegated leaves; 'Mun-
tead Purple', 3 feet, is a cultivar. *L.
ediviva,* 2–3 feet, hardy perennial,
urple, fragrant, May–June.

ultivation *L. annua* needs the standard
eatment for biennials (see Biennials),
nd the final planting positions may be
ightly shaded, though they will grow in
ull sun. Plants make quite large

The papery seed heads of Honesty or
Moneywort, Lunaria annua, persist
through the winter and are useful for
decoration.
2 A pale form of Lunaria rediviva.
3 The purple and white forms of
Honesty, Lunaria annua, flower in May.

1

2

3

specimens and their lower leaves in particular are large and coarse, so that they should be given ample room. They should be planted at least 1 foot apart. The perennial lunaria may be raised from seed, or plants may be divided in March or April.

Lungwort—see Pulmonaria

Lupinus (lu-py-nus)

From the Latin *lupus,* a wolf (destroyer), because it was thought that the plants depleted the fertility of the soil by sheer numbers *(Leguminosae).* Lupin. A genus of over 300 species of annuals, perennials and sub-shrubs, mainly from North America, though there are a few Mediterranean species which, since Roman times, have been used for green manuring. This is surprising since the Roman farmers did not know that within the root nodules were colonies of bacteria capable of utilising nitrogen to produce valuable nitrates. The fine Russell hybrid lupins are among the most showy of herbaceous perennials and have a wide colour range embracing the three primary colours: red, yellow and blue. They do not, however, thrive on alkaline (chalky or limy) soils.

Species cultivated Annual: *L. densi-florus,* 1½–2 feet, yellow, fragrant, July–August, California. *L. hartwegii,* 2–3 feet, blue, white and red, July–October, Mexico. *L. hirsutissimus,* 1 foot, with stinging hairs, purple flowers, July, California. *L. hirsutus,* 2–3 feet, blue and white, July–August, Mediterranean

1 Named forms of Lupins can be propagated by taking cuttings with a sharp knife in March.
2 The top foliage needs to be trimmed but the roots are left intact.
3 The cuttings are inserted in a sharp sandy mixture and can be left out of doors or be protected by a cold frame.
4 Lupin 'Serenade' has sturdy columns of closely spaced flowers.
5 The yellow flowered Lupinus arboreus.
6 The bicolor Lupin 'Vogue'.
7 A Lupin border in June has every colour of the rainbow. Here, at Pyrford, England, plants such as Lychnis, Catmint and Geranium are planted in front.

region. *L. luteus,* 2 feet, yellow, June–August, south Europe. *L. mutabilis,* 5 feet, white, blue and yellow, summer, Colombia. *L. pubescens,* 3 feet, violet, blue and white, summer, Mexico. *L. subcarnosus,* 1 foot, blue and white, July, Texas to Guatemala.

Perennial: *L. nootkatensis,* 3 feet, blue, purple and yellow, May–July, Washington to Alaska. *L. polyphyllus,* 4 feet, blue, white or pink, June–August, California.

Shrubby: *L. arboreus,* 8 feet, short-lived, yellow, white or violet, fragrant, summer, California. *L. excubicus,* 1–5 feet, blue, violet, summer, California; var. *hallii* (syn. *L. paynei*), larger flowers.

Russell hybrids: These well-known hybrids have developed from a cross made at the end of the last century between *L. arboreus* and *L. polyphyllus.* Some years later a seedling with rose-pink flowers appeared, *L. p. roseus,* and with the help of this, Mr George Russell was able to develop and select the superb colours and strong spikes that are available today in the now famous Russell strain.

Some good cultivars are: 'Betty Astell', 3 feet, deep pink; 'Blue Jacket', 3 feet, deep blue and white; 'Fireglow', 3 feet, orange and gold; 'George Russell', 4 feet, pink and cream; 'Gladys Cooper', 4½ feet, smoky blue; 'Joan of York', 4 feet, cerise and pink; 'Josephine', 4 feet, slate blue and yellow; 'Lady Diana Abdy', 3½ feet, blue and white; 'Lady Fayne', 3 feet, coral and rose; 'Lilac Time', 3½ feet, rosy-lilac; 'Mrs Micklethwaite', 3 feet, salmon-pink and gold; 'Mrs Noel Terry', 3 feet, pink and cream; 'Thundercloud', 3 feet, blue and rose-mauve.

Cultivation The most popular section is that of the perennial species, which are easily grown in any sunny border that has not too much lime or chalk. Mulch with compost in spring, and cut down the old flower stems in October.

The Russell lupins are now available from seed. In England named forms are still raised from cuttings of young

1

2

3

1 There are several types of annual Lupins useful for cutting.
2 Lupin 'Lilac Time' has mauve and white spikes of flower.
3 Lupin 'Tom Reeves' just coming into flower in mid-June.
4 Lupin 'Fireglow' is a sturdy cultivar with orange and gold flowers.
5 The cultivar 'Wheatsheaf' has rather flat-topped columns of flowers which appear at first and mature to a golden orange.
6 The long spikes of apricot-pink flowers of Lupin 'Harvester'.

4

5

growths in March. These are not among the longest lived plants and it is wise to renew them from time to time. Since they are hardy they may be raised from seed sown in drills ¼ inch deep in April and put in their final places in the autumn. Many will flower during the following summer.

The annuals are also treated as hardy and seeds are sown in drills in April. In May the seedlings must be thinned out to 9 inches apart. It is important with both annual and perennial lupins to remove the forming seed pods before they can grow large enough to retard the flowering capacity of the plants.

The tree lupin, *L. arboreus*, may be raised from seed with extreme ease. These shrubs make rapid growth and will flower in their second season. They are not long-lived out of their range, but manage to renew themselves by self-sown seedlings. The shrubby lupin, *L. excubicus*, makes a fine large plant, but needs some frost protection. Like most lupins this has very fragrant flowers.

Luronium (lur-o-ne-um)
Derivation uncertain *(Alismataceae)*. A genus of one species of hardy aquatic plant, a native of western Europe including Britain, commonly called the floating water plantain and closely related to *Alisma*, the water plantain. *L. natans*, also known as *Elisma natans*, a variant of *Alisma*, has dainty little, three-petalled, white flowers floating on

6

the surface of shallow water in early summer. The floating green leaves are up to 1 inch long.

Cultivation Plant the fibrous roots in spring in any type of soil in shallow water at the edge of a pool. This plant is quite useful as an oxygenator. Increase by division of the rootstock in spring.

Lute

This is a device (sometimes called a true lute) which enables the gardener to work in top-dressings or to level the ground. It usually takes the form of a simple wooden or metal frame or grid about 2 feet wide and 18 inches long. Several parallel cross-pieces connect the sides and it is these which work top-dressings in or level undulating ground as the grid is pulled backwards and forwards by its long handle.

A modern version is made of metal and the grid is reversible with two working sides. One is smooth-edged for levelling and spreading operations the the other is sharp-edged for rubbing in materials or for the production of a fine tilth.

Lutyens, Sir Edwin Landseer

Sir Edwin Lutyens (1869–1944) was the last and one of the greatest British architects to work on the grand scale in traditional styles. His connection with gardening was fortuitous and was due to meeting, while still a young and little known man, Miss Gertrude Jekyll. For her he built a house, Munstead Wood in Surrey, around which, and in consultation with Lutyens, she designed the garden which was to become a famous, much-copied example of her style.

Henceforth, when a garden designer was needed by Lutyens, Miss Jekyll was called in. In many of his houses, around the building he planned, often most beautifully and ingeniously, a formal, architectural area to link it with the garden proper. For such a place, as well as the garden itself, Miss Jekyll would join with him and in particular arrange the planting.

Lutyens was, however, responsible for some garden designs of his own, such as at Ashby St Ledgers in Northamptonshire and above all, the vast formal garden round the President's Residence in New Delhi, a supreme achievement.

Luzula (lu-zu-la)

Possibly from *Luciola,* a glow-worm, application doubtful *(Juncaceae).* Woodrush. A genus of herbaceous perennials of moderate size, decorative in appearance, with grass-like foliage, which may

1 A lute is used to work in top dressings and is useful on an established lawn.
2 The true lute is made of metal.
3 The Yew Garden at Ammerdown Park, Bath, a garden designed by Sir Edwin Lutyens.
4 A typical Luzula, one of the decorative wood-rushes.

well be planted with rock plants to give an alpine appearance to the rock garden. Many luzulas are, in fact, alpine plants, and six species are found among British flora. Others are found widely distributed over temperate regions but a very few only of these have ever been deliberately planted in gardens. The late E. A. Bowles had the trick of planting chosen woodrushes and grasses among his (mainly alpine) flowering plants.

Species cultivated *L. lutea,* 6 inches, yellowish leaves and flower spikes, Alps, Pyrenees. *L. marginata,* 1 foot, silver lines edging the leaves, Europe. *L. maxima,* 1–2 feet, tufted, grassy leaves, brown flower spikes, Europe, including Britain. *L. nivea,* 2 inches, creamy white flower spikes, European Alps.

Cultivation These very easy plants will grow in any soil, in sun or partial shade, on dry banks or by the sides of streams. The great barrier to their popularity is that they can (and do) so easily harbour unwanted grasses which quickly become impossible to disentangle from a carefully cultivated clump of woodrush.

Luzuriaga (luz-u-re-a-ga)
Named to commemorate Don Ignatio M. R. de Luzuriaga, a Spanish botanist *(Philesiaceae).* A genus of 3 species only, natives of New Zealand and South America. They are low-growing shrubs with small, stalkless, and conspicuously-veined leaves. The flowers are white, bell- or star-shaped, borne singly, or a few together in the leaf axils.

Species cultivated *L. erecta,* 1½ feet, a much-branched, semi-climbing shrub, flowers white, occasionally dotted reddish brown, drooping, bell-shaped, Chile. *L. marginata,* 6 inches, creeping habit, flowers white, fragrant, followed by white berries, Falkland Islands, Patagonia, Tierra del Fuego, New Zealand. *L. radicans,* 4–6 inches, wiry-stemmed shrub, flowers starry, pure white, larger than in above species, Chile, Peru.

Cultivation These may be treated as half-hardy shrubs and grown in blocks of upland peat in a very slightly heated greenhouse, or they may be grown as epiphytes on logs or tree ferns. *L. radicans* may be grown out of doors in the milder regions, in moist soil and shady places. Propagation is by cuttings of half-ripened wood taken in summer and inserted in sand with gentle bottom heat. Very rare in the United States.

Lycaste (ly-kas-tee)
Commemorating *Lycaste,* a Sicilian beauty *(Orchidaceae).* A genus of terrestrial and epiphytic orchids, from tropical America and the West Indies, with plump pseudobulbs and in most species plicate (pleated), deciduous foliage. The flowers are mostly large and showy and are borne singly on the spikes, which appear at or near the time of the new growth, from the base of the pseudobulbs.

1 The deep yellow flowers of Lycaste crinita are on comparatively long stems.
2 Lycaste 'Wyld Court' has pale pink petals with a white reverse.
3 The pale green and whitish petals of Lycaste candida are flushed and spotted pink and purple.

Species cultivated *L. aromatica,* smallish, orange-yellow flowers, very fragrant, winter and spring, Mexico. *L. candida* (syn. *L. brevispatha*), pale green and whitish, flushed pink, spotted rose-purple, spring, Guatemala. *L. costata,* large ivory-white flowers, summer, Peru. *L. cruenta,* orange-yellow with a reddish blotch at the base of the lip, spring, Guatemala. *L. deppei,* green, white, yellow and red spotted, winter, spring, Mexico. *L. dyeriana,* plant and flowers pendent, green, summer, Peru. *L. gigantea,* green with brown and low lip, summer, Ecuador. *L. lanipes*, ~~wh~~ite and greenish-white, autumn, ~~Br~~azil. *L. lasioglossa*, reddish-brown, lip ~~ye~~llow very woolly, winter, Guatemala. ~~L.~~ *leucantha*, greenish and creamy-white, ~~va~~rious, Costa Rica. *L. locusta*, green, ~~ti~~p with white hairs, summer, Peru. *L. ~~lo~~giscapa,* green, spring. *L. x lucianii,* a ~~na~~tural hybrid, rose-mauve, spring, ~~Gu~~atemala. *L. macrobulbon*, orange-~~ye~~llow, tinged green, summer, Colombia. ~~L.~~ *macrophylla*, greenish, white, rose and ~~cr~~imson spotted, various, Brazil. *L. ~~sk~~inneri*, very large, beautiful flowers, ~~so~~ft rose and purplish, somewhat vari-~~ab~~le, winter and spring, Guatemala; ~~va~~rs. *alba*, pure white; *delicatissima*, ~~wh~~ite and pink; *hellemensis*, deep rose-~~pu~~rple; *picta*, rose and creamy-white; ~~Pi~~nk Pearl', rose-pink and crimson; ~~re~~ginae, white and red; *superba*, rose-~~cr~~imson and bluish white; *virginalis,* ~~wh~~ite, flushed rose, tinged lemon. **~~Cu~~ltivation** Provide a mixture of 3 parts ~~of~~ fibrous loam, 1 part of osmunda fibre, ~~an~~d 1 part of sphagnum moss in well-~~dr~~ained pots. Fibrous peat can be used ~~as~~ a substitute for osmunda fibre, but ~~gr~~eater care with watering will be ~~ne~~eded. Moist and well-aired conditions, ~~at~~ a temperature of 60°F (16°C) in

summer are preferred, together with light shading. Water should be given sparingly when the new growth appears and freely afterwards. A decided rest should be given in the winter at 55°F (13°C), or lower if the atmosphere is kept drier. In autumn, matured plants can be exposed to full light. As with all orchids with plicate foliage, syringeing should be avoided, at least until the leaves have become fully grown. Propagation is by division at potting time in spring, and by removing sound back bulbs and placing them singly in well-crocked pots, topped with sphagnum moss.

Lychee—see Litchi

Lychnis (lik-nis)
From the Greek *lychnos,* a lamp, alluding to the brilliantly-coloured flowers *(Caryophyllaceae)*. This small genus from

1 Lycaste leucantha from Costa Rica has green and creamy white flowers, the lower petals always green.
2 The large flowers of Lycaste lasioglossa are cinnamon brown in colour.
3 The bright red flowers of Lychnis chalcedonica, a fine herbaceous perennial.
4 The Red Campion, Lychnis dioica, is a British plant with deep pink flowers.

the north temperate zone of the Old World contains some good herbaceous perennials and one good hardy annual. Two impressive British wild plants, the red and the white campion belong here, and, in fact, are worthy of garden cultivation, the white one in particular for its extreme fragrance in the evening. There is a natural hybrid between these two plants which has delicate pink flowers. The ragged robin, *L. flos-cuculi,* is also a British plant quite worth growing in the wild garden. It is interesting that *L. chalcedonica* gives us the brightest scarlet in the herbaceous garden, while *L. flos-jovis* (syn. *Agrostemma flos-jovis, A. coronaria flos-jovis*) gives us the most saturated magenta to accompany its greyish foliage.
Species cultivated *L. alba* (syn. *Melandrium album*), white campion, 3 feet, May to August, Europe. *L. alpina* (syn. *Viscaria alpina*), 6 inches, pink, summer, Europe. *L. arkwrightii*, 1½ feet, scarlet, summer, hybrid. *L. chalcedonica*, 3 feet, scarlet, summer, Russia. *L. coeli-rosa* (syn. *Silene coeli-rosa*), rose of heaven, 1 foot, purple and various other colours, annual, Levant; *L. coronaria*, 2½ feet, magenta, July and August, south Europe. *L. dioica (Melandrium rubrum),*

the red campion, 3 feet, strong pink, summer, Britain. *L. flos-cuculi,* 1½ feet, ragged robin, rose-pink, May and June, Britain. *L. fulgens,* 9 inches, vermilion, May to September, Siberia. *L. grandiflora* (syn. *L. coronata*), 18 inches, salmon, summer, Japan. *L.* x *haageana,* 9 inches, very large scarlet flowers, hybrid. *L. lagascae* (syn. *Petrocoptis lagascae*), 3 inches, rose and white, summer, Pyrenees. *L. viscaria* (syn. *Viscaria vulgaris*), catchfly, 1 foot, reddish-purple, summer, Europe.

Cultivation Most lychnis are very easily grown in any kind of soil and can withstand dry conditions better than many other herbaceous plants. However, *L. alpina* and *L. lagascae* need rather richer soil. Some of these herbaceous plants are rather short-lived perennials —*L. alba* is almost biennial. All may be readily raised from seed sown in March in the open garden, as they are supremely hardy. The one annual species needs the standard hardy annual treatment.

Lycium (ly-se-um)

Supposedly from the Greek *lykion,* a plant of Lycia, in Asia Minor *(Solanaceae).* Box thorn. The lyciums number 80 species, but very few are worthy of cultivation. They are mostly quite hardy evergreen or deciduous shrubs from temperate or sub-tropical regions, generally climbing or scrambling through other shrubs in a mixed hedge. In many species the branches are thorny. The flowers are not large or brilliant in colour, but are succeeded by decorative coloured fruits, for the sake of which these plants are grown. *L. chinense* is known to many people as a hedge scrambler at a number of seaside resorts, as it has the great advantage of standing up to salt-laden winds.

Species cultivated *L. afrum* (D), 8–10 feet, flowers purple, fragrant, May and June, berries red to black, South Africa, needs wall treatment. *L. chinense,* tea-tree, quick-growing climber, flowers purple, June to September, fruits orange, 1 inch long, August–October, China. *L. grevilleanum* (D), 4–6 feet, flowers purplish, June to August, fruit orange-red, small, Argentine. *L. halimifolium* (D), 9 feet, flowers dull purple, June to August, fruits scarlet, south Europe; this is scarcely distinguishable from *L. chinense. L. pallidum,* 6 feet, flowers greenish-yellow, purple-tinged, more showy than in other species, hanging below the branches, scarlet fruits not always formed, Utah to Mexico.

1 The scarlet flowers of Lychnis haageana make a good splash of colour in June and July. The flowers are large for the genus.
2 The greenish-yellow flowers of Lycium pallidum hang down from the branches, and are followed by scarlet fruits when grown in favourable conditions.

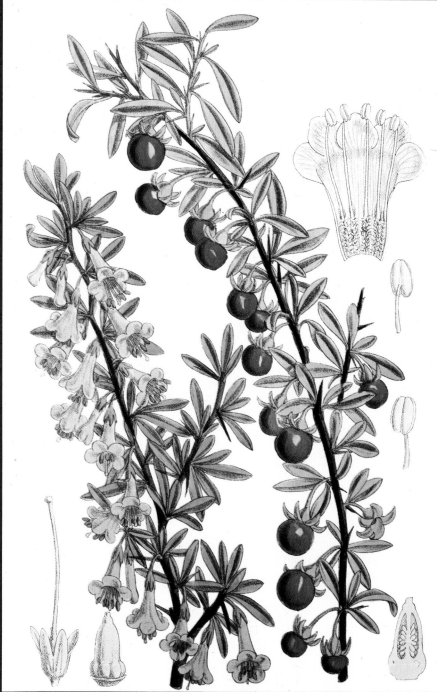

the company of their near relations, the ferns. A fine powdery substance is obtained from some species having properties which make it useful in surgery, and for certain other purposes.
Species cultivated *L. clavatum*, common club moss, stag's horn moss, a creeping form 3 inches high, Arctic, north and south temperate regions, including the US. *L. selago,* fir club moss, 3 inches, north and south temperate regions, including Britain. *L. squarrosum*, 2 feet, tender species, India. *L. taxifolium* 9–12 inches, tender species, West Indies. *L. verticillatum,* procumbent, a widely spread tropical species.
Cultivation Deep moist peaty soil is the best growing medium for hardy species. These may be grown on the shady side of a rock garden. They may also be placed in a carboy or Wardian case, when some charcoal and a liberal amount of limestone chips should be added to the soil mixture. Water once or twice a week, during spring and summer, once a fortnight in autumn, once a month in winter. Provide a little ventilation each day. Tender species should have a soil mixture containing equal parts of loam, peat, limestone chips and silver sand. Water generously from March to September and shade from direct sunlight. The temperature from March to September should be 65–75°F (18–24°C), and from September to March 55–65°F (13–18°C). Propagate by division from February to April.

Lycoris (ly-kor-is)
Named after a beautiful actress in Ancient Rome, the mistress of Mark Antony *(Amaryllidaceae)*. A small genus of Japanese and Chinese bulbous plants, some of which require greenhouse treatment. As with the closely related *Amaryllis belladonna* the leaves are produced first and the funnel-shaped flowers later. In most species the leaves are long and narrow, or strap shaped.
Species cultivated *L. aurea* (syn. *Amaryllis aurea*), golden spider lily, 1½ feet, yellow flowers borne in an umbel, August. *L. radiata* (syn. *Amaryllis radiata*), 1½ feet, flowers red, June. *L. sanguinea*, 2 feet, flowers red, summer. *L. squamigera*, 2 feet, flowers rosy lilac, fragrant; summer.
Cultivation Two common species which may be grown in the open garden, in light, well-drained soil, well mulched in the North, are *L. sanguinea* and *L. squamigera*. The others need greenhouse treatment in North, should be potted in an equal mixture of loam, leafmould (or peat) and sand and put in a light, sunny, cool position. The pots must be specially well-drained. Water moderately while plants are in leaf, but afterwards keep the soil quite dry. Re-potting should be done each year after flowering is over and before new leaves appear. Propagate from offsets, treated as bulbs, September to December. All hardy in South.

1 The flowers of Lycoris squamigera, a Japanese bulbous plant, are carried in a wide umbel, which has given rise to the common name of Golden Spider Lily. The white flowers are tinged rosy-lilac and are fragrant.
2 A typical Lycopodium, one of the Club Mosses, decorative flowerless plants.

Cultivation In general these shrubs will grow in any kind of soil and in sun or partial shade, although the best results are obtained when the plants are set against a wall in rich soil. The box thorns make suckers freely, and these provide a ready means of propagation.

Lycopersicon—see Tomato cultivation

Lycopodium (ly-co-po-di-um)
From the Greek *lykos*, a wolf and *pous*, a foot; the rhizomes are said to resemble a wolf's paw *(Lycopodiaceae)*. Club moss. These mosses, and the related genus *Selaginella,* are among the most decorative non-flowering plants. Tender and hardy species are cultivated, and they look particularly well when grown in

1 A climbing fern for the cool
greenhouse, Lygodium japonicum grows
up to 10 feet. It is native of an area
stretching from Japan to Australia.
2 The white flowers of Lyonothamnus
floribundus, a graceful tree.

Lygodium (ly-go-dee-um)

From the Greek *lygodes,* twining, referring to the habit of the plants *(Schi-
zaeaceae).* A genus of about 40 species of
climbing ferns, found in sub-tropical,
tropical and temperate parts of the
world. They climb clock-wise by means
of their fronds and in nature scramble
over shrubs and small trees.
Species cultivated *L. japonicum* (syn.
Ophioglossum japonicum), 8–10 feet,
pinnules to 8 inches long, Japan to
Australia, cool greenhouse. *L. palmatum,*
4 feet, Hartford fern, handsome fronds,
maple-like appearance, Massachusetts
to Florida, outdoors or greenhouse.
Cultivation The most useful species for
pot cultivation is *L. palmatum.* It
requires a very porous soil consisting of
equal parts of leafmould and chopped
sphagnum moss. Copious watering is

necessary from March to September, a
little less at other times. Most species
are much more vigorous and make a
large amount of fibrous roots so they
need to be planted into a bed of soil, or a
pocket made with rocks and grown on
the greenhouse staging.

The ferns can be shown off to the best
advantage by using thin wires fixed from
the roof to the soil, and each frond can
climb on its own wire. These fronds can
can be trained in different ways, which-
ever is the most suitable for the house or
area to cover. They may also be trained
on sticks, trellis-work or pillars.

These plants are semi-deciduous but it
is advisable to cut the old fronds off when
the young ones start to appear otherwise
they will be difficult to separate.

Lygodiums can remain in the same
position for three or four years, but a

liquid nitrogen feed must be given once
a week during their growing season.
They should be given a shady position in
the greenhouse; the winter temperature
should not fall below 45°F (7°C).

New plants can be raised from spores
which can be found on the upper part of
the fronds. These are sown on the
surface of a mixture of fine sand and peat
in a propagating case, in a temperature
of 75–85°F (24–29°C) at any time. Otherwise plants may be divided at potting
time, from February to April.

Lyme Grass—see Elymus

Lyonia (ly-o-ne-a)

Commemorating John Lyon, a diligent
collector of North American plants who
introduced many to the British Isles
(Ericaceae). A genus of some 40 species
of evergreen or deciduous shrubs or
small trees, closely resembling *Pieris,*
widely distributed over the world. The
only species normally found in cultivation is *L. ligustrina* (syn. *Andromeda
ligustrina, Arsenococcus ligustrinus,
Lyonia paniculata*) Maine to Florida to
Texas, a hardy deciduous shrub, 5–8
feet in height, with panicles of tiny
white, urn-shaped flowers in summer.
Cultivation A lime-free soil is essential
and the plant thrives best in a moist,
peaty or sandy loam. Plant in autumn
or spring. Pruning is unnecessary.
Propagate by seed sown in pans on the
surface of mixture consisting of sandy
peat in spring or autumn and stood in a
shaded cold frame, or by layering in
September or October.

Lyonothamnus (ly-on-o-tham-nus)

The name commemorates W. S. Lyon
who discovered this tree on the island of
Santa Catalina in 1884, and from the
Greek *thamnos,* shrub *(Rosaceae).* There
is one species only, *L. floribundus,* a

ative of Santa Cruz and other islands off the coast of California. It is a graceful, slender, evergreen tree from 30–50 feet in height, bearing large panicles of small, five-petalled, white flowers in May and June. The leaves are fern-like and luxuriant. The form cultivated is *aspleniifolius*, with distinct, pinnately-divided leaves with stalkless leaflets about 4 inches long. It is hardy only in mild climates like its native country.
Cultivation Plant in a well-drained loamy soil and in a sheltered position. Propagation is by seed or by cuttings of half-ripe wood inserted in sandy soil with gentle bottom heat.

Lyperanthus (ly-pe-ran-thus)
From the Greek *lyperos*, mournful, *anthos*, flower, referring to the dark colour of the dry flowers of some species *(Orchidaceae)*. A genus of about 2 species of seldom-grown terrestrial orchids with fleshy or tuberous roots, natives of Australia, New Caledonia and New Zealand. The upper sepal is helmet-

1

1 The evil-smelling Skunk Lily, Lysichitum americanum, a good bog-garden plant, has a pale yellow spathe.
2 The white spathe of Lysichitum camtschatcense, an odourless species.
3 Two older spathe-less flowers and a young bloom of Lysichitum americanum.

shaped; the flowers have large basal bract.
Species cultivated *L. nigricans*, whitish, striped red or crimson, Australia. *L. serratus*, green, yellow, streaked crimson, Australia. *L. suaveolens*, reddish, green and yellow, Australia.
Cultivation Plants should be grown in a mixture of loam, fibre, peat, and sand. Maintain a minimum temperature of 55–60°F (13–16°C). Keep the mixture dry when the flowers have faded. Propagation is by division at potting time.

Lyre Flower—see Dicentra spectabilis

Lysichitum (lie-see-ky-tum)
From the Greek *lysis*, loose, *chiton*, cloak, referring to the spathe which is cast off as the flowers age *(Araceae)*. A genus of 2 species, hardy vigorous plants found growing in marshy places in their native habitats. They belong to the same family as our native *Arum* and have large ornamental spathes and spadices. The large leaves develop fully

2

3

1 The golden leaves of Creeping Jenny, Lysimachia nummularia aurea, make a useful but invasive ground cover.
2 Lysimachia punctata reaches 3 feet, spreads quickly, and has yellow flowers.
3 The tall, white-flowered spikes of Lysimachia ephemerum.

after the flowers are over. They are popularly known as skunk cabbages though this name really applies to a closely related plant, *Symplocarpus foetidus*.

Species cultivated *L. americanum*, yellow skunk lily, spathes up to 6 inches high, pale yellow, flowers in a spadix, greenish to golden-yellow, evil-smelling, to 6 inches long, April, leaves to 2½ feet long when fully developed, Northwest North America. *L. camtschatcensis*, like *L. americanum*, but spathes white, flowers appearing in May, odourless, Japan, Kamtschatka. (Often one species.)
Cultivation These are striking plants for the bog garden or the sides of streams or pools in shallow water. Plant in spring. Propagation is by division of the rhizomes in spring. *L. americanum*, unlike *L. camtschatcensis*, sets seed readily in some places and these may be sown in moist soil when ripe.

Lysimachia (lis-e-mak-e-a)

Probably from either *Lysimachus*, King of Thracia, or from the Greek *luo*, to loose, and *mache*, strife, hence the common name of *L. vulgaris*, *(Primulaceae)*. This genus, most species of which in cultivation are hardy herbaceous perennials, has some species which have long been cultivated. There are about 120 species in all from temperate and sub-tropical regions of the world, some of them being natives—not cultivated. The yellow loosestrife and creeping jenny are cultivated in gardens the latter plant making an excellent specimen for a hanging basket, with its neat leaves and abundance of yellow flowers. Some naturalized in the US.
Species cultivated *L. atropurpurea*, 2 feet, purple, summer, Greece. *L. clethroides*, 3 feet, white, summer, foliage

brightly coloured in autumn, Japan. *L. ephemerum*, 3 feet, white, summer, Europe. *L. fortunei*, 3 feet, white, summer, China and Japan. *L. leschenaultii*, 1 foot, rose-red, summer, India, does best in light, sandy soil. *L. nemorum*, creeping, yellow, summer, Britain. *L. nummularia*, creeping jenny, yellow, summer, Europe; var. *aurea*, golden leaves. *L. punctata* (syn. *L. verticillata*), 3 feet, yellow, summer, Europe. *L. thyrsiflora*, 3 feet, yellow, summer, north Europe. *L. vulgaris*, yellow loosestrife, 3 feet, yellow, summer, Europe and Asia.

Cultivation Rich moist soil is appreciated by these plants, and many species do best by the sides of pools or streams. They will tolerate some shade. The soil needed in hanging baskets or pots for *L. nummularia* consists of 1 part of leafmould and coconut-fibre and 1 part of sand. The baskets should be suspended in partial shade. This plant also makes useful ground-cover under trees etc., particularly in its golden-leaved form. Propagation is by division of plants in spring or autumn.

Lysinema (lie-sin-ee-ma)

From the Greek *lysis,* freeing, *nema,* a filament, in reference to the free stamens *(Epacridaceae).* A genus of 6 species, all natives of Australia, closely related to *Epacris*. They are pretty evergreen shrubs with long, tubular, yellowish-white, creamy or pink flowers borne singly in the leaf axils. The common name, curry-and-rice, is probably due to the over-lapping brown bracts at the base of the white flowers. The only species known in cultivation is *L. pungens,* an erect shrub, 2–3 feet tall, with long branches and small leaves tapering to a rigid point. The flowers are white, pale pink or occasionally red.

Cultivation This is a shrub for the cool greenhouse, which should be grown in a compost of fibrous bracken peat and sharp sand. Watering must always be carried out with care especially when the plants are pruned back after flowering. Otherwise cultivation is as for *Epacris*.

Lythrum (lith-rum)

From the Greek *lythron,* black blood, in reference to the colour of the flowers of some species *(Lythraceae).* Loosestrife. This is a small genus, mainly consisting of hardy herbaceous and shrubby perennials from temperate regions. One of them, *L. salicaria,* makes beautiful the banks of many streams in the US, and grows abundantly in wet meadows, its

1 Lysinema ciliatum, a native of Australia has overlapping brown bracts at the base of the white flowers, earning the plant the name Curry and Rice.
2 Lythrum salicaria, the Purple Loosestrife, from Europe, has several cultivars such as 'Rose Queen'.

long flower spikes coming in late summer when flowering wild plants are getting scarce, but is too aggressive.

Species cultivated *L. alatum*, 3 feet, crimson-purple, July–October, Northeast to Arkansas. *L. salicaria*, purple loose-strife, 3 feet, crimson-purple, July, Europe; cultivars include 'Modern Pink'; 'Prichard', rose-pink; 'The Beacon', deep crimson. *L. virgatum*, 2–3 feet, crimson-purple, summer, Taurus; 'Rose Queen', rosy-red, is a less tall cultivar.

Cultivation Ideal spreading plants for borders of ponds and streams. However, provided the soil is moist, these loose-strifes will grow in any border. It is as well to lift and divide the plants periodically, and this is, in fact, the best method of propagation for colour. It is

---

1 Maackia amurensis, a hardy tree with light pinnate foliage, is native to Japan, Korea and Manchuria.
2 The fruits of the Queensland Nut, Macadamia ternifolia, have a delicate flavour and are occasionally imported into this country. Unfortunately, although the plant may be grown under glass in the North, it rarely fruits.

---

best carried out in October or April.

Maackia (maa-ki-a)
Commemorating Richard Maack, 1825–86, a Russian naturalist *(Leguminosae)*. A genus of 6 species of which one only is generally in cultivation. This is *M. amurensis* (syn. *Cladrastis amurensis*), a hardy tree with pinnate leaves, a native of Manchuria, Korea and Japan, closely related to *Cladrastis*. Though in its native habitat it makes a forest tree

of 40 feet, it sometimes grows to bit more than a shrub. The leaves and flowers are not very attractive. I racemes of pearl-like flowers are quit generously produced in July and Augus but they are dingy white in colour. The are followed by slightly winged seed pod

Cultivation No special soils or sites a required. Propagation is from seed sow in late winter or early spring in wel drained soil in the greenhouse in temperature of 55–60°F (13–16°C). addition the tree can be increased b root cuttings in pans or boxes of a sand loam in March. A temperature of 60° (16°C) should be maintained.

Macadamia (ma-ka-dam-e-a)
Named after John Macadam MD, wh was Secretary of the Philosophica Institute, Victoria, Australia, *(Prote ceae)*. There are about 10 species in th genus; most have a restricted distribu tion and occur in east Australia, Ne Caledonia, Celebes and Madagasca They form small trees, with insignifican flowers, but the fruits of *M. ternifoli* the Queensland nut, are so esteemed fc

1162

ating that they have been cultivated
or years in Florida and California.
Commercial plantations have been form-
d in Hawaii and bear one or two crops
year. Young trees usually start
ropping when about seven years old,
nd a mature tree may yield 300 pounds
f nuts a year. The spherical seeds are
bout the size of a walnut and super-
cially resemble a nut, and the crisp,
hite, oily kernel has a very agreeable
aste. They are occasionally imported
nd sold in Europe. However, the shells
re very hard and this has limited their
opularity. The only species likely to be
ound in cultivation in botanic gardens
a Britain is from Queensland and New
outh Wales which grows to 50 feet in
ature but, under glass in Britain it is
ery slow-growing and rarely reaches
tore than 12 feet; inconspicuous flowers
nd fruit with a fleshy coat surrounding
thick shell.

ultivation In North a plant for cool
reenhouse, usually grown with a 45°F
°C) minimum winter temperature, with
o additional heat in summer. As a
orest plant it can tolerate very moist
hady conditions, and it is easy to grow
nce it is established. However, it rarely,
ever, flowers or fruits under glass in
ome areas, possibly from lack of light.
prefers an acid, organic, well-drained
ixture; a suitable one would be made
p of 1 part of loam, 2 parts of peat and 1
art of sand. Propagation from cuttings
difficult, but semi-ripe stem cuttings
serted in a sandy mixture and placed
1 a closed case have a reasonable
hance of success if they are carefully
reated. Since the seed is oily, its
iability is short lived, and unless it is
easonably fresh it does not germinate.

Macartney Rose—see Rosa bracteata

Mace—see Achillea decolorans and
Myristica fragrans

Macedonian Oak—see Quercus
ojana

Macedonian Pine—see Pinus peuce

Machaerocereus
(mack-ay-ro-seer-ee-us)
rom the Greek *machaira*, a short
word, and *Cereus*, referring to the
attened sword-like central spines
Cactaceae). Two species of greenhouse
ucculent plants, one of which forms
rge prostrate clumps, the other has
rect thick stems branching from the base.
pecies cultivated *M. eruca*, creeping
evil, thick prostrate branches, tips
urve upwards, strong downward point-
g central spines, flowers yellow,
alifornia. *M. gummosus,* stems erect to
feet, flowers red, California.
ultivation The medium should consist
light potting mix to which has been
ded ¼ part of coarse sand, grit or
oken brick. A position in full sun is

required for both species. *M. eruca*
should be grown horizontally. In summer any normal greenhouse temperature
will suffice, and the medium should be
kept moist. From October to March keep

1 The long, hanging creamy-white
racemes of Macadamia tetrophylla
which belongs to the same family as the
Proteas.
2 The horizontal growth of Machaerocereus eruca, the Creeping Devil Cactus.

it dry, in a minimum temperature of 45°F (7°C). Propagation is by seed sown in a well-drained seed mix and kept moist and shaded at 70°F (21°C) until germination, then give more light. Cuttings taken from the branches root easily in a mixture of coarse sand and peat.

Machilus (mack-ill-us)

From *makila,* a native name used for the plant in the East Indies *(Lauraceae).* Some authorities now place *Machilus* within the genus *Persea* of which the avocado pear *(P. americana)* is most familiar. They are mainly evergreen trees or shrubs from south-east Asia, China and Japan. The flowers are not showy and the tropical species are rarely cultivated in the North. The genus is only really represented in cultivation by one or two half hardy Chinese introductions.

Species cultivated *M. bracteatus,* 6–12 feet in cultivation, bushy in habit, dark shiny leaves, smelling of camphor, flowers rarely produced, Yunnan. *M. ichangensis,* 8–16 feet in cultivation, aromatic leaves, China.

Cultivation Planted in sheltered situations and reasonably well-drained sites in gardens in the Deep South and the West Coast, these tolerate quite hard frosts. Seeds can be sown in spring and the plants grown on in a cool-house or cold frame until they are ready for planting out. Semi-ripe stem cuttings will root in a closed case, but they are not easy and require particular care.

Machinery in the garden

At the end of World War II, garden mechanisation was in its infancy, to be considered seriously only by people with an acre or two, probably with a commercial interest. To-day even the small town garden can be mechanised to some extent.

Despite the comprehensive range of equipment available, mechanisation is not necessarily as simple as one would expect. For one thing, the capital cost is comparatively high, and for another it is also possible to purchase gadgets which prove to be more trouble than they are worth. Mechanisation can be worth while if it saves sufficient time to provide more leisure, in other words the leisure is being bought. Mechanisation is, perhaps, even more worth while for older people or those who are incapacitated in some way. Under these circumstances it can well mean the difference between being able to have a garden or not.

Mechanisation may cost $40 or $1,000 according to the extent it is taken. Some will be content with no more than an electric grass edge-cutter, or hedge-cutter; others may equip the entire garden for powered cultivation, grass-cutting and greenhouse control. Either

1

2

3

1 The Scotts Compact Rotary Spreader distributes fertiliser in 6 foot swaths. It can cover an acre per hour.
2 Scotts' spreaders are specifically designed to distribute their own products. This standard spreader model has an accuracy gauge.
3 The Jacobsen 4-Blade Rotary lawn mower with attached grass bag.
4 Gang mowers towed by a tractor are used on large expanses in parks, estates and golf courses.
5 A mechanical seed-sower can be useful for planting vegetable crops.
6 The Scotts lawn mower with grass catcher has a cutting width of 19 inches. The height of cut can be changed without the use of tools.

surrounding hedge would justify an electric hedge-cutter but would not, under normal circumstances, qualify for a motor cultivator.

Equipment Powered mowers and grass-cutters apart, there is quite a range of small equipment for cutting grass. There are electric long grass cutters, priced about $40 up and only about six inches wide, which can quite readily be adapted to cut lawn edges. They have electric motors operating through transformers to ensure that the maximum voltage to earth is only 50 volts. They consist of little more than a small electric motor, mounted at the lower end of a convenient handle and driving a guarded rotating blade at high speed that is light to use. It is intended for work under trees and odd corners rather than for a large area of rough grass. Not very much bigger is an electric cultivator, but in this instance a heavy duty electric motor unit forms the upper part of the handle and drives a small rotary cultivator at the lower end. The tool is detachable from the motor unit, which can then be used to drive a saw or hedge-cutter.

Hedge-cutters are probably the most popular of the small tools since they do really save a tremendous amount of time and labour. For the average gardener the 12-inch blade suffices, and it is the lightest, but 18-, 24- and even 36-inch blades can be obtained. The most expensive cutters work at a very high speed and have a 36-inch blade. The operating voltage is usually 50 volts above earth, through a transformer from cables, but 12-volt battery-operated models allow greater flexibility of use away from the house. Inexpensive double-insulated wire models have just recently made their appearance. If you already have a motor cultivator or lawnmower with a power take-off, the hedge may be cut by a cutter bar attachment driven through a flexible mechanical drive from the power take-off.

Other garden mechanical aids include the flame gun (see Flame guns). Jobs such as sweeping up leaves, or even collecting the grass after a rough grass cutter has been over, can be simplified and speeded up many times by using a rotary broom and catcher, in other words, a mechanical leaf-sweeper. To-day even these are available, propelled by a small gasoline engine.

Fertiliser spreading has not yet been motorized for the gardener, but the hand-propelled spreader for lawns is really a tremendous time-saver and well worth its cost, particularly as it gives a more even spread than spreading by hand; selection of openings is provided to allow adjustment of the spreader to suit the type of fertiliser being applied. There are small rotary dusters for those who prefer dusting to spraying. Log-sawing can be mechanised by electric

way, the equipment can be expected to last, on average, ten years and the capital cost may, therefore, be written off over this period against the value of the leisure or the cost, and inconvenience, of hired labour.

Various kinds of equipment that can be obtained are: gasoline motors, electric and battery-electric lawnmowers and rotary grass-cutters (these are dealt with at some length in the article Lawn-mowing machinery); various types of powered cultivators for tilling the soil and hoeing (these too have their own article—Cultivators). There is also a considerable amount of smaller and

relatively inexpensive equipment, such as mechanical lawn edge-trimmers, small long grass cutters, leaf sweepers, flame guns, powered sprayers, lawn aerating attachments, long-handled pruners and fruit pickers, powered drills with hedge-cutting attachments and powered log saws.

It is possible to make an unwise investment in garden machinery. For example, although the flame gun as a means of clearing weeds is valuable in the large garden, in the tiny garden the use of a suitable chemical weedkiller would be cheaper and more practical. By the same token, the small garden with a

1 For larger gardens with trees and lawns, this lawn sweeper takes the drudgery out of autumn.
2 The use of a wheeled spreader ensures an even distribution of fertiliser over the lawn.
3 The hard Nylon brushes of the lawn sweeper rotate, sweeping the dead leaves into a collecting box.

power, a gasoline engine or a flexible drive from cultivator or lawn-mower.

Spraying equipment is dealt with elsewhere, but it can be included in mechanisation in that it ranges from simple hand syringes to pressure-retaining sprayers which hold their air pressure even when the liquid has been discharged. Finally, for the really ambitious there are powered sprayers operated by gas engines.

Laying out the garden Mechanisation can only be a sound investment if the garden has been laid out to suit it. This entails setting out the plants so that mechanical cultivation can be carried out around them (see Cultivators).

No special planning is needed for mechanical hedge-cutting and grass cutting, but remember there is a limit to the distance from the house that wire operated machinery can be used. For more distant parts a battery-powered machine may be necessary, or one operated through a mechanical flexible drive driven by the motor mower or cultivator.

Machinery maintenance The potential life of ten years applied to mechanical appliances, assumes regular and adequate maintenance. Most of this will be done in spring, although the more conscientious may well carry out most of the major maintenance before the equipment is put away for the winter.

The gasoline engine is the common denominator for both cultivators and lawn-mowers, and it is also usually the most expensive part of the machine, so there is every reason for giving this priority in the maintenance programme.

Engine maintenance Engines today do not need much servicing. At the beginning of the season drain the gas tank and refill with fresh fuel in case any gumming has taken place. Fit a new or cleaned sparking plug, the gap of which has been set to suit the requirement of the engine manufacturers, and check the functioning of the contact breaker by removing the plug and laying it on the top of the engine so that you can see the electrodes. As the engine is turned with the recoil starter, or rope and pulley, there should be a regular spark at the plug points. Defective contact breaker points are not worth renovating it is best to replace them. A pulley drawer will probably be needed if this job is done at home.

Have a look at the carburettor air intake filter and clean it in accordance with the maker's recommendations (there are several different types) because dust is an abrasive and must be excluded from the engine.

When an engine is new, a complete oil change is recommended after the first five hours use (except, of course two stroke engines). Thereafter the recommendations are to change the oil after every 25 hours, although, in practice most people change the oil at the beginning of every season.

Gear-boxes do not normally need draining every year if a good quality oil has been used, but when they are

drained it should be done while the oil is warm. Do not, on any account, wash out either the gearbox or engine sump with kerosene.

Battery operated equipment The battery should be filled with distilled water and thoroughly charged. Allow it to stand for a week and then take a hydrometer reading of each cell. A good battery will still give a fully charged reading for each cell. Make sure that the top of the battery is perfectly dry, clean the connectors and see that they are smeared with petroleum jelly (Vaseline).

The pillar or top hat connectors are somewhat temperamental and are best not removed unnecessarily. Many people find the old clamp-type connectors more reliable and less likely to give the impression of a run-down battery when the real trouble is a high-resistance connection. The nature of the fault can be proved by trying to use the machine. The faulty connector will become hot in use, although it may not be passing sufficient current to operate the electric motor.

Do not allow the surface of the battery to remain wet as this causes a slow but continuous discharge. Any corrosion at the terminals should be wiped off at once and the terminals covered with Vaseline. Corrosion due to acid spillage on any part of the mower should be washed off with a solution of washing soda, followed

1 A powered saw has many uses in the garden including the lopping and felling of trees.
2 Careful attention to the maintenance of equipment and machinery can greatly increase their longevity and usefulness. Accumulated dirt should frequently be cleaned off the blade and the surrounding surfaces of lawn mowers.
3 The wheels of lawn mowers such as those on this Lawn Boy model should be kept well-oiled.
4 The application of a small amount of engine oil in the cylinder will help to prevent corrosion.

by a rinse of clear water. Incidentally always remember to remove the lid covering the motor and electrical 'works' when charging the battery.

Lawn mowers The side-wheel mower barely scrapes in under the heading of garden machinery but nevertheless it does require maintenance. In addition to sharpening the blades and oiling the rollers, remove the split pin and take off the driving wheel to check the driving pawl of the ratchet mechanism. This should always be kept well lubricated and if the pawl is worn, causing the drive to slip intermittently, renew it before it causes damage to other parts.

The roller type mower is more complicated and usually needs more attention if it is to function properly. Oil the bearings of the driving roller. If the

cutting reel does not run in bearings which are sealed and packed with grease, these too should be lubricated. For all this work consult the maker's instruction book. Check the gap between the cutting reel and the fixed blade: if this gap is not constant, movement of the cylinder in its bearings is indicated; on some machines slack in the bearings can be taken up.

Examine the belts for wear. If they set too deeply in the pulley groove, if they are frayed or if they slip, renew them. They are not expensive and it is as well to have spare belts ready. A few of the more expensive machines still employ chain drive in which case the chains should be examined for excessive wear (indicated by the free movement being slight at some points and considerable at others); renewal is the only remedy. Otherwise adjust the chain to give a free movement of half to three quarters of an inch. The chains should in any case be lubricated liberally, preferably with a graphited oil. Best of all, remove the chains and soak them in graphited grease which has been warmed up sufficiently to make it run easily. A chain so treated will need no more lubrication during the season and, if enclosed, will run for more than one season without further attention.

The cutting reel should be cleaned using an old toothbrush and a tin of kerosene, after which the cutting edge may be checked. Light sharpening can

To get the full value and life out of your garden machinery, you must take care in adjusting the various components correctly. Some designs, usually the more expensive ones, are more sophisticated in this respect than others.
1 It is important to ensure a correct setting of the mowing blades.
2 Coating the blade with oil or grease will promote its efficiency.
3 The roller is set to give the right height of cut.
4 The height of cut on some models must be adjusted with a wrench.
5 A simple knurled knob alters the roller height on this model.
6 The plug on this model must be removed before oil can be injected.

sometimes be done in position by applying carborundum paste and turning the cutter backwards (where this is possible) but usually the only thing to do is to have the reel reground on a lathe. Many modern machines have quickly detachable cutter units. Setting of the reel blades to the fixed blade needs care and patience. The method of operating the reel adjustment varies from one type of mower to another, but whatever the method of adjustment, the reel should be set in such a way that the blades just 'kiss' the bottom blade, and this equally on both sides. A blade set too tight will wear quickly and will absorb a great deal of power from the engine; one set too free will cause the grass to be bruised rather than cut.

Sometimes it seems that one rotating blade only is fouling the fixed blade: this could be due to uneven blade wear but is more likely to be caused by wear in the bearings.

Check the front roller for wear whether of wood or metal, as excessive bearing wear will cause uneven cutting. Apply plenty of grease to the moving surfaces, preferable one with a graphite or molybdenum disulphite additive which tends to leave a lubricating film actually in the surface of the metal.

Oil the more specialised parts of the mower such as handlebar adjustment fulcrum points and the clutch mechanism. These vary from make to make, and details should be given in the maker's instruction manual. Check that the throttle cables have not rusted in their sheaths. New cables need no lubrication, but later on it is advisable to lubricate with a graphited oil, or moly-impregnated oil. Check that the throw-plate is correct and the grassbox fitting correctly.

Damp is the main enemy of machinery. Where the shed has no floor one should be improvised: planks on bricks can be used to keep machinery off the ground. Under such conditions all unpainted metal and chromium-plated parts should be wiped over with a rag soaked in light oil, or a car wax could be used. Cutting blades of mowers, in particular, should be oiled. Nuts and bolts should also be oiled so that they do not rust solid.

ıring the winter. Old engine oil is ;eful for this purpose but better 'eparations are the new rust preventaves widely available. Such attention the autumn makes for easier handling hen machinery is brought out of store r the spring.

Some people pack their machinery in normous polythene bags during the inter, but this is not recommended. A 'arm front following a cold spell will ause condensation to form and the bsence of air circulation will cause the ampness to remain and create rust, so hat the final result is worse than if they ad been stored in an open shed.

Reference has been made in this article to oils and greases impregnated with molybdenum disulphite. This additive ensures that a protective surface remains even after ordinary oils have drained away or evaporated. It tends to build up in the grain of the surface of the metal, particularly after a long period of use, and so provide a semi-permanent protection.

Battery-operated equipment needs even more care when stored for the winter. Wire-driven electric mowers will not need any special attention, but

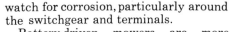

The Plume Poppy, Macleaya cordata, reaches 8–12 feet and has filmy coral coloured flowers in summer.

watch for corrosion, particularly around the switchgear and terminals.

Battery-driven mowers are more scarce than wire-driven: since batteries are expensive they should be well cared for. Always put the machine away for the winter with the battery fully charged and correctly filled up with electrolyte.

It is worth removing the battery about every six or eight weeks and giving it a refreshing charge. A garden shed is not a good place to store a battery: dampness on the surface of the battery can cause invisible electrical leakage and a slow discharge, and an exceptionally severe frost could cause the electrolyte to freeze and burst the case. Any signs of corrosion on the terminals should be dealt with immediately before it spreads.

Mackaya (mak-kay-a)
In honour of Dr J. F. Mackay, once keeper of the University Botanic Garden, Dublin, and author of *Flora Hibernica (Acanthaceae)*. Handsome greenhouse shrubs, usually evergreen, natives of tropical Africa and India. The only species cultivated in the South is African *M. bella* (syn. *Asystasia bella,* the derivation of this name which is now current is unknown), which grows 6 feet tall and has large bell-shaped, lilac flowers with red-pencilled throat, borne on erect stems in May and June.

Cultivation In the North it requires a winter temperature of 55°F (13°C) and in summer a sunny, well-ventilated house. It thrives when planted in the greenhouse border, but may be grown in a 10-inch pot containing a fibrous sandy loam. Cut it back after flowering and give it very little water in winter, but liberal watering and liquid manure during the growing season in early spring. Propagate by cuttings of half-ripened shoots, taken June–August and inserted in sandy soil in a propagating frame with gentle bottom heat.

Macleaya (mac-lay-a)
Commemorating Alexander Macleay, 1767–1848, Secretary of the Linnean Society *(Papaveraceae)*. This genus, sometimes listed under the synonym *Bocconia*, consists of two Chinese species of perennial herbaceous plants very valuable in the garden. Their most outstanding virtue is their great height (8 feet or more) which lifts their large airy heads of tiny petal-less flowers and unusual rounded and lobed leaves above less statuesque plants. Because of their bold and dignified appearance they are useful specimen plants to stand as an isolated eye-catcher, although a group of them is even more impressive.

Species cultivated *M. cordata* (syn. *Bocconia cordata*), plume poppy, tree celandine, 8–12 feet high, leaves 8 inches across, white beneath, and containing an orange coloured sap which oozes out of any cut or broken surface, buff flowers in graceful panicles, summer. *M. microcarpa* (syn. *Bocconia microcarpa*), similar to the former, but the flower plumes are somewhat yellower in colour, and the plant is somewhat less tall; 'Kelway's Coral Plume' is a cultivar with coral-pink buds.

Cultivation Rich soils, suits these plants which should also have full sun. They do very well on well-drained limey soils. They should not require staking, except in very exposed situations, as they have stout hollow stems. Since they sucker rather freely, detachment of suckers in early summer provides the most suitable method of propagation. If a clump is being dug up for transplanting it is essential to remove every piece of root, otherwise new plants will eventually appear even from quite small pieces of root left in the soil.

Maclura (mac-lur-a)

Commemorating W. Maclure (d. 1840) an American geologist *(Moraceae)*. This genus has one species only, *M. pomifera* (syn. *M. aurantiaca*) the Osage orange, or gage orange which is a hardy deciduous tree related to the mulberry. It is grown for the sake of its orange-like fruits, up to 5 inches in diameter, which are not edible and which it frequently produces in this country. The leaves of this North American prairie tree, which reaches 60 feet in its native habitat, have been used to feed silkworms and its strong timber is of some use (the Indians made their bows of it). The flowers are greenish and inconspicuous and the two sexes are borne upon separate trees, so that in order to obtain fruit it is necessary to plant specimens of both sexes or to graft upon a tree of one sex some wood from a tree of opposite sex. When closely planted *M. pomifera* makes an impenetrable hedge, as its branches are armed with spines; it is used for this purpose in the Middle West and in Europe.

Cultivation Even poor soil satisfies this plant, and it is of easy propagation, either by seed, cuttings of young growth, or root-cuttings under glass, all of which give reasonable success.

Macodes (mak-o-deez)

Derivation unknown *(Orchidaceae)*. A small genus of terrestrial orchids closely related to *Anoectochilus* and, like them, grown for their very beautiful foliage. The single species in cultivation, *M. petola,* from Java and Malaya, has broadly oval leaves, 3 inches long and 2 inches broad, which are of a light velvety green and have fine golden veins forming a well-defined network over the whole leaf. Unlike many of the *Anoectochilus* this plant is of easy cultivation and can be readily increased.

Cultivation A mixture of equal parts of osmunda fibre, sphagnum moss and leaf-mould is required, placed in well-drained shallow pans. A warm, moist atmosphere

1 **Maclura pomifera, the Osage Orange, is grown for its orange-like fruits.**
2 **Macodes petola, one of the orchids grown for their beautiful leaves.**
3 **A plant from South-west Australia, Macropidia fuliginosa or Black Kangaroo Paw, reaches about 4 feet and has yellow and black flowers.**

and protection from bright light produce the finest leaves; the spikes carrying the small, insignificant flowers are best removed. Propagation is by separation of the fleshy stems, but not after September. The winter temperature should not fall below 60°F (16°C).

Macropidia (mak-ro-pi-dee-a)

A corruption or typographical error from the Latin name for the Kangaroo, *macropodia,* meaning long foot. It refers to the shape of the flowers which also give rise to the common name of black kangaroo paw *(Haemadoraceae* or, according to some authorities *Amaryllidaceae).* There is one species only, *M. fuliginosa* (syns. *M. fumosa, Anigozanthus fuliginosus),* which is restricted in its distribution to south-west Australia. It is an attractive flowering plant, 3–4 feet high, with iris-like leaves up to 2–3 feet long. The flowers are borne on a long slender stalk and are like those of the related *Anigozanthus* except that they are yellow and black and are normally produced in midsummer.

Cultivation The plant grows very slowly, taking several years to flower from seed. Since it grows in desert areas with limited rainfall, it is very important to keep the plant on the dry side in winter as it can easily be over-watered and killed. It is rare in cultivation, perhaps because of this susceptibility. The medium should be freely draining, as used for cacti. Normally grown in a cool greenhouse with sufficient heat in winter to avoid a stagnant atmosphere, in summer the pots may be plunged out of doors. Propagation is by seed which has to be imported.

Macropiper (mac-ro-pe-per)

From the Greek *macros,* large, and *peperi,* pepper, in reference to their resemblance to *Piper,* the pepper *(Piperaceae).* A genus consisting of about six species of shrubs and small trees. They are found from Tahiti to New Guinea and down to New Zealand. The single New Zealand species is the one most likely to be met with in cultivation. It is at the best a half-hardy shrub and apart from greenhouses it can be expected to succeed only in the most favoured parts of the southland and perhaps southern California. Species cultivated is *M. excelsum,* the kawa kawa or pepper tree which grows from 15–20 feet in cultivation. It forms a bushy shrub with handsome, dark green heart-shaped leaves, and blackish stems swollen at the nodes. The insignificant flowers are borne in unisexual spikes which usually stand out above the foliage. On the female spikes they are followed by yellow to bright orange fruits. Flowering can be expected to occur from late spring to late summer.

Cultivation This shrub will grow in sun or partial shade and should be given a rather rich, well-drained soil. In any except the most favoured locations, it should be given the protection of a wall or overhanging trees. Young plants are particularly susceptible to frost damage. Propagation is by seed sown under glass with gentle heat, or by semi-hardwood cuttings in a closed frame with bottom heat.

Macrozamia (mak-ro-zam-e-a)

The name arises from the Greek *makros,* long, and *Zamia,* to which it is related *(Zamiaceae* or *Cycadaceae).* A genus of some 14 species, confined to Australia, both the tropical and the temperate zones. The genus, like *Lepidozamia,* was at its peak during the time of the coal-forming carboniferous forests, some 50 million years or more ago. They are primitive, wind-pollinated, cone-bearing seed plants resembling tree ferns in appearance. It is said that if the leaves of some species are eaten by cattle, it can cause rickets.

Species cultivated *M. communis,* trunks 3–6 feet high, leaves 3–6 feet long, leaflets numerous, narrow, cones form in October, coastal and eastern mountain slopes. *M. corallipes,* trunk almost round, 8 inches in diameter, leaflets about 50, 5–7 inches, reddish at base, male cones 7 inches long, female cones about 4 inches, seeds orange-red, New South Wales. *M. miquelii,* stout trunks rarely above ground, leaves 2–3 feet, 60 leaflets up to 10 inches long, male cones 6 inches, female cones shorter, Queensland, New South Wales. The down from the leaf bases is collected by the aborigines and used for stuffing pillows. *M. spiralis,* trunk to 3 feet, but usually sunken, leaves 4–5 feet with the lower 18 inches of the petiole (leaf stalk) without leaflets, leaflets 80–100, 6–9 inches long.

Cultivation If grown in beds these plants require a rich porous loam. For

The Kawa Kawa or Pepper Tree, Macropiper excelsum from New Zealand. It is hardy only in warm regions.

pot cultivation a mixture of 1 part of loam, 1 part of peat, 1 part of sand, and 1 part of broken brick is suitable. They need plenty of water during the growing season and a rest in winter. An occasional spray over with water during warm weather is beneficial. Propagation is by seed or by offsets formed at the top of the trunks, if the trunk has been damaged or broken off.

Madagascar Chaplet Flower, Madagascar Jasmine—see Stephanotis floribunda

Maddenia (mad-den-e-a)
Commemorates Colonel E. Madden, died 1856, who collected plants in India *(Rosaceae)*. A small genus of trees and shrubs from China and India, having female flowers on one individual, males on another, that is, the plants are dioecious. The only species cultivated is *M. hypoleuca*, from China, a deciduous shrub or small tree up to 20 feet tall. The inconspicuous flowers with prominent yellow anthers are borne in April and May. The cherry-like, oval leaves are up to 6 inches long, and white beneath. The shrub is curious rather than beautiful.
Cultivation This shrub is hardy in the North where it can thrive in a loamy soil. Propagation is by cuttings of half-ripe shoots inserted in sandy soil in a cold frame. Rare.

Madeira Broom—see Genista virgata

Madeira Vine—see Boussingaultia baselloides

Madeiran Whortleberry—see Vaccinium padifolium

Madonna Lily—see Lilium candidum

Madrona—see Arbutus menziesii

Madwort—see Alyssum

Maerua (may-ru-a)
Possibly derived from *meru*, an Arabian name *(Capparidaceae)*. A genus of about 50 species of shrubs from tropical Africa and Arabia, occasionally grown as warm greenhouse plants. The only species likely to be found in cultivation is *M. oblongifolia* from Abyssinia which grows 4 feet and bears white flowers in terminal racemes in June. The glaucous leaves are oblong, lance-shaped and about 2 inches in length.
Cultivation This plant requires a minimum winter temperature of 60°F (16°C) and a mixture consisting of sandy loam and peat in equal parts. Propagation is by cuttings of nearly-ripe shoots inserted in sandy soil in a propagating frame with gentle bottom heat.

Magnolia (mag-no-lee-a)
Named after Pierre Magnol (1638–1715), Director of the Montpellier Botanic

Garden *(Magnoliaceae)*. A genus of about 80 species of deciduous and evergreen trees and shrubs, many of which are hardy, grown for their large beautiful flowers.
Species cultivated *M. acuminata* (D), cucumber tree, hardy tree to 100 feet, greenish flowers, May–July, prominent dark red fruits, to 3 inches long, NY to Ga. and Ark. *M. campbellii* (D), tree to 150 feet in nature, large pink fragrant flowers before the leaves, from February onwards, needs a protected situation, Sikkim Himalaya. *M. dawsoniana* (D), tree to 30 feet, large leaves, flowers pale rose, flushed purple, April, needs mild conditions, Szechwan. *M. delavayi* (E), to 30 feet with exceptionally large leaves up to 14 inches long, creamy-white flowers to 8 inches across, fragrant, June, grows well on lime, needs mild conditions, western China. *M. denudata* (syn. *M. conspicua*) (D), yulan or lily tree,

1 The terminal racemes of white flowers of Maerua oblongifolia a plant with sword-like glaucous leaves.
2 The large flower of Magnolia sargentiana robusta bends downwards when fully open in March and April being often 1 foot in diameter.

Many attractive Magnolias are grown for their superb flowers. The name commemorates Pierre Magnol, Director of the Montpellier Botanic Garden in the late sixteenth century.
1 Magnolia x soulangeana rustica rubra.
2 Magnolia tripetala has greenish-white flowers with an unpleasant odour.
3 Magnolia x soulangeana makes a small tree of bushy habit.

large bush or tree to 50 feet, flowers white, to 6 inches across, bell-shaped, March onwards, will not tolerate lime, China. *M. fraseri* (D), to 50 feet, leaves to 15 inches long, flowers opening pale yellow, ageing to white, to 8 inches across, fragrant, May and June, fruits cone-shaped, to 5 inches long, Virginia, Georgia, Alabama. *M. grandiflora* (E), laurel magnolia, handsome tree to 100 feet, large white flowers, cup-shaped to 10 inches across, late summer, reasonably hardy but often grown against walls to protect foliage, Washington–Florida–Texas; var. *undulata*, leaves with wavy edges. Cultivars are: 'Exmouth Variety' which flowers much earlier than the type; 'Goliath', leaves broader, flowers larger, produced earlier than the type. *M. x highdownensis* (D), hardy shrub, white scented flowers, May, thrives on lime, hybrid. *M. kobus* (D), small tree to 30 feet, flowers small, about 4 inches across, white, April, Japan. *M. liliflora* (D), spreading shrub to 12 feet, flowers erect, bell-shaped, purple on the outside, white within, Japan; var. *nigra*, larger and deeper-coloured flowers. *M. x loebneri* (D), shrub 8–10 feet, much like *M. stellata,* but with larger leaves and flowers, does well on lime, hybrid. *M. macrophylla* (D), to 50 feet in nature, leaves to 2 feet long and 1 foot wide, flowers creamy-white with purplish centres, to 10 inches across, appearing early summer with the leaves, Kentucky, Florida and Louisiana, needs lime-free or neutral soil in a sheltered woodland position. *M. mollicomata* (D), tree to 50–80 feet, similar to *campbellii*, but hardier and flowering at an earlier age, south-east Tibet, Yunnan. *M. obovata* (syn. *M. hypoleuca*) (D), hardy tree to 100 feet, leaves to 1½ feet long, creamy-white flowers to 8 inches across, June, Japan. *M. officinalis* (D), 20–50 feet in nature, leaves to 21 inches long, 9–10 inches wide, flowers cup-shaped, white, to 10 inches across, fragrant, fruits to 5 inches long, scarlet, western China; var. *biloba,* leaves deeply notched. *M.* × *proctoriana* (D), 10–15 feet, leaves narrow, to 4 inches, long, flowers white with narrow, strap-shaped petals, spring, before the leaves, hybrid. *M. sargentiana* (D), large hardy, tree to 60 feet, pink flowers before the leaves, April and May, western China; var. *robusta,* a better form. *M. sieboldii* (syn. *M. parviflora*) (D), hardy shrub to 10 feet, pendent, cup-shaped, fragrant white flowers, midsummer, Japan and Korea. *M. sinensis,* similar to foregoing but larger, June flowering, China.

M. × *soulangeana* (D), very hardy large shrub to 30 feet, flowers goblet-shaped, white flushed rose-purple at base, April, hybrid origin; vars. *alba,* pure white flowers; 'Alexandrina', similar to the type, but flowers flushed purple at the base; *amabilis,* flowers white; *lennei,* large tulip-like flowers rose-purple without, white within; *rustica rubra,* more vigorous, flowers flushed rosy-purple; *speciosa,* smaller leaves, white flowers freely borne. *M. sprengeri* (D), tree to 30 feet, leaves to 7 inches long, flowers rosy-carmine, fragrant, April, before the leaves, western China. *M. stellata* (D), spreading hardy shrub to 18 feet, flowers white, many-petalled, March and April before the leaves, Japan; var. *rosea,* pink-flowered form. *M.* × *thompsoniana* (D), leaves to 10 inches long, flowers creamy-white, fragrant, to 6 inches across, June and July, summer, hybrid. *M. tripetala* (D), umbrella tree, hardy tree to 40 feet, large leaves, to 20 inches long, so arranged to give popular name, creamy flowers to 10 inches across, May and June, red fruits, Pennsylvania–Alabama–Mississippi. *M. virginiana* (syn. *M. glauca*) (SE), sweet or swamp bay, shrub or tree to 60 feet, small leaves, fragrant creamy-white flowers from June–autumn, Mass., Fla., and Texas. *M. watsonii* (D), tree to 25 feet, rose-tinted fragrant flowers to 6 inches across, June, July, Japan. *M. wilsonii* (D), hardy shrub or small tree to 25 feet, large white, cup-shaped, pendulous flowers, June, west Szechwan, China.
Cultivation Magnolias in their natural habitats are woodland plants and prefer

Natives of northern and central America and of Asia and the Himalaya, Magnolias produce the most magnificent flowers, the buds of which are large, dark in colour and usually stand upright from the branch. The plants vary in form from shrubs to quite sizeable trees, some deciduous and others evergreen.
1 The evergreen Magnolia grandiflora has flowers up to a foot across, and forms a pyramidal tree.
2 The Yulan or Lily Tree, Magnolia denudata, has large white bell-shaped flowers in March.
3 Magnolia kobus, a deciduous tree from Japan.
4 The deep reddish-purple flowers of Magnolia liliflora nigra.
5 M. wilsonii flowers in June at the same time as the leaves appear.
6 Magnolia obovata makes a large deciduous tree and has creamy-white flowers.
7 The purplish-white flowers of Magnolia 'Charles Raffill'.
8 The fragrant, cup-shaped flowers of Magnolia sieboldii.

moist, woodland soils with some surrounding, but not overhanging, shelter. The Asiatic tree-growing species, except *M. mollicomata,* take many years to flower when raised from seed. Those kinds which will grow on lime are specially noted, otherwise a neutral or acid soil is desirable. Plants benefit from an annual mulch with a peaty compost until they are fully established. Little pruning is needed except to remove dead or dying wood or to preserve the shape. With evergreen species this should be done in spring, with deciduous kinds when flowering ends. In colder climates like those of Canada, *M. campbellii, M. soulangeana* and *M. stellata* may be grown as specimens in the cool greenhouse or conservatory, in large pots or tubs, in a mixture consisting of 2 parts of sandy loam, 1 part of peat or leafmould, and sand. They should be syringed daily during spring and summer, watered freely from March to September, moderately at other times.

Propagation is from seed, often freely produced in this country, sown as soon as ripe, usually slow in germination, or by layering, grafting, and cuttings in mist. Plant out in May.

Magnolia Lotus—see Nelumbo nucifera alba

Magpie moth—see Moth

x **Mahoberberis** (ma-ho-ber-ber-is)
A name coined to fit the bigeneric hybrid between *Mahonia aquifolium* and *Berberis vulgaris (Berberidaceae).* The single species, *M. neubertii,* is a 6-foot, semi-evergreen shrub without spines. The leaves vary considerably in shape, some being simple and some pinnate (there is a variety, *latifolia,* with broader leaves). This plant has not been known to produce bloom.
Cultivation This shrub needs similar treatment to that given to the evergreen berberis. Propagation must be by vegetative means, i.e. by cuttings of firm shoots of the season's growth, rooted in sandy soil in a propagating frame in September or by layering shoots in spring.

Magnolias are woodland plants and prefer cool sheltered positions with some summer shade. They benefit from a summer mulch of a peaty compost, especially when they are young. Little pruning is required, except to remove the faded flowers and any dead wood.
1 Magnolia mollicomata is one of the Asiatic tree-growing species, with attractive rose-pink flowers.
2 The dark flowers of Magnolia x soulangeana nigra, a hybrid.
3 The deciduous Magnolia campbellii flowers in February and March before the leaves unfurl.
4 Magnolia x highdownensis does well on limey soils.
5 The starry flowers of Magnolia stellata are borne on young plants.

Mahonia (ma-ho-ne-a)

Commemorating Bernard McMahon, 1775–1816, an American horticulturist (*Berberidaceae*). At one time the mahonias were included in the same genus (*Berberis*) as the barberries. The chief distinguishing character of these evergreen shrubs is the pinnate leaf (lacking in *Berberis*) and the fact that the leaves are spiny, while the branches lack spines. When *M. aquifolium* was first introduced from North America in 1823, it had a great vogue and plants were sold for £10 each. Now in certain coverts in southern England the plant has naturalised itself, easily ousting native woodland undershrubs.

Species cultivated *M. aquifolium*, to 4 feet, leaves with 3–7 pairs of leaflets, yellow flowers in winter, bluish fruits (this is called the holly-leaved barberry and, quite wrongly, the Oregon grape). *M. bealei* grows to 12 feet and has pinnate leaves with 5–9 pairs of leaflets, 6-inch racemes of yellow flowers in winter held more or less erect, China. *M. fortunei*, 6 feet, 3–8 pairs of leaflets, racemes of yellow flowers 6 inches long, China. *M. haematocarpa*, 4–6 feet, 2 or 3 pairs of narrow leaflets, flowers yellow in short, few-flowered inflorescences, fruits scarlet, New Mexico, California. *M. japonica*, much like *M. bealei*, but the long racemes are lax and the flowers are

1 The long racemes of sweetly scented flowers of Mahonia japonica.
2 The leaves of Mahonia bealei colour well in autumn.
3 The blue-black berries of Mahonia aquifolium are glaucous.

pendent and sweetly scented, winter, Japan; var. *trifurca*, leaflets sea-green, flowers in erect spikes. *M. lomariifolia*, 6–12 feet, 10–20 pairs of sea-green rigid leaflets, flowers deep yellow, in erect racemes to 10 inches long, with up to 250 flowers per raceme, November and December, Formosa, Yunnan, the finest of the genus and one of the most striking of all flowering shrubs. *M. nepalensis*, to 10 feet, 5–11 pairs of leaflets, racemes of yellow flowers 1 foot long, Himalayas. *M. nervosa* (true Oregon grape), to 2 feet, 3–9 pairs of leaflets, leaves to 18 inches long, racemes of yellow flowers 8 inches long, California. *M. nevinii*, similar to *M. haematocarpa* but with smaller leaves and black fruits, California. *M. pinnata*, to 16 feet, similar to *M. aquifolium*, but more handsome, racemes of yellow flowers not confined to the top of a branch (not hardy in the north) primarily California and Mexico. *M. repens*, less than 1 foot, 2–4 pairs of leaflets, racemes of yellow flowers, 3 inches long, fruit black, North America; var. *rotundifolia*, 2–3 feet, leaves bluish-green, spineless. *M. trifoliolata*, to 8 feet, 1 pair of leaflets, plus one terminal leaflet, glaucous white in colour, flowers in short corymbs, yellow, Texas, New Mexico, Mexico. *M.* × *wagneri*, 5–8 feet, similar to *M. aquifolium*, but with 7–11 pairs of leaflets.

Cultivation Though *M. aquifolium* is not in any way particular about soil or situation, some of the others are not so accommodating and most need a well-drained growing medium and a sunny aspect. *M. fortunei, M. fremontii, M. pinnata* and *M. trifoliata* are hardy in milder sections only and even there should be given the protection of other shrubs or trees or of a wall. Elsewhere they do better in a cold greenhouse, where they can be protected from frost. Propagation is from seed sown in a frame in spring, suckers detached from the parent plant in autumn or spring or half-ripe cuttings rooted in sandy peat under glass.

Maianthemum (may-an-the-mum)

From the Greek *Maia*, the mother of Mercury (Greek mythology) to whom the month of May was dedicated, and *anthemon*, a flower *(Liliaceae)*. A genus of two or three species only, related to *Smilacina*. They are hardy herbaceous perennials with creeping root-stocks, and racemes of small white flowers. The leaves are rather like those of the lily-of-the-valley *(Convallaria majalis)* and the flowers resemble those of the smilacinas. The maianthemums are useful colonisers of shady places, and once established will need little or no attention. They make excellent flowering groundcovers in partial shade.

Species cultivated *M. bifolium*, May lily, twin-leaved lily-of-the-valley, 9 inches, racemes of white flowers 2 inches long, widely distributed over the north temperate regions, Europe and Asia. *M. canadense*, 7 inches, white, Canada. *M. dilatum*, larger in all its parts than the preceding, California to Alaska and Japan. All are May-flowering.

Cultivation No special care is needed, although shade from strong sun is desirable, and the plants thrive in thin woodland clearings. Detaching pieces of the creeping rhizomes provides a simple method of propagation (see also Smilacina).

Maid of the Mist—see Gladiolus primulinus

Maiden

This is a term used to describe a grafted or budded plant in its first season of growth. It is generally applied to roses and fruit trees but also to strawberry plants in their first year. Some of the finest exhibition roses are grown on maiden plants.

Maiden Pink—see Dianthus deltoides

Maidenhair Fern—see Adiantum

Maidenhair Spleenwort—see Asplenium trichomanes

Maidenhair Tree—see Ginkgo biloba

1 **Mahonia aquifolium** has deep yellow flowers during the spring months.
2 A useful plant for woodland gardens, **Maianthemum bifolium**, sometimes known as Twin-leaved Lily-of-the-Valley, has creamy white flowers and is a good ground cover plant.

Maiden's Wreath—see Francoa

Maihuenia (ma-hoo-ee-nee-a)

Derivation unknown, possibly a native name *(Cactaceae)*. A small genus of greenhouse succulent plants from South America belonging to the same group a the opuntias. They form low, many branched bushes. The flowers appear a the tips of the branches. Glochids ar absent from the areoles.

Species cultivated *M. patagonica*, cylindrical joints, central spines to 1½ inches long, white and yellow flowers, Patagonia. *M. poeppigii*, oval spiny joints central spines to 1 inch, yellow flowers Chile.

Cultivation In their native habitat thes plants grow on high mountains an during winter are often covered with snow. In cultivation the medium shoul be very porous (a well-drained porous cactus mixture with a third part added coarse sand, grit or broken brick). The require full sun in summer at norma greenhouse temperatures, and the com post must be kept moist. In winter the will withstand temperatures down t freezing point, provided the compost i dry. Propagation is by seed, or the joints can be removed and rooted in a coarse sand and peat mixture. See should be sown in well-drained cactus mixture and kept moist and shaded a about 70°F (21°C) until the seedlings appear. These should be pricked ou when the spines begin to appear betweer the cotyledons.

Maintenance of machinery—see Machinery in the garden

Maize—see Zea mays and Sweet corn

Majorana (ma-jaw-ra-na)
Derivation uncertain *(Labiatae)*. Marjoram. A genus of naturally herbaceous plants or sub-shrubs, perennial, sometimes included under *Origanum,* grown chiefly for their aromatic leaves and used for flavouring. Sweet marjoram can be used in salads.

Species cultivated *M. hortensis* (syn. *Origanum majorana*), garden marjoram, knotted marjoram, sweet marjoram, sub-shrub, 1–2 feet, flowers purple or white, summer, Europe. *M. onites* (syn. *Origanum onites*), common marjoram, pot marjoram, sub-shrub, 1 foot, white, summer, south-east Europe.

Cultivation Because it is not winter hardy, sweet marjoram is treated as an annual. Seeds are sown $\frac{1}{16}$ inch deep in boxes in a temperature of 55–65°F (13–18°C). Seedlings, when 2 inches tall, are transplanted outdoors in April, 6 inches apart in rows 9 inches apart. Seed may also be sown in a warm border in April. The tops are cut in July when the shoots are coming into flower, slowly dried in shade and stored for use in winter. Pot

marjoram is a hardy perennial, if given a warm position in light, well-drained soil. Sow seed in a sunny spot in March–April, finally setting out the plants 1 foot apart. Thereafter increase by division in spring. The tops may be used fresh in any season or dried in the same way as sweet marjoram.

Malacocarpus—see Wigginsia

Malathion
This is an organophosphorus compound very useful for controlling most sucking insects such as aphides, scales, whiteflies, also some sawflies, weevils and thrips, as well as possessing acaricidal properties against red spider mites. It is obtainable in the form of sprays, dusts or aerosols, the latter being especially suitable for use in mixed greenhouses where their use entails less danger of damage to sensitive plants than the spray form. Plants liable to be damaged

1 The annual Sweet Marjoram, Majorana hortensis, has purple or white flowers in summer and aromatic foliage which can be used fresh or dried.
2 Virginian Stock, probably the simplest of all hardy annuals to grow, comes in many shades of pink, mauve and white. Its name is Malcolmia maritima.

by malathion include antirrhinums, crassulas, ferns, sweet peas and zinnias. Malathion has the advantage that edible crops may be harvested one day after spraying, though it is as well to leave four days if there is considered to be a chance of taint.

Malay apple—see Eugenia malaccensis

Malcolmia (often spelt Malcomia) (mal-ko-me-a)
Commemorating William Malcolm, nurseryman, botanist, and associate of the naturalist Ray *(Cruciferae).* Though there are 35 species in this genus of hardy annual and perennial plants, and many quite decorative plants among them, there is one only which is commonly grown, the Virginian stock, *M. maritima.* The vernacular name is a misnomer as this plant is a native of Southern Europe and has been grown in many gardens since its introduction in 1713. *M. maritima,* which is perhaps the simplest of all hardy annuals to grow, is a 1-foot tall plant with a colour range including white, pink, red, yellow and lilac. There is a 6-inch tall variety in various colours, known as *nana compacta.* It is sometimes used to edge beds

of annual plants and may be sown quite thickly where it is intended to grow, thinning the seedlings to ½–1 inch apart when they are 1 inch tall. The seeds may be sown in spring for summer blooming, in early summer to flower in late summer and autumn, or in September to bloom in the following spring. Plants may also be grown in 5-inch pots to decorate a sunny windowsill or cold greenhouse.

Male

Because of its great importance in flowering plants, the arrangement and number of sex organs was used by Linnaeus in his sexual system of classification. The majority of plants have hermaphrodite flowers in which both male and female organs are found. In those plants known as monoecious each plant bears both male and female flowers. An example of this is provided by the genus *Begonia*. The term dioecious is used to describe those plants which are exclusively either male or female, such as the skimmia or the holly. A single male organ of a plant is called a stamen and consists generally of an anther containing the pollen and carried upon a slender stalk called a filament. The symbol ♂ is used to indicate a male in botany as well as zoology, and in botany the male system of the flower is called the androecium.

Male Fern—see Dryopteris filix-mas

Malephora (ma-le-for-a)
From the Greek *male,* meaning arm-hole, and *pherein,* to bear *(Aizoaceae)*. A small genus of small shrubby succulents from South Africa, with attractive flowers, similar to those of *Mesembryanthemum.* They are rare in cultivation. Several of the nine species have been cultivated from time to time, the stock having been raised from imported seed, but the plants do not appear to have been continuously maintained in cultivation. **Cultivation** A cool greenhouse is suitable, with a minimum winter temperature of about 40°F (4°C). The medium should be freely draining as it is for cacti. Propagate normally from seed; if several are raised they can be cross pollinated so as to set seed. Suitable south California.

Malope (mal-o-pe)
The old Greek name for a kind of mallow, meaning soft or soothing, from the leaf texture, or the plant's medicinal properties *(Malvaceae)*. This is a small genus of hardy annuals from the Mediterranean region, with showy rose or purple flowers.
Species cultivated *M. malacoides,* 1 foot, rose-pink and purple, June, Mediterranean region. *M. trifida,* 2–3 feet, purple, summer, Spain; vars. *alba,* white; *grandiflora,* large rosy-purple flowers; *rosea,* rose.
Cultivation Good soil and full sunshine

1 The staminate male cones of Pine produce the pollen or male element of the plant.
2 The shining purple flower of Malope trifida, a plant from Spain which is sometimes included in the herb garden because of its medicinal properties.

are appreciated and water should be given in dry periods. Soluble stimulants should be given occasionally when the plants are in full growth. Propagation is by seed sown in boxes or pots under glass in March in a temperature of 50°F (10°C), potting the seedlings on as necessary and planting them out 6

inches apart in their flowering position in May or June. Or seed may be sow ½ inch deep out of doors in April of Ma where the plants are to flower.

Maltese Cross—see Lychnis

Malus (ma-lus, may-lus)
From the Latin word for apple-tre *(Rosaceae)*. Apple, crab apple. A genus c about 25 species, mostly hardy decidu ous, rarely semi-evergreen, small o moderate in size, very twiggy trees o large bushes, cultivated primarily fo their fruit (see Apple) but specie (usually called crab-apples) and thei cultivars grown for the beauty of thei flowers, foliage or small, brightly coloured fruit. The species and hybrid described below are all deciduous. A flower in April and May.
Species cultivated *M.* x *aldenhamensis* 15 feet, rosy-crimson flowers, purplis leaves and fruits, hybrid. *M. angust. folia,* small tree, flowers salmon-pink Virginia, Florida, Mississippi. *M. atro sanguinea,* 15–20 feet, rosy-crimson hybrid. *M. baccata,* 40–50 feet, flower white, eastern Asia; var. *mandschurica* flowers white, fragrant, fruits red, th size of cherries. 'Cashmere Crab', flower pale pink, fruits yellow, hybrid. *M coronaria charlottae,* 25–30 feet, lat flowering, semi-double, soft pink, larg leaves colouring in autumn, garde origin. 'Crittenden', small tree, pale pink fruits bright scarlet, freely borne an persistent. 'Dartmouth Crab', white

1 Malus floribunda, the Japanese Crab, in full flower. The tree has arching branches smothered in flowers.
2 The striking yellow and red plum-shaped fruits of Malus 'John Downie' make it a decorative and popular Crab Apple.
3 The erect-growing Malus lemoinei has large wine-coloured single flowers, followed by small red fruits.

fruits large, plum-like. Native NY to Ala. to Mo. *M. eleyi*, to 20 feet, wine-red flowers, purplish leaves, numerous small purple-red fruits, hybrid. *M. floribunda*, Japanese crab, to 30 feet, arching branches with numerous carmine flower buds opening to white, small red fruit probably Japan; 'Excellens Thiel', is a small weeping form. *M. fusca*, Oregon crab, 20–30 feet, white or rosy-pink, fruits small, red or yellow, Alaska to northern Calif. 'Gibb's Golden Gage', 20–25 feet, fruits medium-sized, golden-yellow. 'Golden Hornet', erect to 25 feet, white flowers, prolific yellow, cherry-sized fruit. *M. halliana*, 15–18 feet, flowers pink, fruits small, purplish, China, Japan; var. *parkmanii*, flowers semi-double. *M. hartwigii*, 15–20 feet, flowers pink, ageing to white, to 2 inches wide, late-flowering, hybrid. 'Hopa Crab', flowers purplish red, large, hybrid. *M. hillieri*, to 20 feet, arching branches, semi-double pink flowers, crimson in bud, hybrid origin. *M. hupehensis* (syn. *M. theifera*), Hupeh crab, large white flowers, orange-pink in bud, later in

1 Malus purpurea is a rather spreading small tree with rosy-crimson flowers in May, and numerous dull crimson fruits later in the year.
2 Malus 'Marshall Oyama' has a profusion of pink buds followed by creamy-white flowers in early summer.
3 The wine-red flowers and purplish leaves of Malus eleyi.

pinkish; Europe (including British Isles) and South-west Asia; vars. *niedzwetzkyana,* reddish leaves, flowers purple-red, clustered, fruits large, dark red covered with purplish bloom, much used in hybridisation; *pendula* (syn. 'Elise Rathke') semi-pendulous branches, large flowers, large sweet fruits. *M. purpurea,* rather spreading small tree, rosy-crimson flowers, dark purplish-green shoots and leaves, numerous dull crimson fruits, hybrid origin. *M. robusta,* Siberian crab, cherry apple, vigorous round-headed small tree, white flowers, fruit prolific, cherry-like; vars. 'Red Siberian', fruits red; 'Yellow Siberian', fruits yellow; all hybrid origin. *M. sargentii,* shrub to 8 feet, white flowers with golden anthers, numerous small red fruits, Japan; var. *rosea,* pink flowers. *M. sieboldii,* 8–15 feet, semi-weeping habit, flowers pale pink, ageing to white, fruits small, red or brownish-yellow, Japan. *M. sikkimensis,* 20–30 feet, flowers white, fruits pear-shaped, dark red, Himalaya. *M. soulardii,* small tree, flowers pink, fruits yellow flushed red, hybrid. *M. spectabilis,* Chinese apple, tree to 30 feet, semi-double, deep pink buds, blush when open, fruits greenish, China; var. *riversii* (syn. *rosea plena*) an improved form. *M. toringoides,* leaves smaller and downier, colour well in autumn, China. *M. trilo-*

season, numerous small, orange-red cherry-like fruits, Western China. *M. ioensis,* Iowa crab, 20–30 feet, flowers fragrant, to 2 inches wide, white, flushed pink, fruits yellowish brown, to 1¼ inches wide, Minn., Ind., to Mo., neutral or acid soil; var. *flore pleno,* Bechtel's crab, flowers double, pink. 'Joy Darling', flowers wine-red, foliage crimson flushed, hybrid. 'John Downie', vigorous tree to 35 feet, inverted pear-shaped fruits, yellow, flushed red, good cooking crab, garden origin. *M. kansuensis,* 20–25 feet, flowers small, white, fruits small, egg-shaped, scarlet and yellow, foliage colours well in autumn, North China. 'Katherine', tree to 20 feet, large double flowers opening pink turning to white, bright red fruits, garden origin, USA. *M. lemoinei,* erect

growing, large wine-coloured single flowers, small red fruit, hybrid origin. *M. magdeburgensis,* small tree, flowers rose, semi-double, hybrid. *M. micromalus,* small tree, flowers pink and white, hybrid. *M. prattii,* 20–30 feet, flowers white, fruits red or yellow, egg-shaped, good autumn leaf colour, China. 'Prince Georges', flowers double, 2 inches across, light-pink, hybrid. 'Profusion', vigorous growth, young leaves at first copper-crimson, flowers wine-red, large, in clusters of six or seven, garden origin. *M. prunifolia,* small tree, flowers white, numerous red fruits hanging long on tree, Eastern Asia; vars. 'Cheal's Crimson', good form with crimson fruits; *fastigiata,* erect growth; *pendula,* weeping form. *M. pumila,* common wild crab, small spreading tree, flowers white or

The Siberian Crab, Malus robusta, is a vigorous round-headed tree with white flowers in May and colourful fruits borne in profusion.
1 The red fruits of M. 'Red Siberian'.
2 Malus 'Yellow Siberian' has golden yellow fruits.

bata, 25–30 feet, columnar in habit, leaves maple-like, flowers white, fruits yellow, small, western Asia. *M. tschonoskii*, 30–40 feet, pyramidal habit, flowers white flushed pink, fruits to 1 inch wide, brownish-yellow, good autumn leaf colour, Japan. 'Veitch's Scarlet', flowers large, white or pink, fruits large, scarlet. 'Wisley Crab', vigorous tree, bronzy-red leaves, flowers wine-coloured, fruit large, shiny red, garden origin. *M. yunnanensis*, 20–30 feet, flowers white or pale pink, fruits small, red, good autumn colour; var. *veitchii*, fruits more brightly coloured, good autumn colour. *M. zumii*, small pyramidal tree, flowers pink fading to white, fruits small, bright red, Japan; var. *calocarpa*, more spreading, smaller flowers, fruits persistent, 20 feet.

Cultivation The decorative species and hybrid crabs are tolerant of a wide range of soils, are extremely hardy and flower regularly, many kinds producing regular heavy crops of fruit. Only the minimum of pruning to shape the trees is necessary. They may be planted in sunny places among other trees or shrubs or make excellent specimen trees. Propagation of the hybrids and named kinds is by budding or grafting. The species may be raised from seeds, sown out of doors 3 inches deep in sandy soil in October, by cuttings 8–12 inches long rooted out of doors in autumn, or by layering in autumn.

Malva (mal-va)

From the Greek *malakos*, soft or soothing, probably in reference to an emollient yielded by the seeds *(Malvaceae)*. A genus of hardy herbaceous perennial and annual plants. *M. moschata*, the musk mallow, is one of the most decorative of our wild flowers, quite suitable for the herbaceous border. It is even more lovely in its white variety. All parts of the musk mallow are said to give off a musky odour when taken indoors, especially in warm dry weather. It is unfortunate that in some areas all malvaceous plants are afflicted by *Puccinia malvacearum,* the hollyhock rust.

Species cultivated *M. alcea*, 4 feet rosy-purple, summer, hardy perennial, often grown as annual, Europe; var. *fastigiata*, flowers red, July to October. *M. crispa*, 8 feet, purple and white, summer, annual, Europe, naturalised in Britain. *M. moschata*, 3 feet, rose or white, summer, perennial, Europe, including Britain; var. *alba*, white. *M. sylvestris*, 3 feet, purple, summer, biennial, Europe, including Britain.

Cultivation In general, these plants will grow in any kind of soil and in most aspects, though the annuals need sunny conditions to give their best. All can be easily raised from seeds sown in sandy soil in spring under glass in a temperature of 55°F (13°C). The perennials will flower in their second season.

---

1 Malva moschata alba, the white form of the Mallow. It is an attractive lax-growing plant easily raised from seed sown in the open.
2 The native Dwarf Mallow, M. neglectus. This little annual is usually a pleasing rosy purple.
3 The foxglove-purple blooms of Malva sylvestris, another European plant.

Malvastrum (mal-vas-trum)

From *Malva*, and the Latin *aster*, a star *(Malvaceae)*. These are herbaceous perennials and sub-shrubs, mostly American, and generally hardy, but some needing protection. Though a position on a sunny rock garden will suit some of these plants, it is safer with others to give them cold greenhouse treatment.

Species cultivated *M. coccineum,* 6 inches, red, summer, Manitoba to Texas. *M. gilliesii,* 6 inches, red, summer needs winter protection, South America. *M. lateritium,* 1 foot, salmon-red, summer, Uruguay, does best in the alpine house.

Cultivation If these plants are grown in the open garden protect from excessive winter rain, and a tilted glass pane will help to prevent this. Well-drained soil is needed, together with a sunny position. They may be easily raised from seed, sown in spring in sandy soil in a warm greenhouse in a temperature of

55°F (13°C), or from cuttings placed in a propagating frame in late summer.

Mamey sapote—see Lucuma mammosa

Mamillopsis—see Mammillopsis

Mammillaria (mam-mil-lar-e-a)
From the Latin *mamma,* the breast, or *mamilla,* nipple, in reference to the teat-like tubercles of many species *(Cactaceae).* A large genus of greenhouse succulent perennials, suitable for window culture. Most species are from the southern parts of North America and Mexico and can be recognised by the

1 Mammillaria bocasana grows in groups and has silky white hairs and red hooks from the areoles all over the plant. The flowers are papery and silver-pink in colour.
2 A group of Mammillaria geminispina.

numerous tubercles covering them; there are no ribs as on many globular cacti. They are mostly dwarf plants forming large groups *(caespitose),* but there are a few taller ones. Mammillarias have areoles between the tubercles from which flowers arise; they also have areoles on the tops of the tubercles from which the species arise. Offsets can form from either type of areole. The flowers are produced in rings near the growing centre between the tubercles (axils). No more flowers will appear at the areole where it has already borne a flower and so fresh growth must be encouraged each year.

Species cultivated There are over 300 species and many varieties—the following is a mere selection: *M. albicans,* densely covered with white spines, red flowers. *M. bocasana,* grouping, with silky white hairs and red hooks, flowers pink. *M. camptotricha,* pale green body with golden twisting spines, white flowers. *M. decipiens,* grouping, large tubercles with red spines, flowers pink or white. *M. elongata,* finger-like stems, many varieties, flowers white. *M. fraileana,* tall-growing with strong hooks, large pink flowers. *M. gracilis,* small type with offsets which fall readily, flowers yellowish. *M. hahniana,* very attractive, with long white hairs, red flowers, *M. innae,* small-growing, white-spined species, red flowers. *M. jaliscana,* globular, freely offsetting with large pinkish-red flowers. *M. karwinskiana,* open type with strong spines, cream coloured inner petals. *M. longiflora,* very long thin tubercles, many thin spines, long tubed pink flowers, central spine hooked. *M. magnimamma,* open type with many varieties, strong spines, flowers cream. *M. nunezii,* columnar growing, many fine spines, red flowers. *M. orcuttii,* dense white wool at top with dark spines, flowers pale red with darker mid-rib. *M. plumosa,* handsome species with feather-like spines, flowers pink, December. *M. quevedoi,* globular with white spines and wool at top. *M. rhodantha,* columnar growth with brassy spines, flowers pink. *M. spinosissima,* tall cylindrical type with many spines, yellow, brown, or red, flowers purplish. *M. tetracantha,* open type, with stiff spines, flowers pink. *M. uncinata,* open type with a hooked spine at each areole, flowers pink. *M. vaupelii,* covered with yellow and brown short spines, attractive. *M. wildii,* common species with yellow spines and hooks, flowers white. *M. xanthina,* rare species with strong hooks. *M. yaquensis,* small type making groups with fierce hooks. *M. zeilmanniana,* the most free-flowering species, with soft tubercles and cerise flowers.

Cultivation Grow mammillarias in well-drained potting mixture with ⅙ part of sharp sand, grit and broken brick added. Repot in March or April, once every year or two; do not use a large pot. Water well from March to October, as

often as the soil dries out, but do not water too much from October–February. The temperature in winter should be 40°F (4°C) and in summer 65–85°F (18–30°C). Some species, from Baja, California and the West Indies, require a higher winter temperature. Some open types need a little shade from strong sunshine. Plants are easily raised from seed sown in pans of well-drained seed mix in February in a temperature of 70°F (21°C). Keep the pans of seedlings at this temperature, moist and shaded. Offsets may also be rooted in a mixture of sharp sand and peat in equal parts. Some species may be increased by detaching and rooting tubercles.

Mammillopsis (ma-mil-op-sis)
From *Mammillaria,* and the Greek *opsis,* appearance, in reference to their resemblance to the mammillarias *(Cactaceae).* A genus of a few species of greenhouse succulent plants, with white spines. They make handsome plants not commonly found in collections. The white spines, many of which are hooked, form a dense covering.

Species cultivated *M. diguetii* has stronger spines and smaller flowers than the following species, Mexico. *M. senilis,* a very attractive plant, globular to cylindrical, with many white spines and hooks, reddish flowers 2 inches across, Mexico. Must have plenty of light and air.

Cultivation Use a well-drained potting mixture with $\frac{1}{5}$ part added of coarse sandy grit and broken brick. Pot every three years in March, and give the plants a very sunny place in the greenhouse. Water very little between October and March, but between March and September water well when the soil in the pot has dried out. The winter temperature should not be less than 40°F (4°C). Propagate from seed sown in pans of a well-drained seed mix, where a temperature of 70°F (21°C) can be maintained. Cover the seed lightly, keep it moist and shaded until germination, then give light but not direct sun. Offsets can be removed and rooted in coarse sand.

Mammoth tree—see Sequoia wellingtonia

Mandarin—see Citrus nobilis deliciosa

Mandevilla (man-de-vil-la)
Named in honour of H. J. Mandeville, one time British Consul in Buenos Aires, who introduced *M. suaveolens* to this country *(Apocynaceae).* A genus of

1 The white spines and hooks of Mammillopsis senilis make the plant look woolly and soft.
2 The Chilean Jasmine, Mandevilla, has sweetly fragrant trumpet-shaped flowers. It requires a warm greenhouse.

Mandragora (man-dra-gor-a)

From the Greek *Mandragoras* (Mandrake), a herb possessing narcotic properties *(Solanaceae)*. This genus contains two species of hardy herbaceous perennial plants, one of which, *M. officinarum*, may be cultivated because of its importance in ancient herbal medicine, and the remarkable ritual which then accompanied the procuring of the plant. It has very little claim to be included in a collection of plants of decorative value. It was believed that digging it up, or removing it from the ground resulted in the death of the person concerned, and an animal, usually a dog, was used. According to legend the operation of capturing the mandrake was undertaken at night, when its whereabouts were easily known, since it was self-luminous. Immediately, a brave man was to rush forward and describe a circle round it with a sword. Next, an unfortunate dog was tied to the plant, and, being offered meat just beyond its reach, wrenched the plant from the ground in its efforts to get the meat. Finally the precious juice was wrung from the roots, which were imagined to resemble a human trunk with its members. The name mandrake has also been given wrongly to *Podophyllum peltatum*.

Species cultivated *M. autumnalis*, 9 inches, violet, September, south Europe. *M. officinarum*, mandrake or devil's apple, 1 foot, greenish-yellow, May, south Europe.

Cultivation Well-drained soil and some light shade suit these plants. They may be propagated from seed sown in the cool greenhouse in March or by careful division of its roots in March.

Mandrake—see Mandragora officinarum

Manettia (man-et-te-a)

Commemorating Xavier Manetti, Prefect of the Botanic Garden at Florence in the mid-eighteenth century *(Rubiaceae)*. This genus of 30 species of plants of tropical America has given us three evergreen climbers with narrowly bell-shaped flowers, suited to greenhouse treatment.

Species cultivated *M. bicolor,* flowers red and yellow, tubular, 2 inches across the mouth, Brazil. *M. glabra,* crimson, 1 inch long, winter–early summer, South America. *M. inflata,* 10 feet, red, tipped yellow, 1 inch long, March–December, Uruguay; though the flowers are small they are continuously produced.

Cultivation Warm greenhouse treatment suits these climbers and a mixture of

about 50 species of tall, tender, climbing shrubs from tropical America, suitable for the warm greenhouse in the North. One species only *M. suaveolens,* is likely to be found in cultivation. This is the Chilean jasmine, a deciduous climber from the Argentine, bearing sweetly fragrant, funnel-shaped white flowers in summer. The leaves are dark green, about 3 inches long and slenderly pointed.

Cultivation This handsome plant does best when planted in a border in a warm greenhouse in a mixture consisting of equal parts of peat and turfy loam with plenty of sharp sand to ensure good drainage. It rarely succeeds when grown in a pot. Maintain a winter temperature of 40–50°F (4–10°C) and give the plant no water from December to February, afterwards watering freely until September, reducing watering thereafter until December. Syringe the plants twice a day from February to July to encourage plenty of new growth. Train the shoots up trellis-work or over the roof of a sunny greenhouse. After flowering is over prune the shoots to within 2 inches of their base. In the mildest parts of the country it may be grown in the open against a sunny wall where it can be given frost protection. Propagation is by cuttings taken of small, stiff side-shoots about 3 inches long inserted in sharp sand in a propagating frame with gentle bottom heat.

1 The legendary Mandrake or Devil's Apple, Mandragora officinarum has whitish flowers in early summer, and is found on dry waste ground.
2 The small orange and yellow flowers of Manettia inflata are produced continuously from March to December.

equal parts loam and peat with a fair amount of charcoal and sand, in pots or beds will give good results. Maintain a winter temperature of 45–55°F (7–13°C), watering moderately only between September and March, freely at other times. Syringe the plants daily during spring and summer to encourage the formation of new growth. The climbing growths should be trained up trellis-work or over the greenhouse rafters. Little pruning is necessary. Propagation is by seeds or cuttings in sandy soil in a propagating frame with a temperature of 65–75°F (18–24°C) in summer.

Mangifera (man-giff-er-a)
From *mango*, the Hindu name for the fruit, and the Latin *fero* to bear (*Anacardiaceae*). A genus of about 12 species of evergreen trees from tropical Asia, of which one only, *M. indica*, the mango-tree from the East Indies and Malaya, is likely to be found in cultivation in botanic gardens or large collections of greenhouse plants. In nature it grows to about 60 feet in height and bears white, yellow-streaked flowers in July, which are followed by kidney-shaped yellow and red fruits, up to 6 inches long, speckled with black as they become ripe. They are juicy and edible and are the mangoes widely grown in the tropics.
Cultivation This tree needs the warm, moist conditions of a warmhouse where a minimum winter temperature of 55–60°F (13–16°C) can be maintained, together with a humid atmosphere at all times. It should be planted in large containers or in the greenhouse border, in a mixture of peat and good loam in equal parts. Propagation is by cuttings taken in late summer and rooted in a propagating frame with bottom heat. Outdoors south Fla. and south Calif.

Mangold fly
The larvae of the mangold fly, *Pegomyia betae*, tunnel in the leaves of beet and mangolds causing blister mines. The first flies emerge from the over-wintering pupae in April and lay eggs on the underside of the leaves of the host plant. The larvae form the mines and, when fully fed, drop to the ground to pupate in the soil. There may be three generations a year. The pest is controlled by spraying with malathion or trichlorphon when the larvae are present in the mines.

Manila Hemp—see Musa textilis

Manna Ash—see Fraxinus ornus

Manna Grass—see Glyceria

Manna Gum—see Eucalyptus viminalis

Manure
Manure may be defined as any substance applied to the soil to make it more

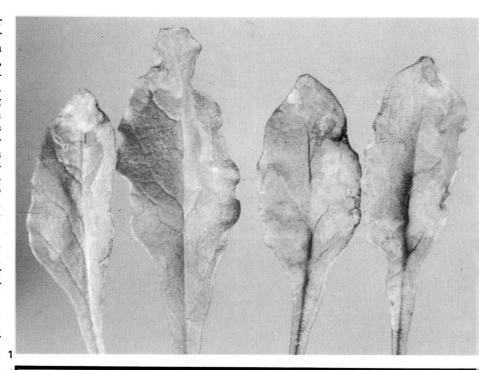

1

2

vegetable and animal waste material

micro-organisms react to release nitrogen, potash, phosphates etc and essential trace elements

humus, the end product, is distributed evenly through the soil layer and releases essential nutrients over a long period

fruitful—a term which may also be applied to fertilisers; so really it is without precise meaning. But we generally think of a manure as a bulky, humus-forming substance that is formed from animal or vegetable origin or in other words, it is a 'natural' manure.

Some bulky manures are inconvenient to handle, usually smelly and expensive to buy. So, will we get better plants, more nutritious vegetables and fruit, and do a better job of conserving soils if we use organic manures instead of relying solely

1 Beet leaves are damaged by the Mangold fly which causes blistery marks when the larvae feed on the leaf tissue.
2 Humus is one of the end products of decay. It absorbs many times its own weight of water thus helping sandy soils to hold moisture better. Substantial amounts of plant foods—nitrogen, phosphates, potash and others including trace elements—are produced in the process of decay. These become available to plants at a slow steady rate over a long period.

Humus may be added to the ground as a top-dressing or mulch in various ways.
1 When manure is used as a mulch, the effect of the release of food materials is slow and lasting.
2 A mulch of peat around Runner Beans not only keeps the roots cool and moist, but also provides food.
3 Wood chippings used as a slow-rotting humus mulch under conifers.

on factory made or 'artificial' fertilisers that supply plant foods alone? The answer is that bulky organic manures add to the content of organic matter, which plays a vital role in building and maintaining soil fertility. Every time you dig, hoe or cultivate a soil you let more air in. Then the soil organisms become more active and these break down organic matter, which is their food, and soils often lose their structure and become more difficult to work and soils on sloping ground often erode.

When first applied, the fibrous material opens up all soils making them more porous, better aerated and drained. Small animals and minute organisms break them down and in so doing produce waste products that bind and cement small particles together to form clusters and in some soils porous crumbs. These have large spaces between them that hold moisture yet allow surplus water to run away. The minute spaces within the crumbs hold moisture and plant foods available for plant use. A soil with a good crumb structure does not fall to paste when rained upon nor does it crush easily when cultivated.

Humus is one of the end products of decay. It absorbs many times its own weight of water and this helps sandy soils to hold moisture better—an effect that is most noticeable in dry periods. Close-grained soils, either silts or clays, which tend to pan or are difficult to work, are much improved. Garden compost, farmyard manure and most other organic manures also supply substantial amounts of plant foods—nitrogen, phosphates and potash and many others including trace elements. But being formed from plant and animal residues they differ from most factory-made fertilisers because their nutrients are not in a form that can be used by plants. For example the nitrogen may be part of a complex protein molecule and as such it cannot be absorbed by a growing plant (see Plant feeding). As the material begins to decay, the nitrogen in its proteins undergoes chemical change and is eventually converted into ammonium and nitrate forms that may be absorbed by plant roots. While these forms of nitrogen are exactly the same, whether they come from an inorganic fertiliser or a manure, they are released at a slow and steady rate over a very much longer period. This long-lasting effect is now being imitated in some of the newer synthetic organic fertilisers.

As 'natural' manures are long lasting in effect they are not exhausted as quickly as inorganic fertilisers, and generally leave useful residues for crops that follow. This is important to remember when planning vegetable rotations; cauliflowers and many other vegetable crops thrive in soils generously manured with organic manures, while others prefer the residues from a previously well-manured crop—a fact that leads to economy in the use of bulky manures.

Apart from the incorporation of manures in the soil before planting or during the life of the plant these materials are of great value when used as surface mulches. Mulches are like a blanket in retaining moisture. Water vapour from the soil surface diffuses very much more slowly through a loose mulch than it does from the bare soil surface. A wet bare soil can easily lose 1 inch of rain in a week, whereas a mulched soil will take about six weeks to lose this amount.

Mulches usually allow water to penetrate soils more easily, the raindrops trickle slowly through the fibrous material and do not compact the soil as badly as they do when falling on bare soil. So mulches are of particular value to silty soils that are subject to surface panning through heavy rain. On such soils even a very light mulch will break the force of rain and prevent compaction and, by protecting the surface from exposure to rain, lessen the chance of cracking.

The best-known organic manure is farmyard manure, but rotting plant remains, usually called composts, are manures too, and undecomposed materials like straw may be included (see Compost heaps). Organic wastes from industrial processes, town refuse and sewage sludges are also offered as organic manures.

All organic manures are not perfect. Some may have a bad effect on plants. For example straw, sawdust and even very strawy farmyard manure. These contain only a very little nitrogen but a lot of carbon and hydrogen, in the form of carbohydrates such as cellulose. But the attacking organisms need supplies of nitrogen while they feed on the carbohydrates and if extra nitrogen is not applied, they will take it from the soil and rob the plants.

This effect can be overcome by adding extra nitrogen to materials of this kind or by allowing them to undergo a partial decay before they are mixed with the soil.

Farmyard manure (FYM) Foldyard manure and dung are names used to describe a mixture of the excreta of farm animals and the straw or other litter used in yards or stalls to absorb the urine and to keep the animals clean.

If you live in a livestock-producing rural area it is easy to get a load of manure delivered to your garden. The average 3-ton truck usually holds about

5 cubic yards of manure which is sufficient for about 500 square yards of soil so that may be too much for your garden and it is necessary to share the load with a neighbour; a cubic yard weighs anything from 10 cwt to 15 cwt according to the amount of straw contained and the age of the manure. The main trouble, of course, is getting the manure into your garden. You need a gate at least 8 feet wide for truck or tractor and trailer access otherwise the manure has to be dumped outside the

Farmyard manure supplies its nutrients in a slowly available form and therefore has a long lasting effect; the benefits of a single dressing can remain for three years, or more.
1 When farmyard manure is fresh, or long, it may be dug into vacant ground or put at the bottom of trenches, at least a spade's depth below the surface When fresh it must not be used in conjunction with established plants as its effect is too caustic.
2 Well-rotted, or short, farmyard manure can be used safely when planting.

yard manure can vary in many ways from load to load, in contrast to inorganic fertilisers that have a fixed and definite composition.

The type of animal producing the dung has a big effect on quality. The dung (the solid excreta) of horses is rich in all nutrients and it is drier than that of cows or pigs, so that the bacterial changes during rotting are much more rapid and a greater amount of ammonia is produced. Horse manure when stacked soon begins to steam showing that fermentation is going on; so it is called a 'hot' manure, specially suitable for mushrooms and for greenhouse work.

Pig dung is the next richest, followed by cow dung; both of these are much wetter than horse dung and in consequence heat up more slowly and are referred to as 'cold' manures.

So far as nutrients are concerned, farmyard manures are weak; for example you need about 50 lb of horse manure to supply as much nitrogen as there is in 1 lb of sulphate of ammonia. The average analysis of most farmyard manures is about ½ per cent nitrogen, ¼ per cent phosphates and ½ per cent potash. All animal manures contain in addition useful amounts of magnesium and calcium and are very good suppliers of trace elements, together with other substances which are believed to have growth-promoting properties.

Quality also depends upon the kind of litter used for bedding. The most commonly used litter is straw, which absorbs about three times its own weight of urine and of course provides additional humus-forming matter. Peat moss is an even better absorber of urine and makes a manure which is easily spread and mixed with the soil. Sawdust and wood shavings are poor absorbers of liquids and are very slow to break down in the soil.

Benefits of manure In view of the foregoing you may well think that in a space age it is an archaic practice to use farmyard manure at all. But the results of experiments with good quality products show that it is the yardstick for comparing all other organic manures. In addition to its content of plant nutrients it is a humus supplier and for every ton you buy you will get about 3 to 5 cwt of organic matter which soon becomes humus in the soil and gives all the benefits associated with humus (see Humus). It supplies its nutrients in a slowly available form and, therefore, has a long-lasting effect; the benefits of a single dressing can last for 3 or more years.

Using farmyard manure If you have some ground ready when the manure comes in, you will lose less of your manure by digging it in right away; but it is often a question of getting a load when you can and storing it until the ground becomes vacant. If you buy a ton of manure now, you will only have about

Well-rotted manure is lighter and easier to handle than fresh manure.
1 Farmyard manure is used at a rate of about 10 lbs to the square yard. Here a plot of 8 square yards is being prepared and the required amount of manure has been wheeled out on to the land for digging in.
2 Well-rotted or short manure can be used at any time of the year and can be worked into the top tnree or four inches of vacant ground. The required amount should be spread evenly over the ground before being dug in.

garden and barrowed in rapidly to prevent it from becoming a nuisance to passers-by.

Town gardeners are hindered by the problems of access and the high cost of transport. Even so, some town gardeners do buy FYM, either directly through local manure dealers or through garden centres. Composted farm manures that are sold in bags are an obvious alternative to the fresh bulky material direct from the farm.

Quality Like all organic manures farm-

1 When stable manure is added while digging it is put at the bottom of the spit and covered with top soil, whether it is old or fresh.
2 One good way of ensuring that well-rotted manure is properly incorporated into the soil is work it in to the top 3-4 inches with a cultivator.

½ a ton in six months time because the microbes change parts of the manure into carbon dioxide and ammonia gases which blow away in the wind; nutrients are also washed out of the manure during heavy rain, forming the brown liquid which you often see round the bottom of a dung heap.

While in the heap it is best kept under cover and always kept trodden down tightly to exclude air, and if the drainings can be collected in a bucket or tank a great waste of precious plant nutrients can be avoided.

In very dry weather, moisten the heap periodically. By stacking fresh manure straight from the stable or piggery for a few months the product is improved; you get a better balance in nutrient content, the nitrogen part becomes slower-acting and is less likely to burn seedlings or the delicate roots of tender plants. The well-rotted manure is much easier to spread and mix in with the topsoil. You can tell if it is well rotted by the absence of unpleasant smell and even texture of the product—the straw part will no longer be recognisable. Fresh manure is much more difficult to spread and mix; if you intend to sow or plant soon after an application you have to bury it deeply otherwise it interferes with operations needed for preparing a plant bed.

Deeply buried manure does not give the best results; ideally it is spread on

well-broken soil and then worked in to a depth of 3 or 4 inches with a cultivator, then turned with a spade or fork. Take care not to turn the soil completely upside down, but rather at an angle wide enough just to cover the surface material. Manure covered with slabs of wet soil merely prevents humus formation. By mixing it with 3 or 4 inches of topsoil, hard crusts which prevent seedlings from pushing through easily, are obviated. To do any real good to soil that is low in humus it is essential to cover the soil with a layer thick enough to obscure the soil beneath it; this will need at least 10 lb of well-rotted manure per square yard. For vegetables this is done every 3 years before you plant crops such as brassicas that respond to generous dressings of manure.

Well-rotted farmyard manure can be applied at any time of the year before sowing or planting, but fresh or 'long' manure as it is called, is best dug in during the autumn or early winter so as to allow it to break down and lose its caustic nature in time for spring plantings.

For mulching during the summer the manure is useful for suppressing weeds and retaining moisture; when dug in at the end of the season it adds to the humus content of the soil.

Since large dressings of farmyard manure supply appreciable amounts of plant nutrients you can reduce your fertiliser dressings by half if 10 lb of well-rotted farmyard manure per square yard has been added.

Composted manures There are a number of products derived from fresh animal manures that are sold in bags under brand names. Large heaps of the fresh manure are allowed to decay under cover for several months during which time the coarse material is broken down and the heat of decomposition drives off much of the moisture.

The resultant dark brown spongy manure is applied at the rate of 6 to 8 ounces per square yard and is lightly forked in or mixed with the topsoil by means of a rotary cultivator.

These products are clean and convenient to handle.

Compost is the term used to describe partially decomposed or pre-digested organic residues. Composting is done before adding organic materials to the surface of the soil as a mulch or mixing with the soil as a manure.

It might be thought that since humus is such a good thing and is made from organic matter, any kind of organic

matter will improve the soil and will obviously give better plants, but this is not always true. Fresh straw, for example, when dug in without the addition of anything else, gives poorer plants not better ones.

In most organic manures there are two common substances—carbon and nitrogen—and both are necessary for humus formation. But straw has a great deal of carbon and very little nitrogen and when this is dug in, the soil microbes which are the humus makers take from the soil the nitrogen that they need for building up their own tissues thus robbing the plants of their requirements. If we add a nitrogen-rich material to the straw this will balance the carbon in the straw and so satisfy the soil microbes.

Other materials contain fairly large amounts of nitrogen and often decompose so quickly that much of the nitrogen and other plant foods are released so quickly that they are often lost before they can be used by the plants.

By combining such variable materials in the compost heap a good product can be obtained and better results achieved than if either kind of material had been used alone.

Well-made compost is equal in value to farmyard manure, but whether your compost heap is a useful source of humus or merely an evil-smelling rubbish dump depends on an elementary knowledge of the process of decay.

A common method of composting that has been practiced since ancient times is a slow process taking up to two years in which the refuse is put into a pit dug in the ground. The decay is brought about by anaerobic bacteria, that is, those that work in the absence of oxygen. Besides being inefficient, it produces evil odours, particularly when the heap is disturbed.

Good modern composting depends on organisms that require plenty of oxygen, known as aerobic bacteria, in order to break down the material quickly without objectionable odours. These are widely distributed in nature and are found in dust and all kinds of refuse so there is no need to add them. If you give them the right materials and their simple needs, air, moisture and warmth, they will do their work efficiently.

Raw materials The soft sappy garden wastes such as lawn mowings, hedge and bank trimmings, weeds and vegetable leaves are ideal. Tea leaves, coffee grounds, eggshells and potato peelings and other kitchen wastes can be added. Less desirable are wood shavings, sawdust, tree bark; these are best composted on their own. Even news-

1 Leaves collected in the autumn can be composted to form leafmould.
2 The site is prepared for a compost heap with a layer of old hedge clippings to ensure drainage and aeration. Wire netting surrounds the heap.

papers that have been thoroughly soaked in water can be used.

Best kept out are thick woody stems, tough weeds and diseased plants.

Making the heap The area should be marked out on a well-drained site; it should never stand in a puddle. But it should be within reach of hose or pipe.

The size of the heap depends upon the amount of material available. You will need very large amounts of material to complete even a small heap in one operation, and you have to plan the size by the amount you have available.

As a general guide for a small garden an area 3 feet by 3 feet should be marked out in a well-drained and sheltered spot away from the house. Making the heap will be much easier if you knock in a stout stake at each corner. Then lay a layer of coarse material such as old prunings, broken up cabbage stalks to help aeration and drainage. Garden refuse should be mixed as thoroughly as possible so that the coarse waste is incorporated with the soft waste; this applies particularly to grass mowings which should not be put in thick layers otherwise air entry will be blocked. Cabbage stalks and woody herbaceous stems will rot quicker if broken up and chopped into short lengths before mixing with the softer material.

The heap is then built up layer by layer to a height of 4 feet, each layer being made 1 foot thick and compacted by treading or with a spade until it goes down to 6 or 8 inches. Each layer should be sprinkled with water; dryness is fatal, but never overwet the heap, particularly during the winter when sodden conditions prevent bacterial activity.

The heap should have straight sides and the top left flat, or with a slight depression in the middle to catch and hold the rain.

It is much more convenient to make a bottomless bin of old planking or heavy gauge wire netting in which the waste can be collected and raked level. Extra stout gauge wire, galvanised, painted or plastic coated bins 3 feet by 3 feet hold one cubic yard of firmed material; when well-rotted the material in a bin of this size weighs about ½ ton.

If the material is very woody or mature sprinkle sulphate of ammonia on each layer at the rate of ½ ounce per square yard and water it in, otherwise special aids are unnecessary; good composting depends on maintaining correct conditions for the organisms that do the work i.e. moisture, air, warmth.

1 Pea vines, cabbage stumps, egg shell and general garden rubbish are added in a thick layer. The sides of the heap must be kept firm.
2 Sulphate of ammonia is lightly spread over the heap at the rate of ½ ounce per square yard to encourage decay and hasten decomposition.

It takes about 6 months to produce good compost, but if you are in a hurry to use it you can get quite good compost in about 3 months, but turning the heap will be necessary to speed up decomposition. Heaps of coarse or woody material would have to be turned three times to speed up decay. A really wet heap would have to be turned more frequently; should there be a bad smell, a good rule is to turn the heap daily until the smell disappears. When turning the heap, always put the drier, outside material into the centre of the new heap.

The temperature of properly managed compost rises quickly even in cool weather as a result of the intense activity of the organisms and it may rise high enough to kill the weed seeds and spores of disease fungi. But there is no guarantee that they will all be killed so it is best to keep diseased material out of the heap.

You can tell when the compost is ready for use by extracting a sample from the middle of the heap with a trowel. It should be fibrous and break into small pieces when squeezed, be a dark brown colour and have a pleasant smell.

Using the compost Well-made composts from vegetable wastes may contain more nutrients and more organic matter than good farmyard manure.

If you know that your soil is very low in humus, about 10 lb per square yard should be mixed with the topsoil for a year or two and in subsequent years give 5 lb per square yard.

Seaweed One of the oldest manures known is seaweed, which is widely used for improving the soils of gardens and farms in coastal districts. The different weeds vary in plant food content; the long broad-leaved species, which is usually found just below the low water mark, is richer than the bladder wrack *(Fucus)* found between low and high tides. It is gathered all the year round but the richest harvest is thrown up by spring tides, or during storms.

About three-quarters of seaweed is water, the remainder being humus-forming material. It contains about ½ per cent nitrogen and up to 1½ per cent phosphates and about 1–1½ per cent potash. Since seaweeds have no roots they obtain all their nutrients from the dissolved substances in the sea, which is constantly being enriched by drainage from the land. So they absorb very large quantities of nutrients and are, therefore, an excellent source of trace elements.

1 Water-in the Sulphate of ammonia to keep the heap moist and thus provide the correct conditions for the bacteria to work: moisture, warmth and air.
2 A bottomless bin can be constructed in which to collect composting material for use as humus.

The actual organic matter consists very largely of alginic acid which, unlike the cellulose which you get in farmyard manure, rots readily in the soil and is an excellent soil conditioner. The other carbohydrates and simple sugars found in seaweed also decompose readily in the soil.

It is best dug into the soil immediately after spreading to prevent it from drying out into a hard, woody mess. The usual rate of application is 10 lb per square yard. Seaweed is particularly suitable for sandy soils in view of its comparative freedom from fibre, thus allowing rapid humus formation. Freedom from weed seeds and disease organisms is an additional advantage of this manure. Its content of common salt is not usually harmful to plants when the manure is used at the normal rates of application.

Dried seaweed products Abroad seaweed dried and ground is now available under brand names. Thus prepared the natural product can be transported inland economically and is four to five times as concentrated as wet seaweed or farmyard manure. The product is dry and pleasant to handle and is sold in small packs. Some manufacturers reinforce their products with fertilisers to give them a higher plant food content and to overcome the tendency of dried seaweed temporarily to tie-up nitrogen in the soil.

The best results are obtained from dried products to which fertiliser has been added when they are applied to the surface of the soil during winter cultivation and left for a few weeks to break down; this time varies according to weather and soil conditions, but about four weeks is sufficient in most instances. A reasonable dressing is 2–4 ounces per square yard.

Products reinforced with complete fertilisers are sold by some manufacturers and are intended to overcome the initial 'tie-up' of nitrogen in the soil. These can be used in the spring and summer on growing plants, at the rate of 2–4 ounces per square yard, for all crops.

Dried seaweeds are also used in soil composts and in topdressings for lawns. The usual rates of application already quoted may seem to be rather low for a bulky organic manure whose main function is to supply humus, but seaweed preparations contain alginates which stimulate the soil organisms to greater activity that results in better tilth formation in heavy soils and greater water-holding properties in sandy soils.

Their trace element content is most valuable and makes this class of manure one of the best and safest means of providing soils with nutrients that are needed in very small amounts.

Spent hops The residue after hops have been extracted with water in the brewery is usually sold to haulage contractors who supply commercial growers with the entire output from many breweries and in consequence the

amounts available for gardeners is somewhat limited. Some of the output purchased by fertiliser manufacturer who reinforce the spent hops wit concentrated fertilisers in order to rais the food content.

In the fresh wet state straight from th brewery, spent hops contain about 7 per cent water, about ½ per cent nitrogen, ¼ per cent phosphates an traces of potash. But since the moistu content varies considerably so does th plant food content. So an analysis base on the dry matter is the best figure. O this basis the nitrogen content range from 2–3 per cent and the phosphat

1 Peat is used as a mulch for Strawberries, and is forked in after picking.
2 Chrysanthemum cuttings rooted, *right* in a seaweed meal compost, and *left,* without the meal in the compost. Although it is not usual to grow cutting in such a compost, there is the advantage that food is available if potting-on has to be delayed.
3 French Beans, *left,* grown with the addition of a seaweed compost, germinate better.

content is about 1 per cent. If you are able to get a good supply of spent hops locally you can improve the plant food content by adding 50 pounds of good, complete fertiliser to every ton of hops. The fertiliser should be sprinkled over the hops and the heap turned over twice to ensure even mixing.

You cannot, as a rule, get small quantities of spent hops; they are usually sold by the truck load which may weigh several tons. If you have large areas of shrub borders to mulch or a very large vegetable garden you will need a truck load to do any real good.

Hop manures are proprietary products prepared from spent hops and reinforced with fertilisers. They are sold in bags together with instructions for use in the garden in the British Isles.

Spent hops are regarded mainly as humus suppliers and are used in the preparation of ground for planting and also for mulching established plants. The best results are obtained when they are incorporated thoroughly with the top 6 inches of soil at the rate of 10 lb per square yard during the winter. For mulching purposes spent hops are very effective in keeping down weeds and retaining soil moisture in shrub borders and soft fruit plots, provided the ground is covered really thickly. If you apply a layer 4–6 inches thick it will last for two years before rotting noticeably. The material gives off an objectionable odour after application but this usually disappears after 2–3 weeks. Although spent hops are slightly more acid than most soils they are used with great success for practically all trees and shrubs except for some of the outstanding lime-requiring plants. The fire hazard from burning cigarette ends is low since spent hops do not burn readily when used as mulches.

Spent mushroom compost The material left after a mushroom crop has been cleared from the beds in which the spawn was planted usually consists of a mixture of well-rotted horse manure and the soil which was used for covering the beds before planting the mushroom spawn. Peat and lime is often used in place of soil in which case the compost will have a proportion of lime in it.

So the quality of the product depends very much upon the proportion of casing soil which it contains. The organic matter of spent mushroom compost is generally more decomposed than in strawy farmyard manure and hence it may be less useful for improving heavy soils.

Being fibrous and well-rotted the compost is an ideal material for mixing in with the topsoil of all soils. The nitrogen content of fresh spent horse manure compost including soil is usually lower than farmyard manure and the phosphate and potash content is just slightly lower.

The lime-rich composts are unsuitable for rhododendrons and other lime-haters, and may contain excessive amounts of lime for fruit crops.

Normal rate of application is 5–10 lb per square yard.

---

1 The addition of such material as spent hops, here used as a top-dressing or mulch, adds humus to the soil.
2 A straw mulch between fruit trees serves to conserve moisture and discourage weeds, and is later ploughed in to add to the humus content.

Manzanita—see Arctostaphylos manzanita

Maple—see Acer

Maranta (mar-ant-a)
Commemorating B. Maranti, an Italian botanist *(Marantaceae)*. This genus contains 30 species, all natives of tropical America. One important economic product, the West Indian arrowroot, is prepared from the rhizomes of *M. arundinacea*. However, those species which are usually cultivated under glass are valued for the sake of their decorative leaves.
Species cultivated *M. arundinacea varie-*

1 Maranta leuconeura kerchoveana has green leaves with deep rosy purple markings. The plant sometimes has small white flowers.
2 Maranta leuconeura massangeana has green leaves with white veins. They are rosy-purple on the underside.
3 The Pearl Berry Margyricarpus setosus is a trailing shrub.

gata, 6 feet, leaves green and white. *M. bicolor,* 1 foot, leaves olive green, Brazil. *M. chantrieri,* 1 foot, leaves grey and dark green. *M. leuconeura,* 1 foot, leaves green, white and purple; vars. *kerchoveana,* green and dark red leaves; *massangeana,* green and rosy-purple.
Cultivation All need warm conditions and

some shade from full sun; under glass o outdoors in South. They are also grow as houseplants and will succeed provide the room temperature does not fall belo 50°F (10°C) and a moist atmosphere i provided round the leaves by standin the pots in other containers filled wit water-absorbent material such as pea which is kept moist. They do best i shady rooms or in shady corners of wel lit rooms. Water in abundance i required from March to October, an plants should be syringed daily durin this period. Keep the soil on the dry sid from October to March. A suitabl mixture consists of 1 part of loam, parts of peat, 1 part of sand, in wel drained pots. The temperature fro February to October should be 60–70° (16–21°C), October to February 55–65° (13–18°C). Repot the plants in sprin after their winter rest. Propagation is b careful division of the rhizomes o tubers at potting time.

March moth—see Moth

Marguerite—see Chrysanthemum frutescens

Marguerite, Blue—see Felicia amelloides

Marguerite, Golden—see Anthemis tinctoria

Margyricarpus (mar-ge-re-kar-pus) From the Latin *margarita,* a pearl, an *karpos,* berry, in reference to the whit fruit *(Rosaceae).* This unusual genus i the rose family has three South America species, only one of which is cultivate in gardens, for the sake of its smal persistent pearly-white succulent fruits *M. setosus,* the pearl berry, from th Andes, is a trailing shrub, about 1 inches tall, suited to a sunny roc garden. It has narrow evergreen leave and inconspicuous green flowers.
Cultivation A soil mixture consisting o equal parts of loam, leafmould, and san suits this rock plant. Propagation is b seed sown in pans of sandy soil in a col frame in spring or autumn, or by cuttin of young growth rooted in an unheate propagating frame in summer, or th trailing shoots may be layered i autumn.

Marianthus (ma-re-an-thus) From *Maria,* Mary and the Gree *anthos,* a flower, the plant is dedicate to the Virgin Mary *(Pittosporaceae).* small genus of Australian shrub, som having a twining, and others a prostrate habit. The flowers are usually i terminal panicles or almost umbellate They all require cool greenhouse treat ment in the North. Only one species i regularly cultivated, *M. procumbens* from New South Wales, a dwarf shrub with small leaves and white flowers either solitary or in twos or threes

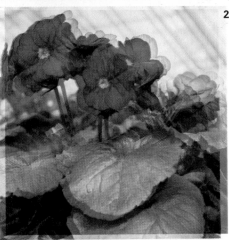

1 **Marianthus procumbens**, a dwarf shrub from New South Wales, has small white flowers in spring.
2 The well-known house and greenhouse flowering plant **Primula obconica** was introduced by Charles Maries.
3 **Iris kaempferi**, of which there are many varieties, was introduced by Charles Maries during the 1870s.
4 **Platycodon grandiflorum**, one of the many introductions attributed to Charles Maries.

produced in spring.

Cultivation This is a relatively slow, weak grower. The twiners are usually trained on wires, or similar supports. It does best in a light medium, i.e. 1 part of loam, 2 parts of peat, 1 part of sand. Propagation is by seed or by semi-ripe stem cuttings inserted in a sandy compost in a closed propagating case in summer.

Maries, Charles

Charles Maries (1851–1902), who was born at Stratford on Avon and first worked in his brother's nursery at Lytham in Lancashire, was the man chosen by Veitch's, the famous Victorian nursery firm, to follow in the footsteps of the French Jesuits whose plant introductions from the east had drawn attention to the rich harvest which might be gained there.

Maries was a foreman gardener with Veitch in 1877 when they sent him to Japan, asking him to concentrate on the sending home of conifer seed and cones and then go on to the Yangtze Valley in China to hunt on a wider basis.

He spent the first year in Japan before going to Formosa for a short stay and then travelled through China to the Yangtze, but severe attacks of sunstroke sent him hurrying back to the coast to recover. In the summer and autumn of 1878 he returned to Japan and was quite successful in his work, but in the spring of 1879 he made for the Yangtze, again travelling as far as the Ichang Gorges, where he came up against trouble with the natives who robbed him of the whole of his baggage, but not before he had

found and was able to introduce that popular house and greenhouse plant, *Primula obconica*.

Maries who had the advantage of having being taught by Professor Henslow, the well-known botanist, was a careful, discerning plant-hunter and, although his finds were not of the same magnitude as those of the people who went before him or after, he introduced many popular plants and conifers, some 38 new plants having been sent home by him from China.

From Japan he sent the two favourite climbing plants, *Schizophragma hydrangeoides* and the colourfully foliaged *Actinidia kolomikta* as well as *Hamamelis mollis*, *Rodgersia podophylla* and the lily, *L. speciosum gloriosoides*. Among others of his introductions were *Platycodon grandiflorum mariesii*, *Styrax obassia*, *Lilium thunbergianum*, *Enkianthus campanulata*, *Azalea rollisoni*, *Iris kaempferi* (many varieties), *Davallia mariesii* and *Osmunda japonica corymbifera*.

His conifer introductions included *Abies veitchii, sachalinensis, mariesii* and *brachyphylla*.

Maries returned home in 1880 but in 1882 he was recommended by Sir Joseph Hooker, of Kew, as Superintendent of the State Gardens and private parks of the Maharajah of Durbhungah. Later he took charge of the State Gardens of the Maharajah Scindia of Gwalior where he remained until his death on October 11th, 1902.

Maries was an original recipient of the Victoria Medal of Honour granted by the RHS and was a Fellow of the Linnean Society.

Marigold, African; French—see Tagetes

Marigold, Common or Pot—see Calendula

Marigold, Corn—see Chrysanthemum segetum

Marigold, Marsh—see Caltha palustris

Mariposa Lily—see Calochortus

Mariscus (mar-is-cus)
The old name used by Pliny for a kind of rush *(Cyperaceae).* A large genus of herbaceous perennial plants, rush-like or grass-like in appearance, closely related to *Cyperus,* in which genus they are sometimes included, all natives of the warmer parts of the world. One of the species grown is *M. umbilensis* (syn. *Cyperus natalensis),* from South Africa, a grassy-leaved marsh plant up to 3 feet high, with globular flowerheads, up to 1 inch long, made up of numerous spikelets, and narrow bracts up to 2 feet long.
Cultivation A heavy loam suits it best, and it should be grown in the cool greenhouse with a minimum winter temperature of 40–45°F (7–10°C), the pots of plants should have some shade. Water generously except in winter. Propagation is by seed sown in gentle heat in spring or by division of the roots at almost any time except winter.

Marjoram—see Majorana and Origanum

Marl
The noun, when used in its strictest sense, means a mixture of clay and chalk. However, the verb to marl has long been used to mean the operation of opening a deep pit down to a stratum of clay which was then applied to fields of exhausted gravelly or sandy soil.

Over parts of the US and among the red sandstone soils of England there are found old marl pits, and sandy soils in the various districts have been marled from pits in the nearby clay.

It is found, however, that the true marl with its addition of calcium carbonate is a far more valuable dressing for excessively light sandy or gravelly soils. The effects of a good marling may last for thirty years, and many ancient town gardens on light soils might well be rejuvenated by marling. The operation is best carried out in autumn and the real benefit does not begin to show till the second year.

2

3

1 A grassy-leaved marsh plant, **Mariscus** from S. Africa.
2 Marrow seeds are sown three to a 5-inch pot in a warm greenhouse in April or early May.
3 The seeds are pushed into the medium to just cover them.
4 The surplus seedlings are pinched out leaving the strongest. Here the seedlings are growing in peat pots, which can be planted straight out in open ground.

A ¼-inch deep top-dressing of marl 4 passed through a fine sieve is sometimes used to bind together the surface of grassed areas, such as cricket pitches, which are subject to hard wear.

Marmalade Fruit—see Lucuma mammosa

Marrow cultivation
The marrow is a popular, half-hardy vegetable. In the North it is often raised from seeds sown under glass in March or early April. Sow two or three seeds in pots of well-drained seed mix. In colder parts of the country extra heat may be necessary to assist germination. Thin the plants to leave one seedling in each pot and wait until all risk of a late spring frost has passed before setting the plants in their growing positions in the open. Alternatively, give the plants Hotkap protection until all

1 frost danger is past.

A very rich bed is essential for a regular supply of marrows between the summer and the autumn. Soil which has received a generous dressing of well-rotted farmyard manure or garden compost is ideal. Planting distances depend on the type of plant. A bush variety needs almost one square yard of surface area; a trailer needs a great deal more if allowed to roam at will over the ground. Trailing or vining marrows may also be trained on tall supports. These may be bamboo canes or even the garden fence.

Water is essential and the plants must on no account be permitted to become dry at the roots. Liquid manure feeds should be given weekly when the first marrows begin to swell. To ensure that both water and liquid manure reach the roots, some gardeners sink a clay pot alongside each plant. The water and the liquid foods are poured into the pots and run directly to the root area. Weeding is necessary until the large leaves shade the surrounding soil and inhibit weed growth.

The plants bear male and female flowers. Bees, flies and other insects transfer ripe male pollen to the female blooms. Where female flowers fall off without setting fruits, natural fertilisation is not occurring. In such cases, hand pollination is advisable. Do this before noon. Pick a male flower for each female to be hand pollinated. Strip the petals from the male and twist its core into the centre of the female. The females may be recognised quite easily because they

1 *Above* the male and *below* the female flowers of the Marrow, with the immature vegetable behind it. Marrow flowers at times are fertilised by hand, in order that the fruit can form.
2 Varieties of Bush Marrows, *left,* 'Bush Green' and *right,* 'Bountiful'.
3 Marrow 'Table Dainty' a popular variety with striped skin.

2

3

carry an embryo marrow behind them.

Bush plants need little attention. Trailers may be guided between other crops or, if they are to be trained to supports, the main shoot must be tied in regularly. Cut the marrows when they are young and tender. They are old if the thumb nail does not pierce the skin easily. Marrows for jam or for storing are allowed to ripen on the plants until September. The storage place should be cool and dry. The marrows are sometimes hung up in nets for storage purposes. Smaller marrows are now preferred. Up-to-date varieties include 'Zucchini F₁ Hybrid' (bush), 'Productive' (bush), 'Prolific' (trailer), 'Cluseed Roller' (trailer). 'Rotherside Orange' is a prolific variety of excellent flavour. 'Cocozelle' (the Italian vegetable marrow), a bush variety, produces dark green, yellow-striped fruits up to 2 feet long.

Courgettes, or French Courgettes, have become increasingly popular in recent years. In the natural course of events the fruits do not grow very large but, in any case, to obtain the best results, they should be cut when not much bigger than thumb size and cooked unpeeled. Constant cutting will ensure the steady production of fruits throughout the summer. Cultivation is otherwise the same as for the larger marrows. For exhibition purposes, 'Sutton's Table Dainty' is a popular variety.

1 A selection from the wide range of marrows.
2 Courgettes, which are like small Marrows, should be cut when they are very small. Regular cutting ensures a long-lasting supply.
3 The White Horehound, Marrubium vulgare, has rough woolly leaves, and is a remedy for coughs.

Marrubium (mar-oo-be-um)
The old Latin name *(Labiatae)*. A genus of perennial herbaceous plants from the temperate and warm regions of the Old World, most species of which are notable for their very hairy or woolly leaves. The only species likely to be found in common cultivation is *M. vulgare*, the horehound or white horehound, 1 foot tall, with woolly leaves and white flowers from June to September, a native of Europe including Britain. This was once grown for the sake of its leaves and young shoots from which an effusion was made and used as a cough cure. Nowadays it is more likely to be used as a bee plant. The variety *cylleanum* has even woollier leaves.
Cultivation The plant is perfectly hardy, but grows best in dry, sunny places. Plant in spring, setting the plants 12–15 inches apart. Propagation is by seed sown out of doors in spring, by division of roots at the same season, or by cuttings rooted out of doors in a shady

lace in April.

Marsdenia (mars-de-ne-a)
Named in honour of William Marsden, FRS, 1754–1836, author of a *History of Sumatra (Asclepiadaceae)*. A genus of some 70 species of evergreen twining shrubs mostly from tropical Colombia, British Guiana, India, and New South Wales. The flowers of most species are bell-shaped or urn-shaped.

Species cultivated *M. erecta*, half hardy, to 6 feet, fragrant white flowers, July, Syria. *M. flavescens,* twining, to 20 feet, yellowish flowers, June and July, New South Wales, warm greenhouse. *M. suaveolens,* erect or twining, to 3 feet, fragrant white flowers, July, New South Wales, warm greenhouse.

Cultivation Twiners are suitable for a warm greenhouse (*M. erecta* outdoors), when planted in a medium of sandy loam with a little peat or leaf soil added. Maintain a minimum winter temperature of around 50–55°F (10–13°C). Propagation is by cuttings taken in April or May and inserted in sand in a frame with gentle bottom heat.

Marsh Gentian—see Gentiana pneumonanthe

Marsh Mallow—see Althaea officinalis

Marsh Marigold—see Caltha palustris

Marsh Speedwell—see Veronica scutellata

Martagon Lily—see Lilium martagon

Martynia (mar-tin-ee-a)
Commemorating John Martyn, eighteenth-century botanical writer and Professor of Botany at Cambridge (*Martyniaceae*). A small genus of herbaceous perennials or annuals, closely related to *Proboscidea*, native to warmer states, Delaware to New Mexico, of which one, *M. louisiana* (syn. *M. annua*) the unicorn plant, or elephant's trunk, is in general cultivation. This is grown as a half-hardy annual. It grows about 2 feet or more tall and the leaves may be up to 1 foot long. The bell-shaped flowers are up to 2 inches long and are strangely coloured. Basically yellowish, with a white tube, they are spotted with green, yellow, violet and white and have violet lines. The lobes are violet and are marked in much the same way. The fleshy fruits are up to 6 inches long, of which half the length consists of a curved beak, with two hooks at the end.

1 The Marsdenias are evergreen twining shrubs from New South Wales.
2 The Unicorn Plant or Elephant's Trunk, Martynia louisiana, is grown as a half-hardy annual. It has large leaves and the flowers are mainly pink.

Cultivation The plant is treated as a half-hardy annual and the seeds are sown in a well-drained seed mix in the warm greenhouse in early spring. The seedlings are potted on into individual pots before being hardened off and planted out in light soil and a warm, sunny place in late May or early June. Alternatively, they may be grown in pots for greenhouse decoration.

Marumi Kumquat—see Fortunella japonica

Marvel of Peru—see Mirabilis jalapa

Maryland Pink Root—see Spigelia

Masdevallia (maz-dev-al-le-a) Commemorating Dr José Masdevall, died 1801, a Spanish botanist *(Orchidaceae)*. A large genus of epiphytic orchids from South America, with short, single-leaved, clustered stems without pseudobulbs. They are mostly small-growing plants, often with attractive flowers, the sepals of which are the dominant feature. In some varieties the sepals are prolonged into tails, in others they are either spreading or joined at the top to form a tube.

Species cultivated A selection only from this large genus: *M. bella*, yellow, spotted chocolate-red, spring, Colombia. *M. calura*, reddish with yellow tails, summer, Costa Rica. *M. chimaera* very striking, yellowish with dark spots, lip slipper-shaped, tails up to 5 inches long, but a very variable species, Colombia. *M. coccinea*, magenta-purple, varied, Colombia. *M. elephanticeps*, large, yellowish with purplish-red marks, various times, Colombia. *M. ignea*, cinnabar red with crimson veins, spring, Colombia. *M. muscosa*, small flowers, yellowish-brown, lip snaps up when touched by an insect, the latter being held for a short time, and then released, various times, Colombia. *M. tovarensis*, pure white, winter, flowers appear in succession, old spikes should not be removed, Venezuela. *M. veitchiana*, very fine large flowers, brilliant orange, shaded with crimson-purple, spring, Peru.

Cultivation A mixture of equal parts of osmunda fibre and sphagnum moss in shallow pans or baskets is suitable. A well-aired but moist atmosphere is essential for good growth. Ample shading should be provided. As the plants have no pseudobulbs, no resting period should be given, but the plants should not be allowed to dry out completely at any time. Maintain a minimum temperature of 55°F (13°C) in winter, rising to 70°F (21°C) in summer. Good ventilation is essential at all times but avoid draughts. Propagation is by division of the plants in spring.

Maskflower—see Alonsoa

1

2

3

1 The neon-pink flowers of Masdevallia coccinea are somewhat variable, though always a shade of magenta.
2 Masdevallia 'Stella' has pink solitary flowers with long stiff tails to the sepals.
3 The upper sepal in Masdevallia coccinnea is markedly narrow and prolonged giving a bizarre appearance.

Masonry

The construction of features in the garden with the use of various types of stone is a very important part of garden-making or improvement. If the design is kept simple, the minimum of skill will produce good results, provided a few basic facts are appreciated.

Any feature made from stone is only as strong as its foundations and the mortar joints. Always make sure that the foundations are well consolidated with rubble, especially if the soil is light. A trench should be excavated about 12 inches deep and slightly wider than the width of the feature which is to be built in it. The rubble should be rammed in to a depth of about 6 inches. A layer of cement should follow, finishing just below the level of the surrounding soil. A suitable mix for this foundation cement is: 1 part of cement, 3¼ parts of sand, and 5 parts of shingle. If mixed ballast is used: 1 part of cement, 6 parts of mixed ballast. For the bonding of joints and courses, a special mix is required and this is made up of: 1 part of cement, 1 part of lime and 5 parts of sand.

Such is the variety of materials available to you for masonry work, that it may be often difficult for you to decide upon the most suitable type. Much will depend, of course, on how much you can afford, but it is false economy to purchase cheap materials. Many colours or shades have been introduced in artificial stone-work. Paving slabs and split stone walling can be obtained in several restful shades—but it is best to avoid the rather bright colours in which some materials are cast. These colours seldom blend with the general garden layout and some tend to fade badly after the first season. It is best to use colour-fast masonry.

Stones and slabs of various shapes and sizes increase the versatility of the material and enable you to produce most attractive patterns. This applies particularly to the modern paving slabs.

1 A wide variety of materials is available. Steps and paving here are of blue stone. The wall is of a somewhat browner tone.
2 A pointed wall of mixed shaped building stone. Many of the stones have been laid on edge.
3 This wall is made of building sandstone mixed with stone of a different blue which is also used for the raised paving. The path and the step are a blue stone.
4 Round stepping stones give an unusual effect. Sink them so that you can mow safely over them.
5 Remove stone and take out turf.
6 Sink stone into cavity so that it is one inch below lawn level.

With these, attractive patios can be constructed (see Patio gardens) and some of the circular stones make unusual stepping stones in a lawn.

Split stone walling is a type which has rough or textured face. This produces a natural or rustic finish to a wall and the use of this type of stone ensures that the design blends well with the rest of the garden. This is not to imply that other walling stones are not suitable, but it is easier for you to produce a successful 'natural' design if you use split stone walling. It is worth wearing gloves when handling split stone as it is quite rough and can scratch the skin badly.

Screen blocks are available in several designs. Most of them are open, but a few are solid with the design in relief. Blocks are usually made in units just under a foot square and a wall can be quickly constructed using such blocks. Special corner stones or pilasters are available, which are necessary for strength and for turning corners where necessary. Capping blocks are also available to finish off the tops of the screen walls. Screen walling is excellent for the making of patios but, used in low proportions (some 3 feet high), very effective dividing walls can be produced.

Bricks can be used for walls and paths but for the former purpose it is necessary to be fairly skilled in brick laying,

especially if heights of more than 3–4 feet are attempted. Used bricks are better for garden use than new, smooth types, unless attractive shades or textured bricks are bought.

Stonework in the garden can play almost as important a part as the flowers and shrubs themselves. Where, for instance, a site is taken over which is on varying levels, or is extremely uneven, walling can be used to form features such as retaining walls. These will solve the problem of dealing with banks of soil and if a series of steps is constructed at key points, access to all parts of the garden will be no problem.

Sometimes a site has extremely poor soil in certain areas. In a situation like this it may pay you to pave it rather than import expensive top soil and manure. A very heavy or wet area could be dealt with in the same way. The elderly gardener or handicapped person could save a considerable amount of labour by using paving in the garden.

Many flowering plants may be grown in cavity walling, which is double-sided walling with the interior filled with good soil. These walls can be used to divide sections of the garden or they can be designed as large containers to hold specimen shrubs or flower displays. The

1 Paving slabs look best if restful shades like these are used.
2 A wall section made up from one of the many screen block designs available. These are relatively simple to assemble.
3 A natural stone sink like this makes an attractive raised bed.
4 Cobble-stones provide one more variation on paving stones, bricks or slabs.
5 Used bricks look better in the garden than new ones. This wall of old bricks is built on the simple herringbone principle.
6 Stone steps are often more attractive than a slope or a bank, and are always easier to maintain.

and patio roofing. They can also be used for archways, gate posts and pillars.

No matter what type of stone is used, a little pre-planning on paper should always be carried out. This will ensure accurate quantity ordering and also it will mean that the best possible layout can be devised for any particular situation.

Massonia (ma-son-e-a)
Named after Francis Masson, an Aberdonian, who was sent by the Royal Botanic Gardens, Kew, in 1772, to collect plants in South Africa. He sailed from Plymouth on Captain Cook's famous ship Resolute and collected more than 400 species of plants which were new to European botanists *(Liliaceae)*. A genus of about 35 species of small bulbous plants from South Africa, which require greenhouse protection in the cooler climates. The flowers are white, borne in umbels.

Species cultivated *M. amygdalina*, almost stemless white flowers with a strong almond scent, April. *M. sanguinea* (syn. *M. latifolia*), known in its native Namaqualand as Veldskoenblaar or Ugly Duckling, stemless flowerheads, white with red-tinged filaments, March, and two large leathery leaves at ground level.

Cultivation These very small bulbs do best in pots of sandy loam with a little leafmould in the cool greenhouse and should be allowed to dry off after flowering as, like many other South African bulbous plants, they are accustomed to a dry, dormant period. Propagate by seed sown in gentle heat in spring or by offsets detached at potting time in spring.

Masterwort—see Astrantia

Matricaria (mat-re-kar-e-a)
From the Latin *matrix*, the womb—the plant was once used for feminine disorders *(Compositae)*. This genus of about 20 species is botanically not very clearly distinguished from *Chrysanthemum* or *Anthemis*. The scentless mayweed, *M. maritima* (syn. *M. inodora*), is a European native and in its double form, with few disc florets, is a useful garden plant, good for cutting. It has finely-divided foliage.

Cultivation Normal garden soil suits this very easy plant, which will grow in sun or shade. Though seed is available, to make sure of fully double forms, the plant should be propagated from cuttings by root divisions.

Matteuccia (mat-u-chee-a)
Named in honour of C. Matteucci, 1800–68, an Italian physicist *(Polypodiaceae)*. A genus of four species of hardy ferns, closely related to *Onoclea* and *Struthiopteris,* natives of China, Japan, North America, and East and Middle Europe. They are graceful, shade-loving plants,

elderly or handicapped gardener will find that raised beds retained by attractive walling will bring the soil to a convenient working level.

With a little patience, skill and ingenuity, you can create attractive walling designs if you mix materials. A section of screen walling blocks framed by ordinary bricks relieves the heaviness of a solid brick wall and at the same time, allows light and air to pass through. It still provides sufficient privacy.

Unusual retaining walls may also be built from broken stone paving (crazy paving), set on edge in a bed of mortar

**1 Massonia cordata, a South African plant which needs greenhouse protection in cool climates.
There are about 35 species of Massonia. But this, M. cordata, and amygdalina and sanguinea are among the few cultivated.
2 Matricaria maritima, Scentless Mayweed, is good for cutting.**

with thick mortar joints for strength. These are very effective for facing raised beds or the edges of a patio which is well above ground level.

Bricks and split stone walling material are excellent for the construction of pillars which support pergola roofing

of great charm for a woodland garden.
Species cultivated *M. orientalis* (syn.
Struthiopteris orientalis), fronds up to 2
feet long, broad, deeply serrated, a
beautiful fern but somewhat slow-
growing, China, Japan. *M. pensylvanica*,
fronds up to 3½ feet in height forming a
graceful funnel, blue-green in colour,
eastern US. *M. struthiopteris* (syn.
Struthiopteris germanica), ostrich fern,
with elegant bright green fronds, almost
3 feet in length, forming a distinctive
funnel, East and Middle Europe.
Cultivation These handsome ferns need
a moist soil consisting of moderately
heavy loam and leaf soil, and partial
shade. They may be increased by division
of the underground root-stock, preferably in the spring just when new
growth is evident, or in the autumn, or
also by spores sown in moist peaty soil
in pans placed in a shaded, cold frame.

Matthiola (mat-te-o-la)

Commemorating Pierandrea Mattioli
1500–77, Italian physician and botanist
(*Cruciferae*). This genus of 50 species is
important for the gardener's benefit
because it contains those annual and
biennial species known as stocks. They
are showy plants and most have the
additional quality of sweet scent. In the
wild state stocks are found in the
Mediterranean, Egypt, South Europe
and in South Africa, and two species, *M.
incana* and *M. sinuata*, are among the
rarer British sorts. *M. incana* is, in
fact, the parent plant from which the
annual ten-week stocks have arisen; it
is also the parent of the biennials: the
East Lothian, Brompton, queen and
wallflower-leaved stocks.

The sweetly fragrant night-scented
stock, *M. bicornis*, looks a dowdy thing
during the daytime but as evening
comes the air is filled with its scent. For
the sake of its fragrance it may well be
grown beneath a window, but not in too
prominent a place as it has no beauty of
appearance. It is sometimes listed as
Hesperis tristis.
Species cultivated *M. bicornis*, the night-
scented stock, 1 foot, purplish, fragrant,
annual, Greece. *M. fenestralis*, 1 foot,
scarlet or purple, biennial, Crete. *M.
incana*, 1½ feet, purple, summer, biennial.
It is from this last species that most of
the showy garden stocks have arisen,
and any seedsman's catalogue will offer
a great choice of colours in various
strains. Named cultivars and strains
include:

Beauty or Mammoth stocks, all 1½ feet
tall 'Abundance', crimson-rose; 'Ameri-

1 The various types of Stock have been
derived from Matthiola incana. They
can be obtained in various shades of
pink and purple, and in white.
2 The erect-growing Matthiola vallesiaca
is a native of Mediterranean regions
and likes dry situations. It produces
unspectacular mauve flowers in summer.

1 The Stocks are useful summer-flowering plants, and lend themselves to informal treatment.
2 The cactus Matucana winteriana has columnar growth covered in short pale green spines.

ean Beauty', carmine rose; 'Beauty of Naples', old rose; 'Beauty of Nice'; flesh-pink; 'Côte d'Azur', light blue; 'Crimson King', scarlet, double; 'Monte Carlo', yellow; 'Queen Alexandra', rosy-lilac; 'Salmon King'; 'Snowdrift', pure white; 'Summer Night', purple; 'Violette de Parme', violet.

Brompton stocks, mainly 15–18 inches tall 'Crimson King'; 'Giant Empress Elizabeth', rosy carmine: 'Ipswich Carmine King', 2 feet; 'Ipswich Pink King', 'Lavender Lady', 'White Lady'; 'Hybrida 'Harbinger', early-flowering.

East Lothian stocks, 15 inches to 2 feet tall, available in lavender, rose, crimson, scarlet and white and in strains such as 'Giant Imperial', 1½ feet, double flowers in various colours; 'Giant Perfection', 2 feet, mainly double, various colours; 'Improved Mammoth Excelsior,' non-branching strain, mainly double flowers, various colours.

Ten-week stocks, 15 inches tall, various colours.

Of both Brompton and ten-week stocks there are available strains known as 'Hanson's Double'. With these it is possible at the seedling stage to select the double varieties as these have light green leaves, whereas those with darker leaves will produce single flowers if grown on. This colour distinction can be emphasised by sowing seeds in a temperature of 54–60°F (12–16°C), lowering it to below 50°F (10°C) when the seedlings have formed their first pair of leaves.

In addition to the above there is a newer strain called 'Trysomic Seven Week Stocks', earlier to flower than all others, which produces plants above 1 foot tall with mainly double flowers in carmine, pink, light blue and white.

Cultivation Ten-week stocks are grown from seed sown under glass in March. Plant out seedlings in April or May, leaving 9 inches between plants. The soil should be deep and well manured. The night-scented stocks are sown out of doors in April where the plants are intended to remain. The biennials of the Brompton group etc, should be sown in frames in June and July. Transplant when 1 inch high to the places where the plants are to flower in the following year, spacing them 1 foot apart. Or, over-winter them in pots in a frame to plant out in the following March. The intermediate and the East Lothian stocks may be given much the same treatment as the Bromptons but will flower much earlier in the year. Though some seedsmen apply the term 'hardy annual' to many of the stocks, it is in fact not advisable to give hardy annual treatment to any but, the night-flowering *M. bicornis*.

Matucana (ma-tu'-ca-na)

The name is taken from the name of the village near which the plant grows in Peru *(Cactaceae)*. A genus of a few species of greenhouse succulents. These plants have globular to cylindrical bodies with many spines. The flowers, borne at the tip of the plant, are usually red.

Species cultivated *M. aurantiaca*, bright green body, short golden spines. *M. comacephala*, long, thin white spines, cylindrical body. *M. haynei*, many thin white spines, darker at the tip, spreading irregularly over the plant body.

Cultivation The mixture should consist of a well-drained potting mixture with a ⅓ part added of coarse sand, grit or broken brick. They require full sun during the growing period from March to September, when the mixture should be kept moist. Frequency of watering should be reduced from the beginning of September and no water at all given from late October to the end of February. The minimum winter temperature should be 45°F (7°C). These plants are rather shy of blooming. Propagation is by seed sown in well-drained seed mix and kept moist and shaded at 70°F (21°C) until the seedlings appear, when they can be given more light. Prick out when the spines appear at the tips of the seedlings.

Maul Oak—see Quercus chrysolepsis

Maurandia (maw-ran-de-a)
Commemorating Mme Catharina Maurandy, student of botany, Cartha-gena, c.1797 *(Scrophulariaceae).* This small genus, mainly of half-hardy climb-ing perennials has a few Mexican species worthy of cultivation in the greenhouse. The climbing kinds climb by the aid of their sensitive leaf-stalks, in the manner of a clematis, and are quite suitable for cultivation in a suspended wire basket. The funnel-shaped flowers are large and showy, and their effect is enhanced by the delicate growth.

Species cultivated *M. barclaiana,* to 6 feet, violet-purple, rose or white, sum-mer. *M. erubescens,* to 6 feet, rose and white, summer. *M. lophospermum,* to 6 feet, rosy-purple, summer. *M. scandens,* to purple and violet, summer.

Cultivation A mixture of equal parts of loam and leafmould or peat and a little sand suits them. Pots or wire baskets are suitable and these climbers need some sort of support upon which to fix their leaf-stalks, such as trellis work or twiggy sticks. In the growing season when plants are flowering, water with a weak liquid fertiliser, but in winter keep the plants nearly dry, with a minimum temperature of 45–55°F (7–13°C). Though perennial, the maurandias are some-times treated as half-hardy annuals.

Plants may also be grown out of door from June onwards in sunny, protecte places, or in our own southwester states. They should be lifted and take into the protection of the greenhouse i September. Propagation is by seed, sow in a well-drained seed mix in March i a temperature of 60–70°F (16–21°C potting the seedlings into individu small pots when they are 1 inch hig Cuttings will root in spring or summe in a closed propagating frame wit bottom heat.

Maxillaria (maks-il-lar-e-a)
From the Latin *maxillae,* the jaws of a insect, referring to the appearance of th column and the lip *(Orchidaceae).* large genus of epiphytic orchids fro South America and the West Indie having a single-flowered spike an mostly ovoid pseudobulbs. The flower are often produced in abundance, thu compensating for their small size though a few species produce large an beautiful flowers.

Species cultivated A selection only: *M acutipetala,* orange-yellow, blotched rec spring, central America. *M. dichrome* white flushed red, fleshy, winter, Per *M. elegantula,* white-yellow, red spot summer, Ecuador. *M. fletcheriana,* large creamy-white, marked red, spring, Per

1 Maurandia scandens, a climbing plant which uses its sensitive leaf-stalks to cling to its support.
2 Maxillaria picta has yellow flowers streaked and dotted dull purple and chocolate brown. The petals curve inwards in a most pronounced way. It flowers under glass in this country.

M. fractiflexa, segments 6 inches long and twisted, white, flushed purple, various times, Ecuador. *M. grandiflora*, very fine white with yellow and purple marks, autumn, Colombia. *M. nigrescens*, brownish-purple, winter, Colombia. *M. ochroleuca*, white and yellowish, summer, Brazil. *M. sanderiana*, very large, whitish with blood-red blotches, spring, Ecuador. *M. tenuifolia*, fragrant, dark red with yellow marks, summer, Mexico. *M. venusta*, large, white, very fragrant, autumn, Colombia, Venezuela.

Cultivation A general mixture of 3 parts of osmunda fibre and 1 part of sphagnum moss is suitable; more moss can be used for some of the smaller growing species. Well-drained pots can be used for the more vigorous types, but for the small species, shallow pans are more suitable. A minimum winter temperature of 55°F (13°C) suits most species and in the summer the temperature can rise to 75–80°F (24–27°C). Frequent watering and syringeing in summer are necessary, but in winter a rest is needed, the degree of which must be determined by the type of plant; the harder-bulbed types should receive a more pronounced rest. Protect them from strong sunlight. *M. sanderiana* appreciates a slightly higher winter temperature and, although a large, vigorous plant, should not be allowed to dry out for long periods. Syringeing of this species should generally be avoided as it induces black spot on the foliage. Propagation is by division at potting time in spring.

May—see Crataegus monogyna and C. oxyacantha

May Apple—see Podophyllum peltatum

May Bug—see Cockchafer

May Flower—see Epigaea repens

May Lily—see Convallaria

Maytenus (may-teen-us)

From *mayton*, the Chilean name for the genus *(Celastraceae)*. A genus of 60 or more species, evergreen shrubs or trees, natives of the southern USA and South America, a few species of which may occasionally be found in this country, one or two grown for the beauty of their seed capsules.

Species cultivated *M. boaria*, shrub to 10 feet or more, flowers greenish-yellow, insignificant, fruits yellow with scarlet arils (seed capsules), Chile. *M. ilicifolia*, leaves holly-like, fruits black, Brazil. *M. phyllanthoides*, 3–10 feet, arils of fruits red, Florida southwards.

Cultivation *M. boaria* and *M. phyllanthoides* may be grown in fertile soil in warm places such as south Florida, southern California. Plant in April. Alternatively, like *M. ilicifolia*, they may be grown in a border in the greenhouse

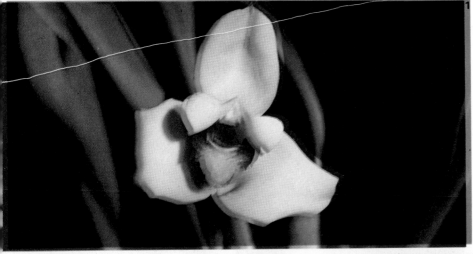

1 Maxillaria grandiflora has very fine creamy-white flowers marked with yellow, brown and purple. The Maxillarias are a genus of South American epiphytic orchids.
2 Maxillaria tenuifolia, a dark red orchid, has yellow and bronze blotches on the petals and rush-like foliage. The flowers are fragrant.
3 Maxillaria picta lindleyi has deep yellow flowers with crimson bars and is a colourful small orchid for the warm greenhouse.

where a minimum winter temperature of 40°F (4°C) can be maintained. Propagation is by seed sown in gentle heat in spring. *M. boaria* produces suckers freely and these may be detached for propagation purposes.

Mazus (ma-zus)

From the Greek *mazos*, a teat, in reference to the tubercles at the mouth of the flowers *(Scrophulariaceae)*. This genus of dwarf perennial plants, related to *Mimulus*, has a few species natives of China, Australia, New Zealand and Malaya. The species cultivated in USA are dwarf hardy plants suitable for the sunny rock garden.

Species cultivated *M. pumilio*, creeping, purplish-blue with yellow centre, summer, New Zealand and Australia. *M. reptans*, prostrate, rosy-lavender, white and brown, May to October, Himalaya. *M. rugosus* (syn. *M. japonicus*), low-growing, lilac-blue, summer, east Asia.

Cultivation Moist sandy soil suits these dwarf plants, which should be grown on a sunny rock garden. Propagation is easily effected by dividing the straggling stems, or seed may be sown in April in a cold frame. The seedlings should be grown on until the following spring before planting out.

Mazzard—see Prunus avium

Meadow Crane's-bill—see Geranium pratense

Meadow Rue—see Thalictrum

Meadow Saffron—see Colchicum

Meadow Saxifrage—see Saxifraga granulata

Meadow Sweet—see Filipendula

Mealy bugs

These insects look rather like pink wood lice covered with a dusting of white waxy substance. They often shelter in the leaf axils and more inaccessible parts of the host plants which makes control difficult. They are mostly pests of glasshouses in North, though they may appear outdoors, too. The eggs are protected by a covering resembling a tuft of cotton wool and when this is teased apart, the tiny brown eggs are revealed.

Many greenhouse plants are attacked, particularly 'woody' stemmed ones, and the insects breed throughout the year. They also occur outdoors in milder parts of the country.

On vines and plants which will tolerate it, the pests are controlled by use of spray oil in the dormant season. On most greenhouse plants, malathion or other approved sprays applied two or three times at 14-day intervals should give control.

There is also a form which occurs in

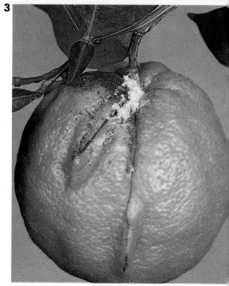

the soil against which watering with diazinon or malathion should prove effective.

Measuring rod

This is a useful device for use when planting vegetable plants or other plants in straight rows at certain distances apart, both in the rows and between the rows. It should preferably

1 Mazus reptans is a prostrate plant with rosy-lavender flowers which continue all summer. It is a good plant for a sunny rock garden.
2 The Mealy Bug looks rather like a pale woodlouse and is covered with a powdery white waxy substance. These pests often shelter in the leaf axils, making control difficult.
3 Mealy Bug on Citrus fruit grown under glass.

be 10 feet long, though satisfactory results can be obtained by using shorter rods. It is made from wood 1¼ inch square or 2 inches by ¾ inch. The first foot on each side should be marked off at 1-inch intervals, thereafter at 3-inch intervals with a longer mark at each foot interval, though it also helps to have the 6-inch intervals marked, too. The marks may be made with paint or may be burned into the wood.

Meconopsis (mek-on-op-sis)

From the Greek *mekon*, a poppy, and *opsis*, like *(Papaveraceae)*. This genus of poppy-like and very showy annual, biennial and perennial plants generally attracts much attention in those fortunate gardens which provide the necessary conditions for their cultivation. Most of the showy Chinese and Himalayan species need light woodland conditions and a moist soil or climate. Very many of these plants are monocarpic, that is, they will die when they attain flowering age whether it be in one, two, three or more years' time. It is probably the bright blue species which are most admired, though some of the delicate yellow ones are extremely fine.

One species, *M. cambrica,* the Welsh poppy, a European plant which, with its

1 The white-flowered Meconopsis superba has a boss of golden anthers which enhances the flower.
2 Meconopsis regia, from Nepal, is attractive in both winter and summer as the basal rosette of silvery leaves remains when the plant has finished flowering.
3 The deep blue flowers of Meconopsis grandis in June. This plant was introduced from Sikkim in 1895.

---

golden-yellow or orange flowers will brighten sunny or shady places in the garden and will successfully seed itself, often in such inhospitable places as between the cracks in paving stones or even between the bricks in old walls where the pointing has decayed.

Species cultivated (monocarpic unless otherwise noted) *M. aculeata,* 15 inches–2 feet, pale blue-violet, summer, western Himalaya. *M. betonicifolia* (syn. *M. baileyi*), blue poppy, blue Himalayan poppy, 4 feet, azure blue, June to July, Himalaya. *M. cambrica,* 1½ feet, yellow, summer, Europe, including Britain, perennial; vars. *aurantiaca,* flowers orange; *plena,* flowers double, orange or yellow. *M. delavayi,* 6 inches, violet, summer, western China. *M. dhwojii,* 2½ feet, primrose-yellow, summer, Nepal. 3 *M. grandis,* 3 feet, blue, June, Sikkim,

1 Meconopsis betonicifolia, the Blue Himalayan Poppy, has flowers of azure blue in June and July. It is generally regarded as a monocarpic plant, and at best is a short-lived perennial.
2 The Welsh Poppy, Meconopsis cambrica, wild, and naturalised in many parts of Britain, has yellow flowers and light green foliage. Western Europe.
3 A red-flowered hybrid Meconopsis.
4 Medicago marina has rather downy leaves, and yellow flowers.

perennial; 'Branklyn' is a form with large, rich blue flowers. *M. horridula*, 3½ feet, blue, red or white, Asia. *M. integrifolia*, 6 inches, violet, Central Asia. *M. napaulensis*, 5 feet, pale mauve and pink, June, Himalaya. *M. paniculata*, 5 feet, yellow, July to August, Western China. *M. punicea*, 1½ feet, crimson, autumn, Tibet. *M. quintuplinervia*, 1½ feet, lavender-blue, Tibet. *M. sarsonii*, 2–3 feet, sulphur-yellow, summer, hybrid. *M. simplicifolia*, 2 feet, purple to sky blue, summer, Himalaya. *M. sinuata*, 2 feet, pale blue, May to June, east Himalaya. *M. superba*, 4 feet, pure white, May and June, Tibet, Bhutan. *M. villosa*, 2 feet, buttercup-yellow, July, Himalaya, perennial.

Cultivation A woodland soil containing leafmould is most suitable, and some light overhead shade during part of the day is appreciated. It is well to sow the seeds as soon as they are available in autumn, but if you get your seeds from a commercial source they will not be available until the spring. A few species, such as *M. quintuplinervia* may be propagated by division; others, for example, *M. grandis*, may be increased

by removing and rooting side-shoots. Many of the species, especially those with rosettes of silvery leaves, are suited to the lower stratum of a rock garden. Water generously in summer but keep dry in winter. In general the meconopsis do better in the moister conditions found in Scotland and western Britain than in the drier east and south.

Medeola (med-e-o-la)

Named after *Medea*, the Greek sorceress, due to its supposed value in medicine *(Liliaceae)*. Allied to *Trillium* this genus of one species, *M. virginica*, is a hardy perennial plant of east North America bearing yellow to greenish-yellow

flowers in June on stems about 9 inches high. The white root has the flavour of cucumber.
Cultivation It thrives in a sandy loam and is best increased by division of the rhizome-like root in the spring.

Medicago (med-ik-a-go)

From the old Greek name *medike*, used for a grass *(Leguminosae)*. This genus of 50 species, closely allied to the clovers, has six British representatives. Most of these plants are south European and two only are of interest to horticulturists.
Species cultivated *M. echinus*, Calvary clover, 3–6 inches, three leaflets marked with red spots supposed to represent

blood, grown principally for the interest of its spirally twisted seed pods covered with bristly hairs, south France, hardy annual. *M. marina,* 1 foot, foliage silvery, flowers yellow, June to August southern Europe, hardy perennial. *M. sativa,* alfalfa, lucerne, 1–3 feet, flowers purplish, pods spirally twisted, Europe, including Britain, grown as a fodder crop, hardy perennial.

Cultivation Plants may be readily raised from seed. Calvary clover is generally grown in a pot, as in that way the plant's peculiarities may be seen at close quarters. Any normal garden soil is suitable, but pots should be very well drained.

Medinilla (me-din-il-la)
Commemorating J. de Medinilla of Pineda, Spanish Governor of the Marianne Islands, in 1820 (*Melastoma-*

1 The flowers of Medinilla magnifica are enhanced by wide pink bracts. It is an evergreen climbing plant with striking flowers, native of the Philippines.
2 Mediolobivia elegans is a cactus of globular growth covered with fine hairs. The flowers are showy and orange-yellow in colour.

taceae). This genus of 150 tropical shrubs, some of them climbers, has several species which are cultivated in the stovehouse or warm greenhouse. They have showy flowers, and sometimes, in addition, coloured bracts and good foliage. A humid atmosphere is needed.

Species cultivated *M. curtisii,* 3 feet, ivory white with purple anthers, spring, Sumatra. *M. javanensis,* 3 feet, pale rose, purple anthers, leaves tinged red beneath, winter, Java. *M. magnifica,* 3 feet, rose-pink, pink bracts, summer, Philippines; this and its variety *superba* are the most strikingly beautiful of these shrubs. *M. teysmanni,* 4 feet, rose-pink, spring, Celebes, New Guinea.

Cultivation A good loam with added charcoal is needed. Pot firmly to encourage short, firm growth, and pot on frequently as the roots increase rapidly. Water and syringe freely during the growing season, but moderately only during the winter. The atmosphere must be kept drier during the flowering period. Propagation is by cuttings of half-ripe shoots placed in a propagating case in a temperature of 70°F (21°C).

Mediolobivia (med-ee-o-lob-iv-ee-a)
From the Latin *medius,* middle, and *Lobivia,* an anagram of Bolivia; this cactus could be said to be between *Rebutia* and *Lobivia (Cactaceae).* Small cacti from Argentina, for the greenhouse or for window cultivation, they have ribs, which rebutias do not, while the flowers are similar to those of *Lobivia,* although smaller. They may still be listed under the generic name *Rebutia.*

Species cultivated *M. aureiflora,* short stem with many small spines, offsets very freely, golden-yellow flowers. *M. duursmaiana,* makes a group of plants, with slender radial spines and long central ones, tube-shaped orange-yellow flowers. *M. elegans,* globular pale green stem, tufted growth with fine short spines, bright yellow flowers with a long tube covered in hairs and scales.

Cultivation Pot in a well-drained potting mix with $\frac{1}{6}$ part added of sharp sand and other roughage. Repot in March every two years. They do best in a sunny position, and need to be watered as the soil dries out from April to September, but for the rest of the year should be kept dry. In winter, maintain a minimum temperature of 40°F (4°C) and 65–90°F (18–27°C) during the growing season while watering. Propagate by seed sown in well-drained seed mix in pans early in the year, keep it moist, shaded and at a temperature of 70°F (21°C). Most plants make offsets, but it is difficult to remove them for cuttings without damaging the plant.

Mediterranean Lily—see Pancratium maritimum

Medlar—see Mespilus germanica

Megacarpaea (meg-a-kar-pay-ee-a) From the Greek *megas*, great, *karpos* fruit, referring to the comparatively large fruits *(Cruciferae)*. A genus of some 7 species of hardy herbaceous perennials, natives of Asia, with much-divided leaves and large, flattened, winged pods. The only species likely to be found in cultivation is *M. polyandra*, a strong growing plant, up to 6 feet tall, its lower leaves up to 2½ feet long. In summer it bears numerous small yellowish-white four-petalled flowers with numerous stamens, but unfortunately does not flower reliably. In Kashmir the leaves are used as a vegetable; elsewhere the pounded roots are used as a condiment.

Cultivation *M. polyandra* does best in sandy soils, in sunny situations. The plants should be set out in spring or autumn, with due regard to their height and the spread of their basal leaves. Propagation is by seed, sown in the cool greenhouse or frame in spring, or out of doors in summer.

Megasea—see Bergenia

Melaleuca (mel-a-lew-ka) From the Greek *melas*, black, and *leukos*, white, referring to the colours of the old and new barks *(Myrtaceae)*. A genus of evergreen flowering shrubs, all confined to Australia or Tasmania except *M. leucadendron* which is also found in Malaya. They are related to the bottle-brushes, or *Callistemon*. In mild southern California these plants have sometimes been grown on a warm wall; they have succeeded in several cooler gardens from time to time, and a number of species are grown outdoors over a fairly wide area on the West Coast. Elsewhere they require greenhouse protection. They are grown for the beauty of their flowers, derived from the bundles of colourful stamens. The woody seed capsules persist on the shrubs for many years. The leaves of some species are fragrant when crushed.

Species cultivated *M. armillaris*, 20–30 feet, white, June. *M. decussata*, to 20 feet, lilac, June. *M. ericifolia*, to 20 feet, yellowish, summer. *M. hypericifolia*, 20 feet, red, summer. *M. leucadendron*, cajeput-tree, 30 feet, cream, Florida. *M. linariifolia*, to 30 feet, white, July.

Cultivation The soil should consist of equal parts of loam, leafmould or peat and sand. Well-drained borders are needed, or the largest pots or tubs. Water freely from April to September but sparingly after this. Maintain a minimum winter temperature of 40–50°F (4–10°C). Prune the tips of the shoots

1 Megacarpaea polyandra is a strong-growing hardy perennial which, when it can be persuaded to flower, makes a tall striking plant.
2 Melaleuca armillaris, an evergreen flowering shrub, has yellowish flowers.

after flowering is over. Out of doors in gardens in the milder regions they may be planted in well-drained borders without problems. Propagation is by cuttings of nearly ripe shoots under glass, during July and August.

Melandrium—see Lychnis

Melasphaerula (mel-ah-sphay-rul-a)

From the Greek *melas*, black, *sphaerula*, a small ball; the corms are small and black *(Iridaceae)*. A genus of but one species, from the Cape of Good Hope *Melasphaerula graminea*, which grows 12–15 inches tall and bears attractive flowers. These are yellowish-green, striped dark purple down the centre of the petals. Each flower which is ¾-inch wide, is held on slender branched panicles in April. Grass-like leaves, up to 1 foot long, are produced early in the year.

Cultivation Insert five or six corms in a pan of sandy loam and peat, covering them with 1 inch of the soil mixture. Keep the pans in a cool glasshouse, watering only when growth has begun. After flowering dry them off gradually. *M. graminea* may be tried in warm or sheltered borders in favourable areas, planting the corms 2–3 inches deep, with some sand placed round the base of the corms in the bottom of the hole. Protect them from frost during the winter with a peat or bracken mulch until March. By delaying planting until mid-March, the plants will flower in June. Propagation is by offsets from the corms which take two years to flower; or by seed, sown in pans of seed mixture in February or March in a warm glasshouse. Flowering corms are produced in three to four years.

Melastoma (mel-as-to-ma)

From the Greek *melas*, black, and *stoma*, mouth, referring to the edible berries which stain the mouth purple-black *(Melastomataceae)*. A genus of some 40 species of evergreen tropical shrubs, usually with rose or purple flowers and fleshy berries.

Species cultivated *M. candidum*, 4 feet, large bristly leaves, hairy beneath, pink or white flowers, summer, southern China. *M. malabathricum*, to 8 feet, large purple flowers, July, East Indies. *M. villosum* (syn. *Pleroma villosum*). 3–4 feet, bearing clusters of rose-pink flowers in May and June, South America.

Cultivation These shrubs need warm house conditions. In summer they should be lightly shaded from the hot sun and syringed daily with tepid water during the growing season. In winter the atmosphere should be kept as dry as possible and the minimum greenhouse temperature should be about 55°F (13°C). They do well in a mixture consisting of equal parts of loam and peat, with sharp sand and charcoal added. Propagation is by cuttings taken in the spring

1 The spiky inflorescence of Melasphaerula graminea. The yellowish-green flowers are marked with purple and the leaves have a dark stripe.
2 Melastoma denticulatum, from Australia has pinkish flowers and leaves in pairs behind each bud.
3 Melia azedarach is called the Bead Tree because of its attractive seeds.

and inserted in sandy peat in a propagating frame with bottom heat.

Melia (me-lee-a)

Derived from the Greek name for ash *(Fraxinus)*, in reference to the ash-like leaves *(Meliaceae)*. A small genus of trees from the East Indies, Australia, India and Asia, with one species, *Melia azedarach*, very commonly grown and now widespread in many warm countries by introduction. Known as the Persian lilac or bead tree (the bony seeds are threaded for use as rosaries) and by several other vernacular names, it is a fast-growing deciduous tree, 30–50 feet high or more, with large deciduous pinnate leaves and panicles of fragrant pale lilac flowers in late spring.

Cultivation In USA this tree is hardy

mainly in southern states, but otherwise may be grown in a cool greenhouse in well-drained compost. Propagation is by cuttings, suckers, or seed. This species is quite often planted as a shade or street tree in warmer climates. *M. azedarach umbraculiformis*, the Texas umbrella tree, has drooping foliage and a shape suggesting a gigantic umbrella. It originated in Texas and is grown in the southern United States.

Melianthus (may-li-an-thus)

From the Greek *meli*, honey, *anthos*, flower, referring to the honey-filled calyces *(Melianthaceae)*. A genus of 8 species from the Cape of Good Hope of semi-woody, evergreen shrubs; the alternate, pinnate leaves produce a disagreeable smell when bruised. The flowers are followed by fruits which are winged, inflated capsules containing black seeds. *M. major* is also found in India.

Species cultivated *M. comosus*, 4 feet, leaves 6 inches long, orange, red-spotted flowers, summer. *M. major*, 7–10 feet, the most ornamental species, with attractive foliage, the leaves up to 1 foot or more in length, flowers red-brown in summer, hardy, given protection in favourable situations, but tender elsewhere. *M. minor*, 2–4 feet, downy young leaves, dull red flowers, early summer.

Cultivation Although *M. major* may be grown out of doors in the milder counties, this and other species are also likely to be seen in representative collections of greenhouse shrubs. *M. comosus* and *M. minor* are occasionally grown in sub-tropical bedding schemes. They are best grown out of doors in rich soil in south California; roots should be protected with good mulch in winter. Under glass they should be grown in a mixture of 2 parts of loam and 1 part of leafmould and sand and the pots should be given a sunny position. Pot in late winter or spring. Maintain a minimum winter temperature of 40–50°F (4–10°C). Propagation is by seeds sown in a temperature of 65–75°F (18–24°C) in late winter or early spring, or in a slightly lower temperature in late summer. Cuttings, taken in spring, will root in a propagating case with bottom heat.

Melica (may-li-ca)

From the Greek *meli*, honey, sweetness, meaning sweet grass *(Gramineae)*. A widely distributed genus of 30 species with several varieties, including two species native to Europe. They are found in temperate regions throughout the world apart from Australia. They are perennials, some with creeping rhizomes, all with soft, flat leaves; their flowers are few, borne in slender panicles, often coloured.

Species cultivated *M. altissima*, 3–4 feet, flowers whitish, early summer; var. *atropurpurea*, purple spikelets, Siberia, east Europe. *M. ciliata*, 2–3 feet, hairy,

1 Melianthus major, a native of the Cape of Good Hope, can be grown out of doors in mild localities.
2 Melicope ternata is a graceful shrub with large shining leaves. The creamy-white flowers are insignificant.

grey-green florets, June–July, Europe, North Africa. *M. uniflora* var. *variegata*, leaves striped green and cream, Europe except north-east. The flowering spikes are often collected and dried as they are useful for winter decorations and floral arrangements.

Cultivation A good loamy soil, preferably limy, is desired. *Melica* species are useful as ground-covering plants, filling in odd corners, planting around shrubs and in open woodlands. Propagate by seeds sown in pans of seed mixture in February or March, in the greenhouse or in the open ground, in drills 1 inch deep in April or May. Older plants may be divided either in the spring or the autumn.

Melicope (mel-e-co-pee)

From the Greek *meli*, honey, and *kope*, cutting or division, in reference to the nectary having notched glands *(Rutaceae)*. A genus of some 20 trees and shrubs ranging from tropical Asia to

Australasia and Polynesia. One only of the two New Zealand species and a hybrid appear to be cultivated. Both are half hardy and can be grown out of doors only in the milder parts of the country.

Species cultivated *M.* x *mantellii*, a hybrid from the species described below, which is perhaps slightly hardier. It has smaller leaves, is more slender in its habit of growth and is not as handsome as its parent. *M. ternata*, the wharangi, an elegant shrub from 6–10 feet tall in cultivation. The flowers are insignificant but it has handsome, shining foliage, the leaflets of which are borne in threes.

Cultivation *M. ternata* should be given a deep soil liberally supplied with humus, while *M.* x *mantellii* is less demanding and will grow in most well-drained soils. Both will tolerate considerable shade and can be grown under woodland conditions. Propagation is by seed, or semi-hardwood cuttings which should be inserted in sand in a frame or greenhouse with gentle bottom heat.

Melicytus (mel-e-see-tus)

From the Greek *meli*, honey, and *kutos*, a cavity, in reference to the cavity below the stamens *(Violaceae)*. This is a genus of four trees and shrubs found in New Zealand, with one species also occurring in some of the other Pacific Islands. All are half hardy and suitable for growing unprotected in the milder parts of the United States such as California and other similar climates. One species only, *M. ramiflorus,* the mahoe, or whitey-wood, appears to have been grown in the British Isles, although both *M. lanceolatus* and *M. macrophyllus* might reasonably be expected to succeed in similar regions. *M. lanceolatus,* to 8 feet, has bright green, willow-like, toothed foliage; *M. macrophyllus* is similar to *M. ramiflorus* but with larger leaves. *M. ramiflorus* grows into a handsome small tree up to 20 feet in height with pleasing foliage, toothed along the margins. The flowers are green and insignificant but they are followed by violet-blue berries which are abundantly produced along the branches. The male and female flowers are borne on separate trees, so that both sexes are needed in order to produce the fruits which usually ripen about November.

Cultivation Any reasonably good and well-drained soil will suit these trees. They will tolerate either sun or shade, and although at their best in a sheltered situation, they are tolerant of a certain amount of wind. Propagation is by seed

1 Melicytus ramiflorus, a shrub from New Zealand of unusual form. The green flowers are somewhat insignificant and cluster thickly along the whole length of the stems.
2 The violet-blue berries of Melicytus ramiflorus which follow the flowers.

which should be sown under glass with gentle heat. Plants of known sex can be easily propagated from semi-hardwood cuttings rooted in sand under glass with a little bottom heat.

Meliosma (mel-i-oz-ma)
Derived from the Greek *meli*, honey, and *osme*, scent, referring to the honeyed fragrance of the flowers of some species *(Sabiaceae)*. A genus of oriental, summer-flowering, small trees or shrubs, the hardy species being deciduous, and the evergreen tender. The flowers are white and borne in large, spiraea-like plumes.
Species cultivated *M. cuneifolia* (D), up to 20 feet, with yellowish-white panicles of hawthorn-scented flowers, July, fruit black and round, about the size of a peppercorn, Eastern China. *M. oldhamii* (D), up to 60 feet in the wild, but liable to damage by spring frost in the cooler areas, where it makes shrub-like growth; flowers white in 1-foot high panicles, June, China and Korea. *M. veitchiorum* (D), small tree with sumach-like pinnate leaves, up to 2½ feet in length, and creamy-white fragrant flowers in 1½ foot panicles, May, fruits almost round, violet in colour, western China.
Cultivation These uncommon trees and shrubs should be planted in a sunny position and in a well-drained loamy soil. They are increased by seed or by cuttings of half-ripe shoots inserted in sandy soil in a propagating frame in July.

Melissa (mel-is-sa)
From the Greek *melissa*, a bee, literally a bee-flower *(Labiatae)*. Balm. Hardy perennial herbs, from southern Europe and Asia, at one time considered excellent for soothing nervous trouble and dispersing melancholy. Of the four or five species, *M. officinalis*, lemon balm, naturalised in parts of US, is the only one usually cultivated. This grows 3–4 feet tall and has lemon-scented, somewhat nettle-like leaves, and small whitish flowers from June onwards, central southern Europe; var. *aurea*, gold-flecked leaves. When dried the leaves may be used in herb mixtures for making stuffing for veal and poultry. For drying, the stems should be cut in late July or August and tied in small bunches and hung to dry in an airy, cool place.
Cultivation The lemon balm is easily grown in ordinary garden soil, but where the soil is light and on the dry side it does better in partial shade. Propagation is by division of the roots in spring or autumn.

Melittis (mel-it-tis)
The derivation is the same for this as *Melissa*, the plant being much loved by bees *(Labiatae)*. A genus of a single hardy species, *M. melissophyllum*, with melissa-like leaves, hence the common name, bastard balm. This grows 1–1½ feet tall and has creamy-white flowers

blotched pink or purple, in May. It is a native of Europe, including the British Isles. The wrinkled hairy leaves retain their fragrance when cut and dried.
Cultivation The plant is easily grown in ordinary garden soil and in partial shade. Plant in autumn or spring. Propagation is by seed sown out of doors in summer, or by division of the roots as soon as the plants have finished flowering.

Melocactus (mel-o-kak-tus)
From the Greek *melon*, the melon, and *kaktos*, spiny plant, a reference to the globular shape of this cactus *(Cactaceae)*. These are greenhouse succulent

1 Melissa officinalis, Lemon Balm, is a plant for the herb garden and has a strong lemon scent.
2 Bastard Balm, Melittis melissophyllum, has wrinkled leaves and creamy-white flowers blotched with purple.

perennials globular to barrel-shaped, with 9–20 ribs. The majority have short spines, but some species have spines 6 inches long. At the top of the plant a 'cephalium' forms to protect the flower buds—it is composed of matted wool or fine hair, and has given rise to the popular name turk's cap cactus. They are very tender plants.

Species cultivated *M. amoenus*, globular, with acute ribs and strong spines, small pink flowers, Colombia. *M. broadwayi*, globular to barrel-shaped, stout awl-shaped spines, small pink to pale purple flowers, West Indies. *M. maxonii*, globular, reddish spines, pink and white flowers, Guatemala. *M. townsendii*, globular, sometimes forming groups, pink flowers, Peru. *M. zuccarinii*, sometimes branches at the base, awl-shaped spines, small pink flowers, Venezuela.

Cultivation Use a well-drained potting mixture with $\frac{1}{6}$ part extra sand, grit

and broken brick. They should be repotted every three or four years in March, and kept in the sunniest position in the greenhouse. Water well during hot weather, but only when the soil has dried out, between March and September; for the rest of the year do not water at all. Some species, especially those from the West Indies, require the addition of a very small quantity of common salt to the water. During the winter the temperature should not drop below 60°F (16°C), but in the summer they will stand the highest temperatures,

---

1 A species of Melocactus, a spiny greenhouse succulent. All of them are barrel-shaped and have a 'cephalium' at the top to protect the flower buds.
2 Water the mound of earth below young Melon plants to avoid dampness at the collar of the plant.
3 The female flower of the Melon needs pollinating by hand.

provided there is adequate ventilation. Propagate by seed sown in well-drained seed mixture in March, kept moist and shaded in a temperature of 75°F (24°C). They are very slow-growing, but the seedlings can be hastened by grafting them on to a *Trichocereus* stock.

Melon

In US 'melon' usually means fruits of the canteloupe or muskmelon type, not watermelons. Give plenty of room, 12–15 inches between plants in rows 4–6 feet apart or hills 6–10 feet apart. They make little progress until warm weather arrives. In the North, start indoors 4–6 weeks ahead of safe planting-out date, or in cold frames 4 weeks ahead. To avoid transplanting set back, sow in peat pots or cubes which are set out 'pot and all'. If planted early, cover with Hotkaps and gradually tear open to harden plants. The soil

As the fruit of the Melon ripens and swells, the weight must be taken by a net, which does not mark the skin.

should be light, well-fertilised and supplied with humus. Melons need all the sun possible and should be kept supplied with water. When vines reach 5–6 joints nip out tips to induce branches. To protect fruits from decay slip a board under each to keep it off the soil. Preferred varieties are: 'Hybrid Mainrock', 'Hybrid Sampson', 'Bender's Surprise', 'Honey Rock', 'Burpee's Hybrid'. In warmer areas also try white-fleshed 'Golden Beauty Casaba' and green-fleshed 'Honey Dew'. Under glass one may copy the British. Start January in warm greenhouses, but in slightly heated or cold ones seeds are sown in May. Sow one seed in each small clay pot filled with a suitable seed mixture. A temperature of around 65°F (18°C) is needed for germination. The bed for melons is similar to that advised for cucumbers, and consists of turfy loam, well-rotted manure, bonemeal and wood ashes. The plants are set out on the bed when they have made three true leaves. Setting the plants on slight mounds is advisable to prevent stem rot. A trellis of vertical and horizontal wires should be erected, to which the plants are tied until they are stopped at a height of 4 or 5 feet. In the meantime, the sideshoots are stopped when a foot long and tied to the horizontal wires. Watering and ventilation must be attended to carefully. Do not permit fruits to set on the main

stem as it is more desirable to have four fruits on separate side-growths. Hand pollination is often necessary and the ripe male pollen should be transferred with a camel hair brush from the male to the female blooms. Pollinate at noon on a bright, sunny day. As soon as the four small fruitlets begin to swell remove all others on plant. Cut away surplus growth at this stage. Top-dressings of well-rotted manure may be applied when white rootlets appear on bed surface. No other feeding is necessary.

Melon Pear, Melon Shrub—see
Solanum muricatum

Mendelism
Mendelism, the basis of modern genetics, takes its name from the Abbé Gregor Mendel an Augustinian Monk at Brunn, Moravia, now known as Brno, Czechoslovakia. His theory, published in 1866 by the local natural history society, is a model of clarity of thought and scientific method, but it was so much in advance of the time that it was not generally recognised until about 1900.

Until then, it was of course well-known that hereditary variations were passed from parents to offspring through the germ cells of the parents. Observing

that the offspring in most cases showed a blending of the characteristics of their parents, it was assumed that the hereditary factors transmitted by the germ cells were blended and altered permanently. The work of Mendel and his many followers has shown that the blending of the characteristics of the offspring is due to the fact that the visible hereditary characteristics of each individual are controlled by pairs of factors, or genes as they are now called, one of each pair being inherited from each parent. Sometimes one gene of a pair, called the dominant gene, completely suppresses the effect of the other called the recessive gene, and since there are many thousands of pairs of genes, the mixture of their effects gives rise to the blending of parental characteristics in the offspring. The important point is that, although one gene may suppress or modify the effect of the other, it does not alter or destroy the other gene, which passes unchanged to future generations, and may show its effect in different circumstances.

This is illustrated in the four o'clock or marvel of Peru *(Mirabilis jalapa)* (see diagram 1 opposite) when a pure white and a pure red are crossed. Because the genes of one carry white factors and those of the other carry red, the seed produced will be the result of either a red pollen grain fertilising a white ovule, or vice versa.

In this case a pink flower is produced. The genes themselves do not blend, however, and a pink flower will carry, half-and-half, white and red genes. If two of the pink flowers are crossed there are four possible permutations of pollen and ovule:

white × white gives a white flower
white × red gives a pink flower
red × white gives a pink flower
red × red gives a red flower.

The F_2 generation will consist of white, pink and red flowers in the ratio 1 : 2 : 1.

A more common type of result is demonstrated by Mendel's famous experiment with peas (see diagram 2). He crossed a yellow-seeded pea with one having green seeds. Although the F_1 generation all carry one yellow and one green gene, all the seeds are yellow. The yellow gene is said to be dominant and the green recessive, as the yellow gene's effect is completely masked by that of the green one.

In the F_2 generation there is a 1 in 4 chance that a green ovule will be fertilised by green pollen. This will produce a green-seeded pea although both parents were yellow. Of the remaining three peas of the F_2 generation, one will be pure yellow (homozygous), and the other two will contain one yellow and one green gene (heterozygous) like their parents. Nonetheless, these two types will both be yellow.

Mendel next observed that if two

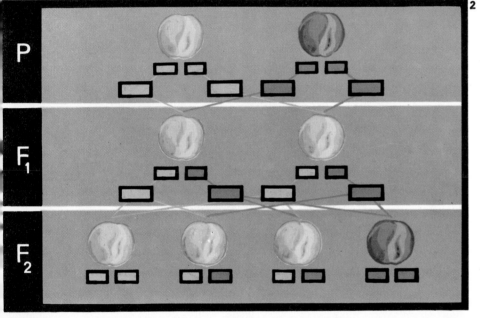

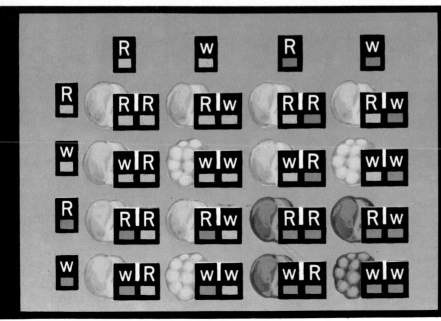

plants differing in *two* of his chosen characteristics were crossed together, the two characteristics each appeared in the second generation in a 3 to 1 ratio, but *independently* of each other.

This formed the basis for his second law, which states that if individuals carrying two or more pairs of contrasted characters are crossed, the characters segregate independently of each other.

To demonstrate this, Mendel crossed round/yellow and wrinkled/green peas, Round is dominant to wrinkled and yellow is dominant to green.

The F_1 generation, containing one gene of each type, were all round yellow, but their gene patterns were of four different kinds and the sixteen possible permutations of genes produced two new types, yellow/wrinkled and round/green, as well as the two original types (diagram 3).

In this case, any crossing of the F_1 individuals always gives the four F_2 types in the ratio; 9 with both dominant genes: 3 with only one dominant gene: 3 with the other dominant gene: 1 with only recessive genes.

Unfortunately, it is very difficult for the ordinary plant-breeder to apply the theory in practice, some of the reasons being as follows:

The ratios in an experiment depend on chance combinations of genes, and are not exact, so that large numbers must be grown to give accurate results.

In every plant there are groups of genes which do not segregate independently of each other as in the above example, being linked together to a greater or lesser extent.

Sometimes a gene controls more than one characteristic.

Sometimes more than one gene is needed to produce a characteristic.

In many pairs of genes, there is no complete dominance and their effects blend.

Often a characteristic is controlled

1 Mirabilis jalapa (the marvel of Peru) is a good example of the action of genetic inheritance. Crossing a red flower with a white flower produces pink offspring, which contain both white and red factors, although the factors are unaltered (the F_1 generation). When the pink flowers are crossed, the results are white, red and pink blooms in the ratio 1 : 1 : 2.
2 Offspring of the cross between a yellow-seeded and a green-seeded pea are all yellow. The yellow gene is dominant in this case, while the green is recessive. The green is not eliminated, however, as is shown by the fact that the second generation contains one green-seeded pea in every four according to the law of averages.
3 Mendel crossed two Peas each with two contrasted characters. The F_1 generation included plants with one characteristic from each parent as well as plants like the parents.

by many pairs of genes, giving apparently continuous variation.

Most plants bred by amateurs are perennials, which are normally propagated by cuttings, offsets etc., and which are not true-breeding from seed, having a great mixture in the various pairs of genes in each individual.

In general, the greatest use of the theory in amateur breeding is to devise sound practical methods of procedure, which are dealt with under the heading Plant breeding.

Menispermum (men-nis-per-mum)
Derived from the Greek *mene,* moon, and *sperma,* seed, the seed being crescent-shaped, hence the common name moon-seed *(Menispermaceae).* A genus of 2 species of deciduous, hardy perennial twining plants of vigorous growth which require ample space to spread. They are suitable for the wild garden as a ground-cover plant. The plant's underground stems can be a menace in a cultivated border. Of the 2 species the only one cultivated is *M. canadense,* Quebec to Georgia to Arkansas, which grows 10–15 feet tall and has greenish-white flowers in June and July of little ornamental value. The large handsome leaves are shiny dark green, 4–8 inches long and the bunches of bluish-black berries resembling small grapes are effective.
Cultivation *M. canadense* will grow in sun or shade, thriving in a moist loam, and will tolerate boggy conditions. It is a quick-growing plant, useful for providing a screen on trellis. It dies almost to the ground in winter and may be cut hard back in the autumn, and strong new growths will appear the following spring. It is easily propagated by division of the underground stems.

Mentha (men-tha)
The Latin name for the mint family; also named after a nymph, Mentha, who is reputed to have been turned into this plant *(Labiatae).* Mint. Hardy perennial herbs remarkable for their aromatic leaves, some of which are much valued for culinary purposes. In all there are about 40 species, and many natural hybrids, which makes identification a problem. They are widely distributed in the temperate zones of the world. Most have purple flowers but a few are grown for ornamental purposes.
Species cultivated *M. citrata,* bergamot mint, 1 foot, with reddish-purple flowers and refreshing aromatic bronzy leaves, Europe, naturalised in USA. *M.* × *gentilis,* 1–1½ feet, leaves and stems hairy, very aromatic, flowers light purple, hybrid; var. *aurea,* leaves veined and mottled gold. *M. piperita,* peppermint, 1–2 feet, with mauve flowers and longish, pointed leaves. Peppermint oil is used in medicinal preparations and the plant is a source of flavouring for confectionery. Europe, including

1 The Bergamot Mint, Mentha citrata, has reddish-purple flowers, and aromatic bronzy leaves.
2 Mentha gentilis aurea with green leaves mottled with gold, is a good ground cover plant to grow for colour effect and aromatic foliage.
3 Mentha spicata, the Green Pea Mint.

Britain. *M. pulegium,* pennyroyal, prostrate, pale purple flowers, autumn, Europe. *M. requienii,* Corsican mint, a carpeting plant with mauve flowers in summer and minute leaves with intense

peppermint scent, for a moist corner, Corsica. *M. rotundifolia,* apple mint, round-leaved mint, 2 feet, strong growing, purplish flowers, summer, Europe. *M. spicata,* spearmint, common green mint, 1–2 feet, purplish flowers in August, leaves up to 2½ inches long with a refreshing spearmint flavour, Europe, including Britain.
Cultivation Menthas are easily grown in ordinary, fairly moist garden soil and partial shade. They are increased by runners in spring or autumn laid hori-

ontally about 6 inches apart in well-dug
ground and covered with 2 inches of
oil and compost (see also Mint).

Mentocalyx—see Gibbaeum

Mentzelia (ment-ze-le-a)
Commemorates Christian Mentzel, 1622–
701, a German botanist (Loasaceae).
Annual, biennial and perennial plants
from North and South America, numbering about 50 species, few of which are in
cultivation.
Species cultivated M. hispida, 1½–2 feet,
yellow flowers in June and July. Per-
nnial which should be over-wintered in
a greenhouse or frame with little water
at that period, Mexico. M. lindleyi (syn.
Bartonia aurea), blazing star. 1½–2 feet,
with golden-yellow flowers and a mass of
feathery stamens resembling a St John's
wort. The slightly fragrant flowers open
only during sunny weather. A delightful
hardy annual to be sown in the open in
April and May where it is to flower,
California. M. nuda, 2–3 feet, with
creamy-white flowers about 2 inches
across borne on slender stems in August
and opening in the evening; biennial,
for a cool greenhouse, Missouri.
Cultivation The hardy annual, M. lindleyi does well in ordinary garden soil and
a sunny position. The tender species
should be grown in pots containing a
well-drained potting mixture and given
little water during the winter. Propagate
by seed sown in the spring in a heated
greenhouse. Cuttings of M. nuda will
root if inserted in sand in a propagating
frame with bottom heat.

Menyanthes (men-e-an-thes)
A name of doubtful origin, possibly from
the Greek men, month, and anthos,
flower, based on the idea that the buck-
bean flowers for one month only, in fact
it flowers for a considerably longer
period. It may also be from menanthos,
moonflower, a name used by Theophras-
us for a plant growing in Lake Orcho-
menos (Gentianaceae). A genus of two
species of hardy perennial aquatics
widely distributed in North America,
Northern Europe, Britain, Asia and
north-west India.
Species cultivated M. crista-gallii, cocks-
comb, 1–2 feet, kidney-shaped leaves up
to 4 inches wide, white flowers in spring,
North America and Alaska. M. trifoliata,
buck-bean, bog-bean, marsh trefoil, 6–12
inches, clusters of pure white flowers,
pink outside, standing above the olive-
green trefoil leaves in spring. The
creeping rhizomes are submerged under
water or in soft mud. The roots are
reputed to be used in medicinal prepara-
ions for the relief of gout and fevers. It
comes from the northern hemisphere and
is common in many parts of USA in
marshes and beside pools.
Cultivation The rhizomes should be
planted horizontally in the spring in a
boggy soil beside a pool where their

1 The yellow-flowered Mentzelia
lindleyi, known as Blazing Star, will
flourish in any ordinary garden soil
and makes a good show of colour early
in the summer.
2 The Bog Bean, Menyanthes trifoliata,
native American plant, has pink buds and
white flowers in late spring.

roots can grow into the water. Propagate
by dividing the rootstock in the spring
into pieces about 12 inches long, each
with a growing tip, and inserting them
in soft mud.

Menziesia (men-ze-ze-a)
In honour of Archibald Menzies, a
surgeon-botanist, who sailed with
Captain Colnett's expedition to the
Pacific coast of North America (1788–90)
and again with Captain Vancouver
(1790–95) (Ericaceae). A small genus of
deciduous, hardy shrubs of slow growth,
closely related to Daboecia and Phyllo-
doce. They are grown for the beauty of
their bell-shaped or urn-shaped flowers.
The Japanese species are garden-worthy
plants, but those from North America
are not widely grown.
Species cultivated M. ciliicalyx, 2 feet,
pale purple to pink waxy flowers in
nodding umbels, May and June, Japan.
M. purpurea, up to 5 feet, purple to deep
red, May and June, Japan.
Cultivation In common with many other
Japanese plants they may prove temperamental in gardens. A lime-free soil
is essential and it should contain plenty
of leaf-soil or moist peat and the roots
should be in partial shade. Plants are
increased by seed, sown in a mixture of
sand and peat in the greenhouse in late
winter, in a temperature of 55–60°F
(13–16°C). Cuttings of the current
season's growth may be taken in July
and rooted in sandy soil in a propagating
frame with bottom heat, but they do not
root easily. Layers may also be rooted
in summer and autumn.

Mercuric chloride—see Corrosive
sublimate

Mercurous chloride—see Calomel

Merendera (mer-en-der-a)

Derived from the Spanish name for colchicum, *Quita meriendas* or *Espanta pastores*, meaning literally flowers that take away the sheep's pasture, for on their appearance in the autumn the time has come for the shepherds to lead the sheep down the mountains *(Liliaceae)*. These dwarf, hardy bulbs, of which there are about 9 species, allied to *Colchicum* are widely spread around the Mediterranean and eastward to Persia.

Species cultivated *M. filifolia* (syn. *M. linifolia)*, 1½ inches, narrow, star-shaped rose-pink petals and thread-like leaves, not reliably hardy, may be grown in a pan in a cool greenhouse, southern France, Balearic Isles, Algeria. *M. montana* (syn. *M. bulbocodium)*, 1½–2 inches, lilac-pink flowers from August to October, followed by linear leaves, Pyrenees, Spain, Portugal. *M. trigyna* (syn. *M. caucasica)*, mauve-pink flowers March and April, the narrow leaves appearing with the flowers, Caucasus, Persia.

Cultivation Owing to their small size these bulbs are more suitable for growing in pans in an alpine house, with the exception of *M. filifolia* which is tender, in a well-drained, loamy soil. They are best propagated by seed as the bulbs increase very slowly.

Mermaid weed—see Proserpinaca

Mertensia (mer-ten-se-a)

Named in honour of Francis Karl Mertens, 1764–1831, Professor of Botany, Bremen *(Boraginaceae)*. A genus of low-growing hardy, perennial plants mostly with blue flowers.

Species cultivated *M. ciliata*, 1½–2 feet, large greyish-green leaves, clusters of bright blue bells, pink in bud, May and June, Rocky Mountains. *M. echioides*, 9 inches, racemes of dark blue flowers, summer, Himalaya. *M. virginica*, Virginia Bluebells, 2 feet, leaves soft bluish-grey, purplish-blue heads of forget-me-not-like flowers on arching sprays, May, New York to Tennessee.

Cultivation Suitable for a deep loamy soil and partial shade, although they will succeed in sun provided the roots are moist. The dwarf species may be grown in partial shade on the rock garden; *M. virginica* is a good plant to grow in light woodland. Propagation is by division of the roots in autumn or by seed sown as soon as it is ripe.

Mertya (mer-te-a)

From the Greek *meruomai*, to furl sails or to roll up, from the characteristic of the male flowers to be in clusters,

1 **Merendera montana, a native of the Iberian peninsula, has lilac pink flowers at the end of the summer.**
2 **The Virginia Bluebells, Mertensia virginica, has arching sprays of Forget-me-not like flowers in May.**

rather like a rolled-up ball *(Araliaceae)*. This is mainly a tropical genus of trees which are found in Melanesia, Polynesia, Queensland, and Norfolk Island. Occasionally they are found in the glasshouse collections of botanic gardens, but they are not common. The sole New Zealand species is perhaps the one most commonly cultivated; this is *M. sinclairii*, the puka, which grows into a round-headed, small tree up to 20 feet in height. It is valued because of its very handsome foliage. The shining, bright green leaves are large, the blade being up to 15 inches in length. It is unfortunately too tender to grow out of doors in the United States, except perhaps in California. However, it makes an excellent pot plant for growing under glass and specimens in 8-inch pots look very well.

Cultivation As a pot plant it can be grown in relatively cool conditions and a minimum winter temperature of 45°F (7°C) will not be too cold for it. Any standard potting mixture will be quite satisfactory. Propagation is by seed which loses its viability rather quickly and should be sown when fresh. Alternatively, semi-hardwood cuttings grown under closed conditions with gentle bottom heat root fairly readily.

Mesembryanthemum
(mes-em-bre-an-the-mum)

From the Greek *mesos,* middle, *embryon,* fruit, and *anthemon,* flower; not from *mesembria,* mid-day and *anthemon,* as is usually suggested. The earliest species known flowered at mid-day, but when night-flowering species were discovered the name was changed to give a change of sense without a change of sound *(Aizoaceae)*. These are succulents, many suitable for bedding in California, or elsewhere in summer with a creeping habit of growth, fleshy leaves and brilliant coloured flowers.

Species cultivated *M. albatum,* branching, green and pinkish-red flowers, Cape Province. *M. crystallinum,* ice plant, spreading branches, white flowers, south-west Africa. *M. fulleri,* annual, white flowers, Cape Province. *M. intransparens,* erect stem, white and pink flowers, Cape Province. *M. macrophyllum,* prostrate, violet-pink flowers, Namaqualand. *M. nodiflorum,* cylindrical leaves, white flowers, Africa, the Middle East and California. *M. setosum,* pink and greenish flowers, Cape Province. *M. striatum,* prostrate, white flowers, Cape Province. The plant popularly known as *M. criniflorum* is now called *Dorotheanthus criniflorum.* **Cultivation** They should be grown in a

very porous mix, for instance a well-drained potting mixture with $\frac{1}{5}$ part added of coarse sand, grit, broken brick and granulated charcoal. The greenhouse kinds require a sunny position, with plenty of ventilation in hot weather. Give them a minimum winter temperature of 45°F (7°C), and normal greenhouse temperature during summer. Water only when the soil has dried out and keep dry during the winter. Propagate from seed sown in well-drained seed mix in March in a temperature of 65–70°F (18–21°C). Do not cover the seed, but keep it moist and shaded until the seedlings are pricked out. Also by cuttings taken during the summer and rooted in equal parts of sharp sand and peat. These can then be put out in a sunny position in well-drained soil as bedding plants, or on a rock garden. (See also Bergeranthus; Cheiridopsis; Conophytum; Delosperma; Dorotheanthus; Drosanthemum; Faucaria; Fenestraria; Gibbaeum; Glottiphyllum; Hereroa; Lampranthus; Lithops; Oscularia; Pleiospilos; Rhombophyllum; Ruschia; Titanopsis; Trichodiadema.)

1 Mertya sinclairii, the Puka, is a round-headed small tree with large handsome shining leaves. In the United States it is hardy only in California.
2 Mesembryanthemums are useful for providing colourful summer bedding.

Mespilus (mes-pil-us)

From the Greek *mesos*, half, *pilos*, a ball, referring to the hemispherical shape of the fruit *(Rosaceae)*. Medlar. A genus which now consists of one species only, a deciduous tree cultivated for its flowers and fruit. *M. germanica* makes a spreading small tree, with large white or pink-flushed flowers in June or July, followed by brown, pear-shaped fruits with flattened, open ends, which are eaten when decay (bletting) has begun. The tree is a native of south-east Europe to Persia.

Cultivation Any fertile soil is suitable, and preferably a sunny situation. They are usually grown as standard trees and may be planted in November or in the spring. The little pruning needed is carried out in winter, merely to shape the tree and to remove dead, diseased, weak or crossing shoots. The fruit is ready for picking in late October or early November, but is not ready for eating for another two or three weeks, when the green colour has been lost, and the flesh is soft. Propagation is from seeds, which are slow to germinate, sown in spring, or by grafting or budding varieties on to pear, quince, hawthorn, or seedling medlar.

Metaldehyde

This substance is used to control slugs and snails. It may be bought as a powder, liquid or in the form of pellets

1 Mespilus germanica makes a small spreading tree with large white or pink-flushed flowers in June.
2 The Medlar, which is the fruit of the Mespilus, is eaten once it has rotted.
3 Mespilus germanica is useful for autumn colour in the garden.
4 Discovered in 1945, Metasequoia glyptostroboides, provides good autumn colour in its fine foliage.

or biscuits.

If powder is used, it may be mixed with bonemeal or bran at the rate of 1 ounce of metaldehyde to 3 lb of bran and should be placed under a broken flower pot or something similar, partly to protect it from the weather and also to prevent this mix from drying out. The bonemeal bait is mixed at the same rate and is used for underground slugs (keeled slugs). The procedure is to bait over as long a period as possible before planting susceptible crops (e.g. potatoes, dahlia tubers etc.), and the slugs come at night to take the bait.

Liquid suspensions of metaldehyde can be used for watering the infested area if preferred. Pellets or biscuits are very effective but should be placed where children and animals cannot reach them. Commercial bran-like baits do not attract children, pets, birds.

Metasequoia (met-a-se-quoy-a)

From the Latin *meta*, next to, in reference to its relationship with *Sequoia*

(Pinaceae). Dawn redwood. A hardy deciduous coniferous tree believed extinct until it was discovered in 1945 in Szechwan Province, western China. The only species cultivated is *M. glyptostroboides*, a quick-growing tree with delightful, feathery light green foliage, turning a pleasant shade of pinkish-brown in autumn before falling. It reaches a height of 100 feet in its natural home, and in due course, specimens may well reach nearly this height in favourable areas.

Cultivation The dawn redwood succeeds in any moderately fertile soil, preferably moist. Propagation is by seed or cuttings —which root easily—of either partly ripe or dormant wood.

Metrosideros (me-tros-id-e-ros)

From the Greek *metra*, the heart of a tree, *sideros*, iron, in reference to the toughness of the wood *(Myrtaceae)*. A genus of about 30 species of evergreen, flowering trees and shrubs, some climbing by means of aerial roots, for greenhouse, or outside positions in mild,

1 Metasequoia glyptostroboides is a quick growing conifer with feathery foliage, and makes a tree of pyramidal form.
2 A native of New Zealand, Metrosideros tomentosa makes a tall tree and is remarkable for its aerial roots.
3 Metrosideros alba from New Zealand produces white brush-like flowers.

particularly maritime, districts. Specimens become extremely tall, grown in their native countries, New Zealand or other islands in Polynesia.

Species cultivated *M. diffusa*, climbing, crimson flowers, late spring. *M. lucida*, to 60 feet, vivid red flowers, late summer, usually takes some time to settle into a regular flowering routine. *M. robusta*, to 100 feet, sombre red flowers, May. *M. scandens*, to 40 feet, white flowers, August. *M. tomentosa*, to 70 feet, dark red flowers, August. All the above are natives of New Zealand.

Cultivation For growth in pots the compost should contain peat, loam and sand. A well-drained potting mix is very satisfactory. The pots should be well-drained and it is best to use large ones. Cool greenhouse borders are also suitable for metrosideros; potting or planting should be done in October or April. The spring to autumn temperature should be 55–65°F (13–16°C), and from autumn to spring; 40–50°F (4–10°C). Water generously during the warm summer months. Potted specimens may be stood outside during the summer. Trim into shape after flowering, if necessary. Plants also thrive in warm seaside localities. They will withstand sea breezes and salt spray readily enough, but not sharp frost. Fine specimens of some of the species of *Metrosideros* described above may be found growing in California and in

1 The Beauty Bush, Kolkwitzia amabilis, a popular flowering shrub, was Introduced by Meyer from China.
2 Juniperus squamata meyeri was found in north-western China by Meyer in relatively unexplored territory.

similar warm coastal climates elsewhere. Propagation is by cuttings of young growth, taken in May and then inserted in sandy soil in a propagating frame with bottom heat.

Mexican Cigar Flower—see Cuphea

Mexican Fire Plant—see Euphorbia heterophylla

Mexican Foxglove—see Tetranema mexicanum

Mexican Nut Pine—see Pinus cembroides

Mexican Orange Blossom—see Choisya ternata

Mexican Poppy—see Argemone mexicana

Mexican Sunflower—see Tithonia

Mexican White Pine—see Pinus ayacahuite

Meyer, F. N.

Frank N. Meyer (1875–1918), a Dutch-man born at Amsterdam, and a collector for the American government, travelled extensively in China and throughout his whole life was an inveterate traveller, having, before he took up plant hunting, walked from Holland to Italy.

He went to the United States in 1900 after having been gardener to Hugo de Vries, the celebrated Dutch botanist, and was walking through the southern United States and Northern Mexico when he first came to the notice of the U.S. Department of Agriculture in 1905. Dr David Fairchild, of the Department, was looking for someone who would travel extensively in China and Meyer was certainly his man. Meyer began a series of almost incredible journeys, walking 1,800 miles during his first,

before his exciting travels ended by drowning in the Yangtze River in 1918.

Meyer was asked to collect new varieties and species of plants of use to U.S. agriculture and horticulture so that his harvest of garden plants was not so great as others who later hunted in similar territory, but he did send home quantities of seed to establish in gardens *Euonymus bungeana, Rosa xanthina* (the canary bird rose), *Actinidia kolomikta* and, introduced into the U.S., *Kolkwitzia amabilis* (the beauty bush), now one of the most popular flowering shrubs there.

His first expedition from September 1905 to May 1908 saw him on the Yangtze as far south as Soochow and he went on to hunt in Manchuria and western Korea collecting varieties of economic plants such as millet, rice and beans of various kinds, particularly soya beans, from which have been bred some of the outstanding varieties in the U.S. today. Later he was in relatively unexplored territory in north-east China and sent home *Acer ginnala, Prunus tomentosa, Aesculus chinensis, Viburnum macrocephalum, Syringa villosa* and *S. meyeri,* as well as *Juniperus squamata meyeri.*

His second expedition, from 1909 to 1912, took him to the Caucasus, Persia, Turkestan and eastern Tibet seeking good varieties of forage plants.

Meyer's third expedition, starting in 1913, saw him travelling in inner Mongolia and, later, visiting Farrer's country around Kansu, Siku and Minchow where he was seeking the seeds of peaches, almonds and plums. He started his last and fatal trip in the

The second species comes from North Africa.

Cultivation This annual grass, although of little garden use, is botanically interesting. It may be grown from seed sown in spring in any kind of garden soil.

Mice

Mice cause occasional damage when they attack beans and peas or strawberries; invade the fruit store or feed on bulbs. There are several ways of dealing with them—by trapping, by the use of Warfarin baits or by means of repellents. If traps are used, care must be taken to avoid harm to birds.

Warfarin baits should be placed in pieces of garden hose or something similar so that only mice have access to them. The bait causes fatal haemorrhage if taken regularly and the bait should be replaced every few days until it no longer decreases, indicating that the mice have been exterminated.

There are various rodent repellents on the market and these should be applied according to the maker's instructions. Some must not be applied to growing plants but are used on labels or pieces of rag placed strategically near the plants to be protected. Other repellents are used as sprays or dusts.

There tend to be 'plague years' of mice and voles in gardens, after which very few may be seen for a considerable time.

Michaelmas Daisy—see Aster

Michauxia (me-sho-se-a)
Commemorating Andre Michaux, the eighteenth-century French botanist *(Campanulaceae)*. A small genus of tall-growing plants which, though strictly perennials, are more satisfactory when grown as biennials. They have whorls of campanula-like flowers.

Species cultivated *M. campanuloides,* 3–6 feet, loose sprays of waxy-white flowers somewhat reminiscent of lilies, July, Levant. *M. laevigata,* 10–11 feet, white flowers, summer. *M. tchihatchewii* (syn. *M. tchihatcheffii*) 5–7 feet, white flowers July to September.

Cultivation These plants grow best in sunny, sheltered borders. The soil needs to be sufficiently moist but well drained. Ordinary garden soil is adequate and the plants do well on limy or chalky soils. Propagation is by seed, which should be sown in a sunny position out of doors, $\frac{1}{8}$ inch deep, during April. Young plants should be ready for transplanting to their flowering sites during the following July and August. Alternatively, seeds can be sown where

autumn of 1916 travelling overland to Hankow and by boat to Ichang, where he remained about a year, using it as a centre for plant hunting in Hupeh. His body was found in the Yangtze on 1st June 1918.

Mezereon—see Daphne mezereum

Mibora (my-bo-ra)
Derivation uncertain *(Gramineae)*. A genus of two species only. The one most usually seen is *M. minima,* a small,

usually spring-flowering tufted annual, 1–7 inches tall, and one of the smallest of British grasses. This species may readily be distinguished by the almost stalkless one-flowered spikelets arranged in two rows on one side of the stem only. A native of Europe but rare in Britain, it occurs naturally only in the Channel Isles and Anglesey and, by accidental introduction in a very few coastal localities on the mainland also. By introduction, also, it is now established in North America and Australia.

1 Micranthus plantagineus has a spike of dark blue flowers and dark grass-like leaves blotched with brown.
2 Michelia doltsopa has creamy white semi-double flowers from April to June. It is an evergreen shrub.

it is intended the plants should flower. Mature plants can be planted during autumn and spring.

Michelia (mitch-ee-lee-a)

Commemorating Pietro Antonio Micheli, (1679–1737), a Florentine botanist (*Magnoliaceae*). A genus of about 50 species of evergreen flowering trees and shrubs, of which a few only are in cultivation. There are about 50 species in the genus. Relationship to *Magnolia* is very close; the main difference is that michelia blossoms are produced from the axils of the leaves.

Species cultivated *M. alba,* 30–40 feet, white flowers, 2 inches or more across, fragrant at first, Java. *M. champaca,* 30–40 feet, similar to foregoing, flowers yellow, India, Java. *M. compressa,* to 40 feet, pale yellow fragrant flowers. *M. doltsopa* (syn. *M. excelsa*) up to 40 feet, creamy-white, semi-double flowers, April onwards, June, Himalaya, China. *M. figo* (syn. *M. fuscata*) to 20 feet, but usually not as tall in cultivation, a small-leaved species, flowers very fragrant, yellowish-green with a purple tinge, June onwards for a considerable time, China. *M. lanuginosa* (syn. *M. velutina*) 12 feet, fragrant yellowish flowers, Nepal, Sikkim.

Cultivation In very mild localities *M. doltsopa, M. figo* and others may be grown outdoors in the Deep South and California. Elsewhere, they require the protection of a cool greenhouse. Out of doors the best soil is a well-worked sandy loam. Plant in spring.

Under glass the plants should be grown in large containers in a mixture of sandy loam and well-rotted leafmould Maintain a minimum winter temperature of 40°F (4°C) rising in summer with normal sun heat, when plenty of ventilation is required.

Micranthus (mic-ran-thus)

From the Greek *micro,* small, and *anthos,* flower (*Iridaceae*). A South African genus containing three species of herbaceous plants with small tunicated corms and small flowers in dense spikes, white to dark blue.

Species cultivated *M. fistulosus,* 9–12 inches, flowers creamy white to pale blue, late summer, appearing after the leaves have withered. *M. alopecurioides* (syn. *M. plantagineus*) 12–18 inches, flowers, dark blue, late summer, the lower ones often replaced by bulbils.

Cultivation As micranthus are semi-tender, they will survive in the open only in warmer south and western parts of the USA. A well-drained loam containing leafmould or peat is desirable. Plant in March or April in a warm, southerly aspect. In colder areas, the corms should be lifted, dried and stored over winter like those of gladiolus. Propagation is from offsets which may take two years to flower; by seeds sown in seed composts in the warm greenhouse in a temperature of 60–65°F (16–18°C) or by sowing the bulbils in seed mixture in a pan or box, covering them with ½ inch of mixture. Micranthus may also be grown in the cool greenhouse or in frames protected from frost.

Microcachrys (my-kro-kak-ris)

From the Greek, *mikros,* small, and *kachrys,* a cone, referring to the small cones *(Taxacaceae).* A genus of a single species, a dwarf, procumbent, rather unruly evergreen shrub. The single species is *M. tetragona,* which grows 18–24 inches tall, from Tasmania. Its somewhat snake-like branches are covered with tiny, scale-like leaves. Each plant bears male and female flowers, but on different shoots. The females develop into little crimson cones.

Cultivation This little conifer is well-suited to alpine house culture, or it may be grown in a cool, sheltered position on the rock garden in loamy, well-drained deeply worked soil. Propagation is by cuttings taken in late summer, made from shortish well-ripened sidegrowths, rooted in sand and peat in a frame or cold greenhouse.

Microcitrus (my-kro-sit-rus)

The name is a combination of the Greek word *mikros,* small, and *citrus,* the ancient name for an African wood *(Rutaceae).* A genus of some 6 species, shrubs or small trees with dense foliage and spiny branches, closely related to *Citrus,* from east Australia and New Guinea. They have been used as rootstocks for citrus grafting and are interesting botanically as they develop differently formed leaves.

Species cultivated *M. australasica,* Australian finger-lime, a tree 30–40 feet tall, bearing thin fruits about 4 inches long which have an acid juice. This can be a useful ornamental shrub or tree for warmer coastal regions of the world and, because of its dense growth, spines, and ease of propagation, makes a good hedge. *M. australis,* Australian round-lime, to 60 feet, the largest native of Australian citrus fruit tree; the variety 'Sydney Hybrid' *(M. australis* × *M. australasica)* is more vigorous than its parents.

Cultivation Microcitrus are grown in the same manner as *Citrus,* using a loamy potting mixture and, if possible, they should be planted out with *Citrus.* There is hope that crosses may bring hardiness to citrus trees. Propagation is by soft wood cuttings of summer growth in sandy soil.

Microclimate

The microclimate of a particular garden is its highly individual and special adaptation of the general climate of the neighbourhood. It makes the daffodils in one garden bloom days earlier than in another; it gives a few extra weeks glory to someone else's dahlias in the autumn; it renders another enviably free from frost damage to blossom. Whereas the general climate, determined by latitude, position relative to land and sea masses, height above sea level etc, is beyond our interference,

microclimate can to some degree be manipulated by the cunning gardener.

Consider first the weather elements from which plants need protection. Hoar frost in spring is one of the worst. It forms on still nights which are cloud free, when long hours of darkness permit cooling of air as far as dew point. If dew point is below the temperature 32°F (0°C), condensation will form as ice crystals. Because cold air is heavier than warm air, it tends to sink as far as it can. The aim must always be to allow it a free exit from your garden if possible. A sloping garden to the river

Microclimates exist naturally in gardens and can be modified to the benefit of some plants.
1 In a greenhouse the glass prevents rapid loss of heat. Ventilation is also used to control the microclimate.
2 The larger Hydrangea appears to benefit from the activities of an overflow pipe above it and has consistently better blooms than its neighbours.
3 and 4 Riverside gardens with similar orientation but different microclimates. In one case the trees afford shelter from wind and night frosts but also make much shade. The other gets sunshine but also wind.

is ideal; an open-work gate or a deflecting hedge may do the trick just as well. If the garden contains an unadaptable hollow, at least adjust the planting scheme to fit in with it by keeping the tenderest plants to the higher edges of the hollow.

The natural protection against frost is a cloud cover. Since one cannot produce that to order, a shelter of tree branches, even where bare, blinds on the cold frames, even wire mesh, can act as substitutes. Such minor adjustments may make all the difference in the short frosts of our spring.

Air frost is not manufactured on the spot, like hoar frost, but is brought in mainly by north or east winds from the continent in winter. When this happens the whole air mass has a temperature below 32°F (0°C), not just the shallow layer near the ground. The air may be dry and there may be no visible hoar frost, but it is nevertheless a merciless killer. Hedges or lattice fencing on the north or north-east of susceptible plants will help for short periods only. The particular snag of winter air frosts from inland areas is that once they come they tend to stay for some time. Glass, polythene or sacking covers will delay freezing but not prevent it. They will, however, deter the rapid dispersal of any heat introduced artificially under the cover. Thus, glass over a plant in the middle of the garden may be useless whereas glass over a plant against a chimney warm wall may be quite adequate. Even a heated glasshouse will benefit by having the shelter of a brick

1 Apricots are grown on a sunny wall in England. Radiated heat from the bricks provides extra warmth, protecting the blossom and encouraging ripening.
2 Deficits of rainfall can be made up by watering, and 'artificial rain' provides a gentle supply of water over a long period.

wall or hedge to the north.

Quite apart from the freezing winds, warmer winds can cause trouble by their sheer persistent battering, particularly on windward coasts or the tops of hills. Hedges and trees make excellent wind breaks but compete with the other garden plants for light and water. Since our prevailing winds and coldest spells come from the same direction as some sunlight, protection by trees may not be as practicable as by low bushes. Fencing is suitable but should be semi-permeable to filter the wind rather than try to stop it. If air comes up against a solid obstruction it will squeeze over the top and produce a vicious eddy on the lee side which may be worse than the constant strong wind itself.

In small urban gardens, narrow passage-ways between houses may prove death traps to plants situated at their extremities. Air blowing on to one end will funnel through at merciless speeds, particularly fatal if from the north or east. Deflect it if possible by fencing, or reconsider the planting zone.

The deficits of rainfall can be made up by artificial watering. Remember that 'long and slow' is the only way to ensure penetration of water to adequate

depths. Rainfall excesses can be minimised by using protective walls, though beware of low eaves which can overdo the protection. The microclimate affecting two almost adjacent plants may vary for surprising reasons. For instance, you may have two hydrangeas growing on a north wall which protects them from a good deal of rain. But one may be underneath a dripping overflow pipe from a cooler, whereas the other may be well away from it. The first specimen, benefiting from the dripping water will flower better and more regularly than the other.

Of the beneficial weather elements, sunshine is the most elusive. The most we can do is to try to trap the heat it generates when it does appear. A south-facing brick wall is a good heat storage unit, glass is another but needs human attention. Excess temperatures may build up under it if ventilation is inadequate at high sun. On the other hand, if covers are removed, then they should be replaced well before sunset if the night is to be started with a good bonus of heat to combat night cooling.

So many factors go towards determining the microclimate of a garden that some are bound to be in opposition to others. The perfect garden is unobtainable: compromise is always necessary.

Microglossa (mi-kro-glos-a)
From the Greek *mikros*, small, *glossa*, tongue, from the appearance of the segments of the corolla *(Compositae)*. A small genus of shrubby plants, some climbing, natives of Asia and Africa,

related to *Aster*. One species only is cultivated, *M. albescens*, the shrubby starwort, a shrub 2–3 feet tall which in July and August has lilac blue or bluish white flowers.

Cultivation Sunny borders and ordinary-to-good garden soil, are suitable for this plant. Planting should be done during October, or March through May. Propagation is either by division of established specimens during spring or, alternatively, by seed sown at a depth of ⅛ of an inch during spring, out of doors, in a sunny position. Seed may also be sown in a cold frame during April.

Microlepia (mi-kro-lep-ee-a)

From the Greek *mikros*, small, *lepis*, scale, referring to the membrane covering the spore cases *(Polypodiaceae)*. A genus of about 45 species of ferns, closely related to *Dennstaedtia* and sometimes included in the genus *Davallia*. Most of them are natives of southeast Asia and Polynesia. They are terrestrial plants with creeping rhizomes. Their fronds, which are usually hairy, vary a great deal in size, texture and form.

Species cultivated *M. hirta* (syn. *M. pyramidata*), fronds to 6 feet long, tropical Asia, Hawaii; sometimes grown as a house plant. *M. marginata*, fronds to 2 feet long and 15 inches broad, Japan to Ceylon. *M. platyphylla*, fronds to 4 feet long, West Indies. *M. speluncae*, fronds to 6 feet long, 2 feet broad, soft in texture, tropics and sub-tropics. *M. strigosa*, fronds to 3 feet long, 1 foot broad, tropical Asia.

Cultivation These are strong growing ferns, which do better if they are planted out in a bed of soil in the greenhouse rather than grown in pots. Their creeping rhizomes cover a great deal of ground. If it is desirable to restrict their growth they may be grown in pans in a mixture consisting of 2 parts of peat, 1 of loam and 1 of sand. The plants need a great deal of water, and should be grown in a shady part of the greenhouse. *M. hirta*, *M. marginata* and *M. strigosa* do very well in a cool greenhouse, with a minimum winter temperature of 40–45°F (4–7°C); the other species mentioned above need more warmth and are usually grown in the warmhouse, in which a minimum winter temperature of 55°F (13°C) can be maintained. Propagation is either by division of the creeping rhizomes or by sowing spores as described in the article Fern cultivation.

Micromeria (mi-kro-meer-ee-a)

From the Greek *mikros*, small, *meris*, referring to their small flowers and foliage *(Labiatae)*. A genus of shrubby, half hardy perennials, mostly natives of the Mediterranean area, but also widely distributed over the temperate and warmer areas of the world.

Species cultivated *M. chamissonis* (syn. *M. douglasii*), trailer, with fragrant

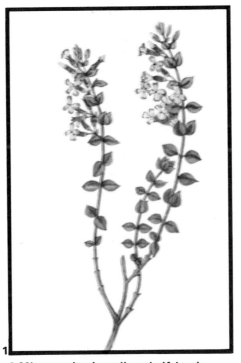

1 Micromeria piperella, a half-hardy perennial for the rock garden with purple flowers in summer.
2 Micromyrtus ciliata is a low-growing heath-like shrub, native of Australia. It bears pink or white blooms.

foliage and inconspicuous flowers, western North America. *M. croatica*, 6 inches, pale rose flowers, spring. *M. piperella*, 4–6 inches, purple flowers, summer.

Cultivation Sunny rock gardens are the best places in which to grow micromerias, which will thrive in any ordinary soil. Planting should be done from mid to late autumn in suitable weather, or during March or April. Some protection for the plants during winter is recommended. For this, handlights or cloches will serve satisfactorily. Propagation is by means of cuttings taken in autumn and inserted in sandy soil in a cold frame. They will root more easily if they are given further protection by placing another glass over them.

Micromyrtus (mi-kro-mir-tus)

From the Greek *mikros*, small, *myrtos*, myrtle *(Myrtaceae)*. A genus of a few species of small-leaved heath-like shrubs, all natives of Australia and closely allied to *Thryptomene*. *M. ciliata* (syn. *M. microphylla*) is the one species sometimes grown. It is a branched shrub about 3 feet tall with small white or pink flowers borne singly in the leaf axils.

Cultivation The plant requires cool greenhouse conditions and a medium of very sandy open loam with added leaf-

mould. Propagation is by cuttings of firm wood taken in summer, rooted in a propagating case with bottom heat.

Microseris (my-kro-ser-iss)
From the Greek *mikros,* small, and the Latin *seris,* chicory, endive, referring to the appearance of the flowers which resemble those of chicory (*Cichorium intybus*) (*Compositae*). A genus of 14 species, British Columbia to California and New Mexico, with 1 species found

in Chile and another in Australia, Tasmania and New Zealand. The latter is also likely to be found in cultivation but only in botanic gardens and the like. This is *M. forsteri* (syns. *Scorzonera scapigera, Phyllopappus lanceolatus*) from south-eastern and south-western Australia and New Zealand. It is a variable plant, sometimes growing up to 2 feet tall, the leaves narrow, up to 6 inches long, sometimes deeply lobed. The flowers are yellow,

chaffy in appearance, about $\frac{1}{2}$ inch across. The roots are tuberous and edible, being sweet and milky with a flavour resembling that of coconut. They were used as food by the Australian aborigines.

Microsperma (Mi-kro-sper-ma)
From the Greek *mikros,* small, *sperma* seed, referring to the minute seeds (*Loasaceae*). A small genus of half hardy annual plants closely related to *Mentzelia,* of which *M.* 'Golden Tassel', is cultivated. This grows 9 inches tall and has bright yellow flowers in summer.
Cultivation This annual will grow in any ordinary garden soil. Propagation is by seed sown under glass during early spring, as with other half hardy annuals. Seedlings are pricked out, grown on and gradually hardened off before being planted out after all risk of frost has passed.

Microstylis (mi-kro-stye-lis)
From the Greek *mikros,* small, and *stylos,* a column (*Orchidaceae*). A genus of orchids from Europe, Asia and the Americas, generally classed as terrestrial though undoubtedly some occur as epiphytes. They are described here as a separate genus though botanically they now belong to the genus *Malaxis.* They are mainly grown for their attractive foliage which in some species is deciduous in winter.
Species cultivated *M. calophylla,* leaves green, marked with rich brown, East Indies. *M. discolor,* leaves metallic brown, bordered with green, Ceylon. *M. josephiana,* leaves coppery-olive and green, Sikkim. *M. lowii,* leaves coppery-brown with a central white line, Borneo. *M. macrochila,* leaves with cream, pale brown and yellow mottlings, Malaya. *M. purpurea,* leaves metallic red, Ceylon. *M. scottii,* leaves shiny, reddish suffused with grey and green, reddish-brown and silver flecks, Burma.
Cultivation A mixture of 2 parts of osmunda fibre, and 1 part of sphagnum moss with the addition of a little leafmould is suitable; for the more vigorous types a small quantity of loam fibre should also be added. Repot each spring. All types require shading and a warm moist atmosphere, and frequent watering in summer. In winter the temperature should be about 65°F (18°C) and for the deciduous types 60°F (16°C) and a decided rest is required. Propagate the stemmed species by removing offsets, and the bulbed types by separation of the new-formed bulbs which are frequently produced either at the top or at the base of the old bulbs.

1

2

1 The yellow flowers of Microseris forsteri, a rare Australian plant, eaten by aborigines.
2 Microstylis scottii from Burma, an orchid with leaves suffused with green and grey, reddish-brown and silver flecks.

Microtis (my-kro-tis)

From the Greek *mikros*, small, *ous*, an ear, probably referring to the shape of the flowers *(Orchidaceae)*. A genus of 10 species of terrestrial orchids, mainly from Australia, Tasmania and New Zealand, but with species found in Malaysia, Polynesia and eastern Asia. Some Australian species are known as onion orchids. Their flowers, borne in dense spikes on slender stems, are small and curious rather than beautiful. They are green in colour with a comparatively large dorsal petal. In height they range from about 6 inches to 2 feet; their roots are tuberous. Few are likely to be found in cultivation.

Midges

These are small flies *(Chironomidae)* which often are found near water. The males have a habit of dancing in swarms. There are over 1,000 species of midges. The so-called 'blood-worms' found in mud at the bottom of ponds are midge larvae. They are harmless and are eaten by other water creatures. There are occasional reports of damage to water-lily leaves by midge larvae mining the tissues.

There are also 'biting midges' well-known to gardeners who are tormented by the minute adult flies. Repellents based on diethyltoluamide give protection against these.

Mid-rib

The mid-rib of a leaf is the central supportive and thickened tissue extending as a continuation of the leafstalk, along the length of the lamina, usually to its tip. The mid-rib contains the main vein from which the branch veins arise; all the veins containing the essential vascular bundles. The leaves and leaflets of dicotyledonous—and a number of monocotyledonous—plants, trees and shrubs possess mid-ribs.

Mignonette—see Reseda odorata

Mikania (mik-an-ee-a)

Commemorating Joseph Mikan (1743–1814), a botany professor at Prague *(Compositae)*. A genus of some 60 species of evergreen climbers, related to *Eupatorium,* mainly from tropical America, of which one species, *M. scandens,* the climbing hempweed, is likely to be found in general cultivation. This reaches 6–8 feet and bears yellow and white flowers in summer.

Cultivation This plant may be grown in a sunny greenhouse or indoors on a sunny window-sill. Plant during early spring, in a mixture containing loam, peat and sand, using well-crocked pots. The growths are trained up trellis-work or other support. Alternatively, this climber can be planted in a hanging basket and be allowed to trail down over

1 The mid-rib or main vein of a leaf is the one extending from stem to tip and is usually prominent.
2 Mikania scandens, the Climbing Hempweed, has pink and white flowers.
3 Downy mildew on Oak leaves.

the sides. Water generously from spring to autumn; sparingly from autumn to spring. Maintain a temperature of 55–65°F (13–18°C) from spring to autumn; from autumn to spring 40–50°F (4–10°C). A little weak liquid manure from time to time is helpful during the summer months. Out of doors the plant may be grown in sunny positions hanging from sheltered walls or trellises. Plant in May. Plants grown out of doors must be lifted in October, and over-wintered in pots in frost-proof frames or greenhouses.

Mildew

This is the name given to a type of plant disease which shows in the leaves, shoots, fruits etc. as a surface covering of a powdery white or greyish fungus growth *(Mycelium)*. The name is often loosely applied to many mouldy or mildewy looking fungus growths seen on wood or paper objects of all kinds under damp conditions, but, strictly speaking, mildews are well-defined and fall into two distinct groups of plant diseases.

Firstly, the powdery mildews *(Erysyphales)* are entirely superficial and grow on the surfaces of leaves, shoots etc., as a white powdery coating and producing spores there in chains to spread infection. Examples of powdery mildew diseases are found on apple, vine, gooseberry, strawberry, rose, chrysanthemum, delphinium and a host of other plants. The winter spores are formed in perithecia (containing ascospores) on the surface of infected tissues.

Secondly, the downy mildews *(Peronosporales)* grow deeply into the inner tissues and send up threads through the

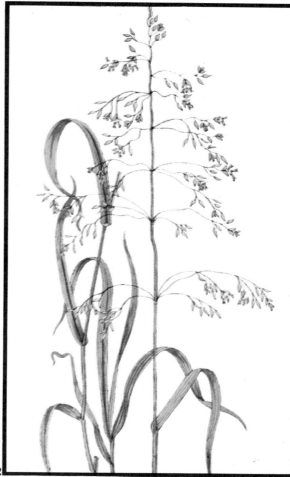

surface only to produce infective summer spores. These mildews are seen on the surface only as a greyish patch of furry growth but they are far more injurious than the superficial powdery mildews. Examples of downy mildews are seen on onions, peas, spinach, lettuces, meconopsis etc., Winter-resting spores are formed deep in the tissues and contaminate the soil as these finally drop off and rot away. Control is by proper ventilation etc., and spraying with Dinocap, Karathane, copper-based fungicides or Zineb.

Mile-a-minute—see Polygonum baldschuanicum

Milfoil—see Achillea millofolium

Milium (mi-li-um)
From the ancient Latin name for millet, the seeds resembling those of the true millet *(Panicum miliaceum) (Gramineae)*. A genus of 3 or 4 species of grasses native to the northern temperate zone, a chlorophyll deficient mutant of only one species being cultivated. This is known as Bowles's golden grass, *M. effusum aureum,* after its discoverer E. A. Bowles (1865–1954). *M. e. aureum* is a decorative loosely-tufted evergreen perennial with leaves up to 1 foot long and flowering stems of 2 feet or more. The whole plant, including the flowers, is strongly suffused golden yellow. This

1 Powdery mildew appears on Roses as a white powdery coating.
2 Milium effusum aureum is a decorative golden-leaved grass. It can be raised from seed sown in summer.
3 The spotted snake millepede on a damaged carrot.
4 Millepedes tend to curl up like watch-springs when disturbed.

---

characteristic is genetically dominant and thus the plant comes true from seeds.
Cultivation Any well-drained garden soil is suitable, preferably in a shady site. Seeds may be sown *in situ* any time from spring to autumn. If grown in an informal position, such as under a tree or in a mixed border, this grass usually freely perpetuates itself from self-sown seedlings.

Milk Thistle—see Silybum marianum

Milk Wort—see Polygala

Milkmaids—see Cardamine pratensis

Milkweed—see Asclepias

Milla—see Brodiaea

Millepedes
There are several species of millepede; the spotted millepede (*Blaniulus*), the black millepede (*Tachypodiulus*) and the flattened millepede (*Polydesmus*).

They tend to curl up like watch-springs when disturbed and have two pairs of legs to a segment, giving the effect of a deep fringe. This distinguishes them from centipedes, which have only one pair of stouter, longer legs per segment.

They lay small clusters of eggs in the soil and from these emerge the young

of all times. Trained as a gardener, he
set up as a nurseryman in London. Here
he was noticed by the distinguished
doctor and scientist Sir Hans Sloane not
only for his exceptional skill as a
gardener but because of his botanical
knowledge of the plants he grew.
Through Sloane he was appointed to the
Chelsea Garden of the Apothecaries
Company and soon made it one of the
outstanding botanical gardens in the
world.

Miller's skill was phenomenal. Using
the gentle heat of a bed of tan bark, he
germinated the seeds of exotic plants
which had formerly proved impossible.
He was the first to flower bulbs, particularly hyacinths, by standing them in
narrow-necked vases of water. His acute
powers of observation made him one of
the first to realise that many flowers
were fertilised by insects. And his fame
brought many famous foreign botanists
and gardeners to Chelsea. His most
memorable work, however, was *The
Gardener's Dictionary* which he first
published in 1724. It was outstanding,
and the first of its kind in Britain.
Frequently revised and enlarged, and
also translated, it remained the standard
work of its kind for nearly a century.

Milletia (mill-ee-sha)

Commemorating an eighteenth-century
French botanist, J. A. Millet *(Leguminosae)*. About 100 species of trees and
climbing shrubs, related to *Wisteria*,.
natives of tropical Africa and Asia, one
species Australian in origin. The pea-like
flowers are followed by thick flat pots.
In their native countries the plants are
used for poisoning fish.

Species cultivated *M. dura* (E), tree to 40
feet, but also making a climbing shrub
up to 10 feet, 6-inch panicles of pink
flowers with blue and yellow markings,
tropical Africa. *M. ferruginea* (E), tree,
9-inch tall racemes of creamy flowers,
Abysinnia. *M. glaucescens,* climber,
metallic blue flowers in 6-inch racemes,
Burma. *M. megasperma* (E), climbing
shrub in the style of wisteria, purple
flowers, Queensland.

Cultivation These are plants for the
warm greenhouse, where a minimum
winter temperature of 45–50°F (7–10°C)
can be maintained. The mixture should
consist of good loam and leafmould in
equal parts. Water freely in spring and
summer, moderately only at other times.
Propagation is by seed sown in heat in
spring, or by half-ripe cuttings rooted in
summer in a propagating case with
bottom heat.

millepedes, which acquire their full
complement of segments and legs as they
grow to maturity.

Millepedes feed mostly on plant tissue
already decaying from other causes,
being found infesting plants such as
potatoes, dahlia tubers, tulip bulbs etc.,
which have quite often been attacked by
slugs or other soil pests in the first place.

They are serious pests of peas and
beans and often occur in large numbers
inside potatoes etc. They are not easy to
control in soils moist and rich in humus.
It is best to keep the soil well cultivated,
because they dislike disturbance, and to
sprinkle approved dust in drills and
dibber holes before planting susceptible
crops to give protection in the early
stages of growth.

Miller, Philip

Philip Miller (1691–1771), son of a Scot
who had settled in England, was one of
the most outstanding British gardeners

Miltonia (mil-toe-ne-a)

Commemorating Viscount Milton, a patron of natural science and lover of orchids *(Orchidaceae)*. A genus of about 20 epiphytic orchids from tropical America. *M. vexillaria* and *M. roezlii* and the many fine hybrids derived from them are known as the pansy orchids. Their large, attractive flowers, with wide lips, are produced in spikes which arise from the base of the very light green sheathing foliage. The pseudobulbs are somewhat flattened. The other types, mainly from Brazil, have harder bulbs and darker foliage and produce long spikes with widely spaced flowers or shortish spikes with single flowers.

Species cultivated *M. candida,* chestnut-brown, yellow and white, autumn, Brazil. *M. clowesii,* brown, yellow, purplish, white, various, Brazil. *M. cuneata,* brown, yellow and white, spring, Brazil. *M. endresii,* white and rose-purple, spring, Costa Rica. *M. flavescens,* starry flowers, white and yellow, summer, Brazil. *M. phalaenopsis,* white with purplish blotches, summer, Colombia. *M. regnellii,* white with rose and rose-purple flushes, summer, Brazil. *M. roezlii,* white and purple, autumn, Colombia. *M. schroederiana,* brown, yellow, rose and white, summer, Costa Rica. *M. spectabilis,* large flowers, single, creamy-white, purplish, rose-flushed, summer, Brazil. *M. vexillaria,* large flowers, very variable, white to pink or deep rose, spring, Colombia. *M. warscewiczii,* reddish-brown, white and rose purple, spring, Colombia. Many fine cultivars are available and are best sought out in nurserymen's catalogues. 'Beethoven', 'Celle', 'Men. Frederick Sander' are fine large reds; 'Solfatari' and 'Prince of Orange' are good yellows, and 'Maiden's Blush' is a delightful pink.

Cultivation A mixture of 2 parts of osmunda fibre and 1 part of sphagnum moss should be used. The winter night temperature should be 55–60°F (13–16°C) and in summer up to 70°F (21°C) with sun heat. Fairly heavy shading is required especially for *M. vexillaria* and its hybrids, as the foliage is delicate. Aim for a warm, moist, well-aired atmosphere. The Brazilian species can receive a little more light and benefit from a slightly higher temperature. Frequently winter growths are present, when watering can be reduced but do not give the plants a long rest. Propagation is by division of

1

4

2

3

5

1 The starry flowers of Miltonia flavescens, a native of Brazil, are white and yellow in summer.
2 The white and purple flowers of Miltonia roezlii from Colombia bloom in autumn under glass in Britain.
3 An un-named cultivar of Miltonia. Many attractive ones can be sought out in nurserymen's catalogues.
4 A hybrid Miltonia raised at the Glasgow Botanic Garden.
5 The blood-brown flowers of Miltonia spectabilis 'Moreliana', from Brazil.

arge plants when potting in the spring.

Miltonidium (mil-ton-id-ee-um)
From the genera *Miltonia* and *Oncidium,* from which these bigeneric hybrids were derived *(Orchidaceae).* The miltonias used so far are mostly the hard-leaved Brazilian species. Plants and flowers are intermediate between the two genera. Cultivars include × *Mtdm.* 'Aristocrat' *M. schroderiana* × *O. leucochilum).* A considerable number of others have been raised by Mr W. W. G. Moir in Hawaii.
Cultivation These orchids need intermediate house conditions with shading from bright sun. Pot in a mixture of osmunda fibre and sphagnum moss.

Mimicry plants
All mimicry, as applied to plants, animals and insects, arises naturally and involuntarily, as opposed to the voluntary attempt made by one human to imitate another.

Theories have, however, been put forward to suggest that additional significance over and above family relationships, natural appearance, or kinds of habitat, may exist in the nature and appearance of various plants and seeds, among other living things.

There are, for example, a number of distinct resemblances between various plants, marked resemblances between certain seeds and insects, even likenesses between plants and inanimate objects.

It is probable that because certain seeds resemble insects, birds are attracted to them. The seeds are eaten and deposited elsewhere. This is therefore an effective means of seed distribution due

---

1 The Bee Orchid resembles a bee, thus attracting real bees and encouraging pollination.
2 The 'mimicry' of the Fly Orchid attracts flies. The plant is also modified to allow pollination by these insects.
3 Lithops, or Pebble Plant, resembles stones, which serves to protect it from grazing animals.
4 The Bee Orchid, a British native, likes chalk and limestone hills.

---

to 'mimicry'.

Defence is a consequence of some plant similarities. So the likeness between the stingless dead-nettles and those which sting, may be interpreted as a means of preservation for the former. Whether this resemblance is chance or design is a matter of dispute but, as gardeners know, the likeness of the one to the other must often defend them and preserve them from the interference of humans.

Resemblances of a very different kind sometimes appear in flowers; in, for example, those of a number of orchids. The bee orchid, *Ophrys apifera,* has flowers looking like a little bee.

This secures effective pollination; bee being attracted to 'bee'. The fly orchid, *Ophrys insectifera,* bears flowers sufficiently insect-like to attract the males of a particular kind of wasp. Again, pollination is effected by the insect as a result of the resemblance.

Lithops and *Pleiospilos,* two succulent genera, resemble stones or pebbles and

no doubt are saved from being eaten by grazing animals because of this effect, a kind of camouflage, for all but their cleft stone-like or pebble-like upper surfaces remain below the ground.

There are a number of instances of resemblances between members of related or unrelated plant species, between plants and objects, seeds and insects. It remains to decide on their true significance.

Mimosa (mim-o-sa)
From the Greek *mimos*, mimic, referring to the way in which these plants 'imitate' animals, as their foliage is sensitive to touch and shrinks when handled (*Leguminosae* or *Mimosaceae*). A large genus, mainly consisting of herbaceous perennials, with a few climbing shrubs and some trees, most of them from tropical America, a few from tropical and East Africa. They need warm or stove greenhouse conditions in cool places. Their foliage is pinnate and feather-like. Their flowers are small and are borne in rounded heads or spikes. The generic name and the common names given below refer to the fact that when the leaves are touched they immediately droop, the leaflets coming together.
Species cultivated *M. marginata*, 5–10 feet, pink flowers, summer. *M. pudica*, humble plant, obedient plant, 12–18 inches, rosy-mauve flowers, summer. *M. sensitiva*, sensitive plant, 3–6 feet, purple flowers, summer.
Cultivation Though strictly perennials,

1 The Cardinal Flower, Mimulus cardinalis, has red and yellow flowers in summer. It is perennial.
2 The perennial Monkey Musk, Mimulus guttatus, has yellow flowers spotted with red in summer.
3 The dainty growth of Mimulus luteus lends itself to natural planting near water.

M. pudica and *M. sensitiva* are best grown as annuals. They require a light position and do best in well-drained pots in a mixture of loam, peat and sand in equal parts. *M. marginata* should be provided with some support as it is a climber. Potting should be done in early

spring. Water established plants freel from spring to autumn, moderately onl from autumn to spring. Propagation i by seed sown in well-drained seed mi: in late winter, in a temperature o 65–75°F (18–24°C), or by cuttings mad from young growths, rooted in sand soil, at any time, in a similar tempera ture. (For the shrub popularly known a mimosa see Acacia.)

Mimulus (mim-u-lus)
From the Greek *mimo*, ape; the flower were thought to look like a mask o monkey's face (*Scrophulariaceae,* Monkey flower, monkey musk, musk. genus of hardy annual, half-hard perennial and hardy perennial plants grown for their showy flowers. They ar found in many temperate parts of th world, particularly in North America.
Species cultivated Annual *M. brevipes* 1½–2 feet, yellow flowers, summer. M *fremontii*, 6–8 inches, crimson flowers summer. Hardy perennial *M.* × *burneti* 1 foot, yellow, spotted bronze; var *duplex,* flowers double. *M. cardinalis* cardinal monkey flower, 1–2 feet, red o red and yellow flowers, summer. M *cupreus,* 8–12 inches, flowers yellow t copper-red, summer; cultivars includ 'Monarch Strain', 1 foot, various colours 'Red Emperor', 6 inches, scarlet flowers 'Whitecroft Scarlet', 4 inches, brigh orange-scarlet flowers. *M. guttatus* (syr *M. langsdorfii*), 1–1½ feet, yellow, re spotted flowers, summer. *M. lewisii*, 1–1 feet, red or white flowers, late summe

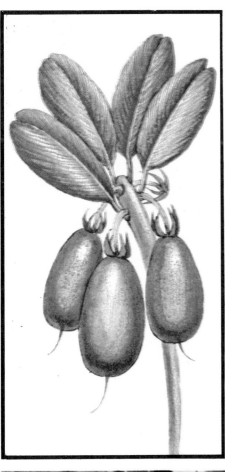

1 *M. luteus*, 1½ feet, yellow flowers, summer. *M. moschatus,* monkey musk, 9 inches, yellow flowers, summer. *M. primuloides,* 2–3 inches, creeping habit, yellow, June and July. *M. ringens,* 2 feet, violet to white flowers, summer. *M. variegatus*, 1 foot, blotched flowers, summer, best grown as a half hardy annual. Cultivars include 'Bonfire', 9 inches, orange-scarlet flowers; 'Queen's Prize', 9 inches, white, cream and yellow, blotched red flowers. (For the plant known as shrubby mimulus see Diplacus.)

Cultivation Annual species do best in moist, shady positions, though they will grow in sunny places provided the soil is sufficiently moist. Propagation is by seed sown under glass in a temperature of 55–65°F (13–18°C) in spring. The seedlings are pricked out, and gradually hardened off, finally in a cold frame, before being planted out at the end of May or the beginning of June. The hardy perennials grow well in sun or shade provided the soil is moist. They should

be planted from spring to early summer. Propagation is by seed sown from spring to early summer, in a temperature of 55–60°F (13–16°C), by cuttings of young growths inserted in sandy soil at almost any time, in a temperature of 55–65°F (13–18°C) or by division of established plants in spring.

Mimusops (mim-u-sops)
From the Greek *mimo,* ape, and *opsis,* like, with reference to the form of the corolla *(Sapotaceae).* About 60 species of evergreen trees and shrubs with milky sap from tropical areas of the world. The sweetish gum of *M. kauki* is eaten by natives in Malaya.

Species cultivated *M. balata,* beef wood, gum balata, up to 50 feet, greyish leaves, slender-pointed up to 4 inches long, flowers white, West Indies. *M. elengi,* up to 50 feet, slender-pointed leaves, fragrant white flowers in drooping clusters. The yellowish fruit is edible, India, Malaya. *M. kauki,* up to 30 feet, blunt, silvery leaves, clusters of white flowers, Burma, Malaya.

Cultivation These trees require a minimum winter temperature of about 55°F (13°C). They thrive in sandy loam and peat with ample water during the growing season, less in winter, but they must not be allowed to get dry at the roots. Propagate by cuttings of strong, half-ripened shoots inserted in moist sand in a propagating frame with bottom heat.

Mina—see Quamoclit

Mind your own business—see Helxine soleirolii

Miniature gardens
The growing scarcity of building land, particularly in towns and suburbs, with the accompanying shrinkage in the size of plots as prices continue to rise, poses difficult problems. Making a worthwhile garden in such restricted areas requires a good deal of careful forethought. In fact, the proverbial pocket-handkerchief plot has almost become a reality, and this at a time when interest in gardening has never been greater.

Where space is really limited, there is only one answer. Design and planting must be scaled down to fit the area available. But gardening on this reduced scale can be just as rewarding. In these pygmy plots, the opportunity for healthy exercise may be lacking, but to many gardeners, especially the elderly and those who prefer to 'putter', this may not necessarily be a great disadvantage.

Miniature gardens can take a number of forms. In the very small plot, you can share the pleasures of those who work on a broader canvas by restricting your planting, not only to single specimens of your favourite plants, but also by growing those that are compact in habit with a slow rate of increase.

1 Mimusops kauki, from Burma and Malaya, grows up to 30 feet. It has blunt silvery leaves and clusters of white flowers.
2 A first-class container for a garden in miniature, is a stone sink or trough where small alpines can be assembled permanently.

1

2

3

4

5

6

The miniature garden proper, however, will not be able to rely on such measures. For its impact, it will have to depend mainly on dwarf plants, some of which may be miniature replicas of their taller counterparts while others will display their own individual characteristics.

A good way of getting horticultural quarts into pint pots is to garden in sinks and troughs. Several of these plant containers, each with its separate planting scheme, can be accommodated in a minimum of space. Many a town forecourt, backyard or balcony could benefit from the inclusion of a feature of this kind.

Unfortunately, genuine stone troughs and sinks are fast becoming collectors' items and, in consequence, increasingly difficult and expensive to come by. The stone sinks of Victorian kitchens and sculleries have long ago been replaced by vitreous enamel and stainless steel, while the larger troughs, formerly used for watering cattle and horses, have given place to galvanised iron tanks.

The occasional specimen still turns up at country sales and in junk yards, but dealers are aware of their value and prices have risen astronomically. As an alternative, concrete or old glazed sinks can be adapted for the purpose. But neither of these will have the charm of the genuine article which, if it has been out-of-doors for any length of time, will

be weathered and decorated with mosses and lichens.

Particular attention must be paid to drainage before planting up any of these containers. A piece of perforated zinc should cover the existing drainage hole and the base of the trough or sink should be covered with broken crocks or stone chippings to a depth of 2–3 inches. On top of this goes a layer of peat moss or chopped turves, the latter grass side down.

The planting mixture should consist of 2 parts of loam to 1 part of peat and 1 of sharp sand, with a dusting of lime or the addition of mortar rubble. The lime content must be omitted where ericaceous plants, dwarf rhododendrons, or other

lime-haters are to be planted.

Among the many plants that can be grown successfully in a sink or trough garden are the hardier small saxifrages, sempervivums (houseleeks), thrift and other alpine plants of tough constitution. In a shady situation, mossy saxifrages, hardy cyclamen and miniature ferns will flourish.

For more permanent effects, use can be made of some of the dwarf shrubs and conifers mentioned below.

Miniature rose gardens Miniature roses have become generally popular in recent years. One of their main attractions lies in the opportunity that they afford of enjoying the beauty of roses where space would not permit the planting of a rose garden of the orthodox kind.

Sometimes known as fairy roses, many of these delightful dwarfs bear a strong resemblance to popular hybrid tea roses and floribundas. Others have equally delightful individual characteristics.

Little interest was shown by gardeners in these pygmy roses until after World War II, when scarcity of garden help and a swing from houses to flats and maisonettes brought their many useful qualities into prominence. These, apart from their compact habit, include permanence and a very long flowering season.

Many of the miniature roses stem from the dainty *Rosa rouletti*, a tiny rose that was discovered in a Swiss cottage garden by a Dr Roulet and named in his honour. From this charming miniature have evolved, directly or indirectly, many of the loveliest miniatures available today, including 'Tom Thumb', 'Pixies' and 'Midget'.

Miniature roses are extremely hardy. They come into flower early—often by the middle of May—and continue to produce their flowers throughout the summer and autumn. They are best planted from pots as they do not like root disturbance. This makes it possible to plant them at almost any time of year although March and April are the best months for this operation. Those planted in summer should be given plenty of water during dry spells in their first season.

The many named forms now available can be used to create a complete rose garden in miniature or can be incorporated as a separate feature of a larger garden. They are also useful for permanent dwarf bedding schemes.

All the features of a full-sized rose garden can be incorporated, scaled down, of course, to suitable dimensions. Pygmy pergolas, trellises and small rustic screens can be used to support climbing varieties, while miniature standards will emphasise focal points and act as central features of miniature bedding schemes.

Miniature roses need only a minimum of attention where pruning is concerned. This operation is best carried out with a sharp pair of nail scissors. It consists mainly of removing weak growths and cutting back dead or diseased shoots to healthy wood. It is carried out in spring.

These small roses thrive best in similar types of soil to those in which the hybrid tea roses and floribundas do well. They like a fairly heavy, slightly acid loam, rich in humus. Lack of humus can be remedied by forking in well-rotted animal manure or garden compost, a few weeks before planting. If neither of these is available, peat or leafmould, laced with bonemeal, make satisfactory substitutes.

1 Small succulents have been planted in a two-inch shell to make a really miniature garden.
2 Miniature gardens made up of Saxifrages, Sedums, Campanulas, Arenarias, Lewisias and miniature Conifers.
3 Androsaces, Houseleeks, Lewisias, Dwarf Conifers and other alpine plants make an interesting small garden.

These dwarf roses will also flourish and look well in the old stone troughs already mentioned; the sinks are too shallow and there would be a danger of the roots drying out. They can be used, as well, for another kind of miniature garden, the window box, provided that the latter is at least 9 inches deep.

Among those most widely grown are 'Baby Gold Star' (golden yellow), 'Bit O' Sunshine' (gold), 'Humoreske' (deep pink,) 'Little Buckaroo' (scarlet with white centre), 'Sparkle' (single scarlet) and the midget rose that started it all, *Rosa rouletti*.

'Baby Masquerade', a newer introduction, is a perfect replica, in miniature, of the favourite floribunda of the same name, with clusters of flowers that produce the typical kaleidoscope of colour of the latter.

This rose, together with 'Cinderella' (pale pink edged white), 'Coralin' (coral-pink) and 'Maid Marion' is obtainable in standard form. There are climbing forms of the bright pink 'Perla Rosa', the yellow and orange 'Little Showoff', which is practically perpetual-flowering and 'Baby Crimson', which is also known as 'Perla d'Alcanada'. 'Pink Cameo', too, makes an attractive climber. None of these climbing miniatures exceeds 4–5 feet in height.

A garden of dwarf conifers Another way of making a miniature garden, of interest the whole year through, is to use dwarf conifers. Many of these are

replicas of their taller counterparts and can be used to obtain similar effects on a reduced scale.

First and foremost are the various forms of Lawson's cypress, which share the useful characteristics of the larger kinds. *Chamaecyparis lawsoniana minima glauca,* with blue-grey foliage and whorled branchlets makes an interesting focal plant in a garden of dwarf conifers. It reaches an ultimate height of 4–6 feet, but this only very slowly. Similar in habit is *C. l. obtusa coralliformis,* with red twisted branches and close-packed bright green foliage. *C. pisifera* 'Boulevard' is a comparatively new introduction with blue-grey sprays of feathery foliage while *C. p. filifera aurea* is practically a golden counterpart of the former.

There are two charming little cryptomerias that will not exceed 2–2½ feet. Both *Cryptomeria japonica pygmaea* and *vilmoriniana* are slow-growing and make dense globular bushes whose form contrasts well with the pyramidal shape of the dwarf cypresses.

One of the most outstanding of these miniature conifers is the dwarf juniper, *Juniperus communis compressa.* This makes a dense blue-grey column, only 2 feet tall. There are also two dwarf spruces with a conical habit in the same pygmy category as this juniper. They are *Picea abies pygmaea,* with close-set dark green needles and *P. a. albertiana conica* whose foliage is a softer green. *Pinus sylvestris beauvronensis* is a dwarf Scots pine, only 4–4½ feet at maturity, that can be planted to simulate a large tree in the scaled-down dimensions of a garden of dwarf conifers.

The remaining space can be filled by the very slow-growing bun-shaped dwarfs such as *Chamaecyparis lawsoniana juniperoides,* a variety that grows only 4–6 inches tall, with a spread of similar dimensions or *Picea abies gregoryana,* which makes a 1½-foot hummock of grey-green foliage and is broader than it is tall.

1 Dwarf Conifers of many kinds are ideal for miniature gardens.
2 The Royal Horticultural Society's garden at Wisley, England, has a splendid collection of trough gardens, each one planted up in an individual way with succulents and miniature conifers.
3 One of the troughs, which contains a selection of Houseleeks.

1 Mentha spicata, the commonly-grown Mint of the kitchen garden, produces fresh growth each year and should be cut before it comes into flower.
2 The mat-forming Minuartia laricifolia has grey-green leaves and white flowers.

growth can be controlled more readily.

Propagation is by cuttings taken in late September or by root division. The latter is the popular method and pieces of root may be planted in 2-inch deep drills in autumn or spring. Mint plants may also be dug from established beds in summer, transplanted elsewhere and kept well watered, should the weather be dry, until they take hold. It is customary to renew mint beds every three years.

For early supplies, mint may be forced in the greenhouse or cold frame. Pieces of the long roots are planted during October in a light mixture. Mint shoots for drying and storing are picked on a dry, sunny day in late June. The maximum height of 1½–2 feet is attained in August when the light mauve flowers bloom. Mint rust, *Puccinia menthae,* can ruin a bed of spearmint. Apple or round-leaved mint. *M. rotundifolia,* is far less susceptible to this fungal disease. It replaces spearmint in some gardens. Apple mint reaches a height of almost 4 feet. The flowers are pinkish-grey.

Other mints, grown principally for their decorative value in the garden and for the aroma of their foliage are: *M. aquatica* and *M. citrata* which may be grown in shallow water in the garden pool or in the bog garden; Eau de Cologne mint (another variety of *M. citrata*), height 2–3 feet, foliage dark green with purple veining, mauve flowers. *M. piperita,* peppermint, is similar but the purple coloration is darker. Pennyroyal, *M. pulegium,* resembles peppermint. Corsican mint, *M. requienii,* is a dwarf plant of use in the rock garden or between paving stones (see also Mentha).

Mint Bush—see Prostanthera

Minuartia (min-u-ar-tee-a)
Commemorating Juan Minuart, Professor in the Botanic Garden, Madrid, in the eighteenth century *(Caryophyllaceae).* A genus mainly consisting of perennial plants, with a few sub-shrubs, most of them from Arctic or north temperate regions. They are low-growing, often cushion-forming or tufted, plants, with small narrow leaves, and small flowers, usually white. They are suitable for rock gardens or the alpine house. The genus is closely related to *Arenaria* and some species mentioned below may still be described in some catalogues under that genus.
Species cultivated *M. caucasica* (syn. *Arenaria pinifolia*), 6 inches, tuft-forming, flowers white, June. *M. imbricata,* 1 inch, forms hard green cushions, white, summer. *M. laricifolia,* 4 inches,

Mint
Mint *(Mentha)* is an aromatic herb mainly grown in the kitchen garden, or in odd beds near the kitchen door, where it can be reached easily when required. The young shoots and leaves are used as a sauce and as flavourings. Spearmint, *M. spicata,* known, too, as common mint, green pea mint and lamb mint, is the most widely grown in American gardens.

A site which is shaded for part of the day is very suitable. The soil should be fertile, retentive of water in dry summer weather and free from perennial weeds. Mint has a spreading habit which can be troublesome. This may be controlled by growing the herb in large clay pots or old pails sunk to their rims in the ground, or in the narrow beds often found at the foot of a wall, where the exuberant

mat-forming, grey-green leaves, white flowers, summer, Europe. *M. parnassica*, 1–2 inches, rosettes of leaves forming hard cushions, flowers stemless, white, spring, early summer. *M. saxifraga*, 3–4 inches, tuft-forming, white flowers, spring. *M. verna*, 3 inches, forms dense mats, white flowers, June to September; var. *caespitosa aurea*, 1 inch, foliage yellow. All these are perennials.

Cultivation Whether they are grown on the rock garden or in the alpine house, these little plants require a very well-drained soil and on the rock garden it is worth making up a special bed for them in which much sharp sand and grit is incorporated. They should be given sunny positions. Propagation is by careful division of the plants in spring, by seeds sown in sandy soil in spring in a cold frame or by cuttings, rooted in sandy soil in spring or summer in the frame or alpine house.

Mirabilis (mir-ab-il-is)

From the Latin *mirabilis*, wonderful, to be admired *(Nyctaginaceae)*. A small genus of annuals and perennials, some with tuberous roots, from the warmer regions of America: all those in cultivation are half-hardy plants. *M. jalapa* is unusual in that flowers of different colours often appear on different stems of the same plant (see also Genes).

Species cultivated *M. × hybrida*, 2 feet, flowers white, summer, opening in afternoon. *M. jalapa*, marvel of Peru, four o'clock plant, 2–3 feet, fragrant flowers, various colours, summer, opening in late afternoon, hence one of the common names; 'Pygmee', 1 foot, is a dwarf strain. *M. longiflora*, 3 feet, mixed colours, fragrant, summer, opening in afternoon. *M. multiflora*, 2–3 feet, rosy-purple flowers, summer, remaining open in sun, unlike other species.

Cultivation Sunny positions and quite ordinary garden soil suit these plants, which should be planted out in May or early June, after the danger of frost is over. The tubers may be lifted during October, to be stored, like those of

1 Mirabilis jalapa, the Four O'Clock Plant or Marvel of Peru, has various coloured flowers which open in the late afternoon.
2 The wide open blooms of Mirabilis jalapa, photographed in the early evening when the flowers are fragrant.
3 Mirbelia dilatata is an erect-growing shrub with Holly-like leaves.

dahlias, in frost-free places in peat, sand, or other material, until they are required for planting again. In the milder localities the black tubers of *M. jalapa* may be left in the ground during the winter and most of them will survive. Quicker results are obtained, however, by growing plants from seed each year. Propagation is by seed sown $\frac{1}{8}$ inch deep during February to April, in a well-drained seed mix in a temperature of 65–75°F (18–24°C). Young plants should be gradually hardened off, completing this process in a cold frame in late spring to early summer, and finally planted out in June. Overwintered tubers may also be divided at planting time.

Mirbelia (mir-bel-e-a)

Named after the French botanist C. F. K. Brisseau-Mirbel *(Leguminosae)*. Small soft-wooded shrubs numbering about 24 species, with pea-shaped flowers

coloured purple-red, blue or yellow, borne either singly or in clusters, natives of Australia, suitable for the cool greenhouse, or out of doors in the mildest places.

Species cultivated *M. dilatata,* erect bushy shrub 3–4 feet, purplish flowers in summer. *M. grandiflora,* 1–3 feet, yellow flowers, May. *M. oxylobioides,* very stiff, tall-growing shrub with slender branches, flowers orange-yellow, spring. *M. reticulata,* low, slender-branched shrub, flowers bluish-purple, early summer. *M. speciosa,* erect shrub up to 4 feet, reddish-purple flowers later fading to pale purple, spring.

Cultivation *M. dilatata* and *M. reticulata* may be grown outside in very mild parts of the United States, otherwise these and the other species need the protection of a greenhouse where they are grown in pots or other containers. The medium must be sandy and well-drained. Propagation is by cuttings of side shoots, 2–4 inches long, rooted in pots in a warm frame. A little sharp sand should be dropped in around each cutting when it is inserted.

Miscanthus (mis-kan-thus)

From the Greek *miskos,* a stem, and *anthos,* a flower, referring to the fan-shaped inflorescence at the end of a long stem *(Gramineae).* Graceful, tall, hardy, perennial grasses whose flowers are in pairs, one in each pair being at the end of the spikelet. They are useful for border planting or as specimen plants and are also cultivated under glass. They make good dried material for flower arrangements. The genus was once known as *Eulalia.*

Species cultivated *M. sacchariflorus* (syn. *M. saccharifer*), 6–8 feet, has almost awnless spikelets; var. *aureus,* 4–5 feet, gold-striped leaves. *M. sinensis* (syn. *Eulalia japonica*), to 10 feet, the green leaves have a prominent white mid-rib; vars. *foliis striatus,* creamy-white stripes; *gracillimus,* narrow arching leaves, a smaller variety; *zebrinus,* zebra-striped rush, alternate green and yellow bands.

Cultivation These ornamental grasses will grow in any ordinary soil provided it is not too dry. Plant in spring in a sunny position. They are also grown as pot plants with or without heat and are sometimes used for bedding purposes, especially the variegated varieties. Water freely when in growth and propagate by division in spring.

Mistletoe—see Viscum album

Mistletoe Cactus—see Rhipsalis cereuscula

Two tall-growing perennial grasses.
1 The tall shining foliage of Miscanthus sacchariflorus reaches 6–8 feet and is smooth in texture.
2 Miscanthus sinensis foliis striatus has prominent, creamy-white stripes on its leaves.

Mistletoe Fig—see Ficus
diversifolia

Mist propagation—see Propagation

Mitchella (mit-chel-la)

Named after an early North American
botanist, Dr John Mitchell *(Rubiaceae)*.
A genus of 2 species of evergreen,
trailing plants with small funnel-shaped
flowers followed by berries. They are
hardy and form good ground cover with
their mat-like habit; they have the added
advantage of growing in the shade.
They are good plants for berry bowl and
alpine house with their persistent red
berries that are decorative in the winter.
Species cultivated *M. repens,* partridge
berry, small white flowers, spring,
followed by scarlet berries that last
through the winter, North America;
var. *leucocarpa* white berries. *M. undulata,* very similar to *M. repens* but with
slightly longer flowers, Japan.
Cultivation Mitchellas prefer peaty soil
with leafmould added and are suitable
for shady positions in the rock garden
or as ground cover plants in shade. Use
equal quantities of peat and leafmould
when potting up for greenhouse cultivation. Plant in the autumn or spring and
propagate by division of the roots at the
same seasons.

Mitella (mit-el-la)

The diminutive form of the Latin *mitra,*
a mitre or cap, in reference to the
shape of the fruit *(Saxifragaceae).*
Bishop's cap. These hardy perennial
herbaceous plants resemble and are
closely related to *Tiarella* but, being
smaller, are useful for planting in
partial shade in the rock garden or in
a moist position in the wild garden.
Only three or four species are cultivated
although about eight species exist,
natives of North America and north-
east Asia. The flowers are insignificant
but well worth a closer examination.
Species cultivated *M. breweri,* 1–1½ feet,
whitish or greenish flowers, May, British
Columbia. *M. diphylla,* mitre-wort, 1–1½
feet, white, April. *M. nuda,* 1 foot,
greenish, eastern North America. *M.
pentandra,* 6–12 inches, yellowish, May.
Cultivation These plants do best in a
sandy, peaty soil and should be planted
in the spring. Propagation is by dividing
the roots in the spring.

1 **Partridge Berry, Mitchella repens,**
is hardy and forms good ground cover.
It has small white funnel-shaped flowers
and red berries.
2 **Fruit tree red spider mite lives on the**
underside of the leaves.
3 **Greenhouse red spider mite has**
caused severe damage on a Datura.
4 **Red spider mites feed by sucking the**
sap and cause browning and eventual
shrivelling on Apple shoots.
5 **Witch's Broom on Birch caused by a**
gall mite.

Mites

Mites are closely related to spiders; they have eight legs when adult. Among those fairly often encountered in the garden are red spider mite of greenhouses, fruit tree red spider mite and gooseberry red spider, all of which cause foliage to become chlorotic and eventually, in severe cases, to shrivel and fall.

Oribatid or 'beetle' mites are blood-red and since they are found in clusters on twigs where they feed on algae etc., they are sometimes mistaken for red spider mite eggs until they move.

Gall mites are microscopic, carrot-shaped creatures with their legs set near the head. They cause a variety of symptoms ranging from swollen buds (black currant gall mite) to red pustules (nail galls on lime) or witch's brooms e.g. broom gall mite.

Red spider mites are controlled by such insecticides and acaricides as azobenzene smokes, derris, malathion, dimethoate, polybutene, etc. Gall mites are reduced in number by spraying with lime sulphur in spring when the buds open. Tarsonemid mites succumb to flowers of sulphur or dicotol and bulb mites to hot water treatment. Tarsonemid mites are microscopic. They cause foliage to become brittle and curl and plants to become stunted.

Bulb scale mites are also microscopic. They cause lack of vigour and scarring. Bulb mites are secondary pests only, and are visible to the naked eye.

Mitraria (mit-rah-re-ah)

Derived from the Latin, *mitra,* mitre, referring to the shape of the seed pods *(Gesneriaceae).* A genus of only one species, from Chile. *M. coccinea* is an ornamental best grown under glass in cooler areas. It is an evergreen climber with stems up to 6 feet tall, the leaves small, oval, sharply serrated and glossy. Solitary scarlet flowers 1½ inches long, are borne on slender stalks from the axils of the leaves from May to October. The fruits are berries. *M. coccinea* will succeed in the open in warm areas, provided that it is not exposed to direct sunshine or to cold winds.

Cultivation *M. coccinea* may be grown on bark or in pots in moist stove conditions in a peat and sand mixture. High humidity is required. A shady situation is essential for the plants. Propagation is by cuttings taken from April to July, 2 inches long, inserted in sandy loam and peat in a propagating case, with a temperature of 65–75°F (18–21°C), or by division of the roots in the spring. A well-drained soil, rich in humus, and a

1 Mitella diphylla, the Mitre-wort has white fluffy flowers in April and usually reaches about a foot.
2 Mitraria coccinea is a plant for the stovehouse, and produces deep red flowers throughout the summer.

sheltered, partially shaded position, should be provided for plants grown out-of-doors.

Mitre Flower—see Mitraria coccinea

Mitre Wort—see Mitella

Mitrophyllum (mi-tro-phill-um)
From the Latin *mitra*, mitre, and the Greek *phyllon*, leaf, referring to the leaf shape (*Aizoaceae*). A genus of a few species of greenhouse succulent plants belonging to the *Mesembryanthemum* group. They are very small shrubs with two types of leaves. One pair is united over most of their length, these are the leaves during the resting period. During the growing season another pair of leaves develops within the united leaves and either push their way out of them or absorb the substance from them until a thin skin only remains, the leaves then bursting out of their skin. The stems are covered with these dried skins.
Species cultivated *M. mitratum*, resting leaves about 3 inches long, the tips free for about $\frac{1}{2}$ inch, secondary leaves 4 inches long, joined only at the base, flowers white, Cape Province. *M. pillansii*, resting leaves 2 to 3 inches long, secondary leaves 4 inches long, very pointed at the tips, flowers white, Cape Province.
Cultivation The medium should consist of a light soil to which has been added $\frac{1}{3}$ part of coarse sand, grit or broken brick. A sunny place in the greenhouse is required at all times. The growing period begins about September when the new leaves begin to burst through the dry skins. Water should then be given with care until the short leaves start to form between the newly-grown leaves. No more water should then be given until the start of the

1 The stems of the South African succulent Mitrophyllum mitratum are covered with dried leaf-skins.
2 The Mole which can cause so much damage to grassland and lawns.
3 Mole-hills are evidence of the work of Moles, and appear overnight. Moles cause damage below ground and unsightliness above.

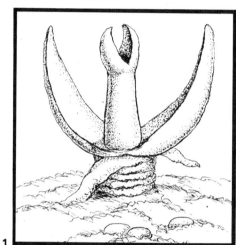

next growing season. Thus it can be seen that watering is carried out for one or two weeks of the year only. At no time should the temperature fall below 60°F (16°C). Propagation is by seed sown in a well-drained seed mix and kept moist and shaded until germination takes place, then more light should be given. If possible, the seedlings should be kept growing without check for the first twelve months, and then the normal resting period should be observed. Cuttings taken from the stems can be rooted with difficulty in a mixture of coarse sand and peat.

Moa Grass—see Gynerium sagittatum

Mock Orange—see Philadelphus

Moldavian Balm—see Dracocephalum moldaivea

Moles
Moles can be a great nuisance in lawns and flower beds. Their runs undermine the grass and the roots of plants; their hillocks are unsightly and surface tunnels may subside causing unevenness in grassed areas.

There are three main methods of control: by trapping, by smoke generators and by repellents. If traps are used, the barrel-trap type is usually the most effective. Smoke generators tend to be less effective on light soils than on heavy.

1 Molinia caerulea variegata, Indian Grass or Lavender Grass, is a cultivated species of grass.
2 The calyces of Moluccella laevis dry and persist, making them useful for floral decoration in the winter.

There are various repellents on the market. Substances such as rabbit smears, which have a rather pungent smell in most cases, may be used to soak rags which are then placed in the runs. Substances such as gamma-BHC dust or pepper dust are used in the runs and there are products sold as mole repellents which should prove equally distasteful to them.

The caper spurge (Euphorbia lathyrus) is sometimes planted in the belief that this will deter moles from the area but it is often found that the creatures will burrow within a short distance of the plants.

Molinia (mol-ee-ne-a)
In honour of Juan Molina, 1740–1829, of Chile, who wrote on the natural history of that country (Gramineae). Two species only are recorded, one indigenous to Japan, the other found in parts of Asia and Europe. This fairly widespread perennial grass is quite hardy and grows on cold, open areas provided there is plenty of moisture present. The single species cultivated in gardens is M. caerulea variegata, Indian grass or lavender grass. It grows to about 2 feet and has leaves edged with silvery-white; the flower spikes have purplish stems.

Cultivation Any ordinary soil and an open or semi-shady position will suit this grass. It should be planted in early autumn or in late spring and early summer. Propagation is carried out by dividing the clumps in the autumn or spring.

Mollis azaleas—see Rhododendron

Moltkia—see Lithospermum

Molopospermum
(mo-lo-pos-per-mum)
From the Greek molops, stripe, and sperma, seed, referring to the colour of the fruit, chestnut and yellow, giving a striped effect (Umbelliferae). Striped hemlock. A genus of a single species, M. cicutarium (syn. M. peloponnesia-cum), a hardy perennial from the mountains of central and southern Europe. It makes a large plant with decorative, fern-like, strongly aromatic leaves and is suitable for a wild or water garden. It grows 3–5 feet tall and has large heads of small, yellowish-white flowers in May and June. The much-divided leaves are shiny and long-pointed.

Cultivation Any reasonably good, deep, moist soil is adequate. Propagation is best by seed sown as soon as it is ripe, or the roots may be divided in the autumn.

Moluccella (mol-u-sel-a)
The name is taken from the Moluccas, islands in the Malay Archipelago, from whence one of the two species is thought to have come (Labiatae). Their flowers are curious, the white-veined and enlarged calyces are pale green in colour and look like petals. One of the species, M. laevis, is treated as a half-

hardy annual and is much sought after by flower arrangers, who grow it specially for this purpose. These flowers are also very useful for winter decoration as they dry well. The 'flowers' have a papery appearance and are green and look like shells, hence the name shell flower or bells of Ireland. The flowers are arranged in whorls along the flowering stem.

Species cultivated *M. laevis,* 3 feet, white flowers cupped in white-veined pale green calyces, August, Syria, treated as a half-hardy annual. *M. spinosa,* to 8 feet, white flowers, spined calyces, summer, eastern Mediterranean, usually treated as an annual.

Cultivation Moluccellas do best in a sandy loam soil and a sunny position. They should be treated as half-hardy annuals, sowing the seed in heat in February or March. The seedlings are then pricked off and hardened off, ready for planting out in May.

Momordica (mo-mor-dik-a)

From the Latin *mordeo,* to bite, in allusion to the seeds which look as though they have been bitten *(Cucurbitaceae).* There are over 30 annual and perennial species but in this country only two species are generally cultivated. The bell-shaped flowers are followed by cylindrical or oblong fruits generally knobbly on the outside, bursting with considerable force when ripe; they are edible and ornamental. In Asia and tropical Africa they are grown for food.

Species cultivated *M. balsamina,* balsam apple, to 4 feet, yellow, June, scarlet fruits, tropics. *M. charantia,* balsam pear, yellow, June, yellow fruits, tropical Africa, SE Asia. Naturalised Florida.

Cultivation These climbers are best grown in a warm greenhouse but they can be planted out in a warm, sheltered border in favourable regions. Under glass they need a rich, light mixture and can be grown in pots or beds in a temperature of 65°F (18°C). They must be shaded from hot sun, and a warm, humid atmosphere is best. They need a trellis or other support to climb on. Feed with a liquid fertiliser when the fruit is forming and water freely, particularly in dry weather. Propagation is by seed sown singly in small pots in February or March in a temperature of 65°F (18°C) or up to 10° warmer. The seedlings are then either grown on in the greenhouse in large pots or borders or they can be planted out of doors if a suitably warm border is available.

Monanthes (mo-nan-thez)

From the Greek *mono,* one, and *anthos,* flower; the flowers were at first thought to be produced singly *(Crassulaceae).* A genus of a few species of greenhouse succulent plants. They are small shrubs up to 5 inches high, the leaves borne at the ends of the very thin branches. The

flowers are small, up to ¼ inch in diameter, on very thin stalks.

Species cultivated *M. anagensis,* to 6 inches, much-branched sub-shrub, yellowish-green flowers, May–June, Teneriffe. *M. atlantica,* leaves small dark green, warty, flowers yellow, North Africa. *M. laxiflora,* brownish-green leaves, wrinkled, flowers red, March–May Canary Islands. *M. muralis,* very small sub-shrub, 3½ inches high, very pale pink flowers, May, Canary Islands. *M. polyphylla,* very dense low cushions, bluey-green leaves, in dense rosettes, reddish flowers, June, Canary Islands.

Cultivation The medium should consist of a light soil with ¼ part added of coarse sand, grit or broken brick. Water sparingly when the compost is dry, otherwise plants will become very straggly. They require shade in summer at normal greenhouse temperatures, or they can be planted in a shady place in the rock garden. Keep dry during the winter at a minimum temperature of 40°F (4°C). Propagation is mainly by rooting stems cut from small shrubs or by division of the plant. Seed should be sown in a well-drained seed mix and

1 The Momordicas are often grown as greenhouse plants although they can survive in very sheltered places out of doors.
2 The pink-flowered Monanthes muralis, a shrubby native of the Canary Isles.

kept moist and shaded at 70°F (21°C) until seedlings appear, then give more light.

Monarch of the East—see
Sauromatum guttatum

Monarda (mon-ar-da)
Named after a sixteenth-century Spanish physician and botanist, Nicholas Monardes *(Labiatae)*. A small genus of annual and perennial herbs from North America, with fragrant leaves and flowers, related to *Salvia*. The leaves are nettle-like and the flowers have a spiky appearance and are clustered together in whorls: the colour ranges from white through pinks, mauves and purples to red.

Species cultivated *M. didyma*, bee balm, Oswego tea, 2–3 feet, scarlet flowers, sometimes in twin whorls, late summer; cultivars include 'Adam', 2½ feet, cerise; 'Beauty of Cobham', purple leaves, pink flowers; 'Cambridge Scarlet', crimson-scarlet; 'Croftway Pink', soft pink; 'Dark Ponticum', dark lilac; 'Melissa', soft pink; 'Pale Ponticum', lavender; 'Pillar Box', bright red; 'Sunset', 4 feet, purple-red. *M. fistulosa*, wild bergamot, 3 feet, purple flowers, summer, not as showy as *M. didyma;* var. *violacea* (*violacea superba*), deep violet-purple. *M. menthaefolia*, similar to *M. fistulosa*, with mint-like foliage.

Cultivation Any ordinary garden soil will suit these plants but there must be plenty of moisture and good drainage.

1 Monarda didyma 'Cambridge Scarlet'.
2 Monardella macrantha has the general appearance of a dwarf Monarda.

They will grow in sun or partial shade. They can be planted in the autumn or spring and like top-dressing. Propagation is by division in March or April or they can be raised from seed sown out of doors in a semi-shaded position in spring or in boxes placed in the greenhouse or cold frame in March. Seeds germinate easily but the plants will need rogueing and any drab coloured varieties discarded.

Monardella (mon-ar-del-a)
The diminutive of *Monarda*, the plants having the general characteristics of a dwarf monarda *(Labiatae)*. A small genus of hardy perennial and annual plants from western North America with aromatic leaves. They are suitable for a reasonably sheltered ledge on a rock garden. The species described below are natives of California.

Species cultivated *M. candicans*, 9–12 inches, small white flowers with greenish-tipped downy bracts, annual. *M. macrantha*, 9–12 inches, with scarlet or orange-red flower heads and whitish or purplish bracts, autumn, tufted perennial with a creeping rootstock. *M. villosa*, 9–12 inches, similar to *M. macrantha*, but the flowers are more numerous, in closer heads, and the plant is softly hairy, perennial.

Cultivation These do best in sandy soil with a little peat or leafmould added to help retain moisture. Good drainage is essential. Propagate the annual species by seed sown in the spring, and the perennials by division in the spring.

Money Wort—see Lysimachia
nummularia

Mongolian Lime—see Tilia
mongolica

Monilaria (mo-nil-ar-e-a)
From the Latin, *monila*, a necklace, as the stems are constructed into bead-like sections *(Aizoaceae)*. A genus of a few species of greenhouse succulent plants belonging to the *Mesembryanthemum* group. They are interesting dwarf plants having two different types of leaves. In the growing season November to March, long thin cylindrical leaves are formed, but during the resting period small leaves occur, which are almost united into a globose body. Inside these are the young leaves being formed for the next growing season. In the resting period, the stems resemble a string of beads. The plants come from Little Namaqualand.

Species cultivated *M. moniliformis*, long leaves about 6 inches, short leaves ½ inch in diameter, white flowers on long stalks, white. *M. pisiformis*, much smaller version of the foregoing, yellow flowers.

Cultivation The mixture should consist of a light soil with ¼ part added of coarse sand, grit or broken brick. No water should be given between March and November, and only sufficient should be given between November and March to keep the mixture moist. In winter the temperature should not be below 50°F (10°C), preferably 60°F (16°C), and at all times the plants should be placed in the sunniest position possible. Propagation is by seed sown in a well-drained seed mixture, kept moist and shaded at a temperature of 70°F (21°C) until the seedlings appear. Some species grow without resting for 12 months, others will grow rapidly for three months and then rest until the following November.

Monkey Flower—see Mimulus

Monkey Nut—see Arachis hypogaea

Monkey Puzzle—see Araucaria araucana

Monkshood—see Aconitum

Monocarpic (bot.)
Although the literal meaning is 'once-fruiting', as far as gardeners are concerned plants which take an indefinite period to reach their flowering age and die afterwards are said to be monocarpic. They represent only a small number of plants, but examples familiar to many gardeners include some meconopsis species, *Saxifraga longifolia, Saxifraga* 'Tumbling Waters', houseleeks (sempervivums), most bromeliads, and the so-called century plant, *Agave americana*, which, although it does not take a hundred years to flower and then die, may at times take fifty years. Annuals and biennials differ from monocarpic plants in that their life cycles are limited to one year in annuals and two years in biennials.

Monochaetum (mono-chay-tum)
From the Greek *monos,* one, and *chaite,* a bristle, referring to the shape of the connective of the stamen *(Melastomataceae).* About 30 species of tender, evergreen, flowering shrubs natives of Central and South America. They are small shrubs with handsome flowers, freely produced, and distinctively veined leaves. They are easily grown in a warm greenhouse.
Species cultivated *M. alpestre,* 1–1½ feet, of compact growth, purple-red, bell-shaped flowers, Mexico. *M. bonplandii* (syn. *M. sericeum*), 1–1½ feet, with purplish-rose flowers, early spring, Peru. *M. hartwigianum,* 1–1½ feet, pale rosy-purple flowers, autumn, Ecuador, New Grenada.
Cultivation These attractive shrubs are easily grown in a mixture consisting of sandy loam and leaf-soil. The minimum winter temperature in the greenhouse

1 Sempervivums, or Houseleeks, are an example of a monocarpic plant, one which dies after its first flowering or first fruiting.
2 Monochaetum bonplandii.
3 The Banana, or Musa, is a mono-cotyledonous plant. The veins of the leaves are parallel.

should not fall below 55°F (13°C). Propagate by cuttings of young shoots inserted in sandy, moist peat in a propagating frame with gentle bottom heat.

Monocotyledon (bot.)
The flowering plants, or angiosperms, are divided into two main groups, the monocotyledons and the dicotyledons. The monocotyledons usually produce one seed leaf only, whereas in the dicotyledons there are two. There are a number of exceptions among the dicotyledons, of more than two cotyledons being produced, and also with the monocotyledons when, on rare occasions, two seed leaves are formed. Examples of monocotyledonous plants are grasses, lilies, irises and onions. The leaves of monocotyledons are often peculiar in form, as in the onion, where they are tubular. In the vast majority of monocotyledons the veins of the leaves are parallel.

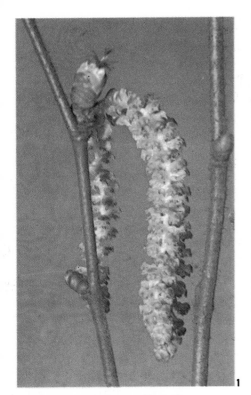

1 The Hazel, Corylus avellana, is mono'ecious, bearing male and female catkins on the same plant.
2 The flowers of Monsonia are red or purple towards the centre and the buds are always green on the outside.

Monodora (mon-o-dor-a)

Taken from the Greek *monas*, one, *dora*, a gift, in reference to the solitary flowers *(Annonaceae)*. A genus of 20 species of tropical trees, sometimes shrubs or climbers, from tropical Africa and Madagascar. The leaves are generally large as also are the flowers which appear vaguely orchid-like in general shape. The flowers are mostly borne singly and are pendulous. Monodoras are widely planted in the tropics, but they are of little ornamental value in temperate climates where they require warmhouse conditions.

Species cultivated *M. angolensis*, calabash nutmeg, to 12 feet tall, fragrant flowers, Angola. *M. myristica*, calabash nutmeg or Jamaica nutmeg, to 20 feet high, flowers have outer petals of bright yellow with purple spots, the inner pale yellow with crimson spots, sweetly scented, fruits several inches in diameter, woody, containing many seeds immersed in a resinous pulp; these are frequently used as a spice, but should not be confused with the true nutmeg, *Cryptocarya moschata. M. tenuifolia*, orchid flower tree, an attractive small flowering tree or shrub, often flowering when leafless, outer petals variegated purple, inner flushed rose, seeds used as those of *M. myristica,* see above.

Cultivation Warm greenhouse conditions are needed to grow these plants successfully, maintaining a minimum winter temperature of 55°F (13°C), with ample humidity, particularly in summer. A mixture of light sandy loam and peat is suitable. Propagation is by cuttings of ripened shoots rooted in sand in a closed propagating case.

Monoecious (bot.)

A plant is said to be monoecious when two quite separate flowers are produced on the same plant: the male flowers carrying the stamens or male organs and the female flowers, the female organs or pistils only. An example of this can be seen in maize. To a large degree this may reduce the proportion of inbred seeds, the inflorescences being widely separated. The well-known hazel tree is monoecious, the catkins being the male inflorescences, while the female flowers are very small and are found in small spikes along the branches. All the pines and most of the conifers are monoecious.

Monsonia (mon-son-ee-a)

Named after Lady Ann Monson, who corresponded with Linnaeus *(Geraniaceae)*. These plants are from tropical Africa and Asia and are grown in this country as ornamental plants for the greenhouse. There are about 20 species, some of them herbs, others sub-shrubs.

Species cultivated *M. lobata,* 1-foot sub-shrub, flowers purple, red and white, the outside of the petals greenish, spring. *M. speciosa,* 6 inches, sub-shrub, larger flowers, red and purple, greenish on the outside, spring.

Cultivation These plants need a sunny greenhouse and a well-drained medium consisting of loam mixed with some sand and leafmould or a well-drained potting mix. Do not overwater these herbs as they like to be kept rather dry. Any repotting should be carried out in the spring. They are propagated by seeds sown in a sandy medium in spring in the warm greenhouse or they may be increased by spring or autumn cuttings rooted in a closed propagating case with bottom heat.

Monstera (mon-ster-a)

Possibly so named because the perforated leaves of some species are rather unusual and may perhaps be considered monstrosities *(Araceae).* A genus of about 30 species of evergreen climbers from tropical America and the West Indies. A few species only are cultivated and one, at least, *M. deliciosa,* makes an excellent house plant where the temperature of the room is suitable. The leaves are very large and in some species there are curious indentations and perforations. Aerial roots are produced along the stems and these attach themselves to supports. They need a warm greenhouse but when established can be transferred to a living room. The fruit of *M. deliciosa* is sometimes obtainable and has a pineapple flavour.

Species cultivated *M. acuminata,* flattened stem, leaves to 10 inches long, Guatemala. *M. deliciosa,* deep green leaves, to 2 feet across, perforated, flowers yellowish, Mexico. *M. pertusa,* very variable species, leaves to 16 inches long, perforated, tropical America.

Cultivation When grown in a warm greenhouse these plants do best in a border and must be provided with some support upon which to climb. They like a mixture of peat, leafmould, loam and some sand, or they can be grown in a fairly well-drained potting mixture. Syringe daily and water freely in the summer months. A temperature of 55–65°F (13–18°C) should be maintained in the winter months. They are best planted in the spring and can be propagated by stem cuttings taken at any time during the year and rooted in a temperature of 70–80°F (21–27°C) using a sandy mix. Outdoors Calif., Fla.

Monstrose (bot.)

A term used to indicate some abnormality in a plant's form, for instance, in the curious comb-like appearance of the cactus *Cereus peruvianus* var. *monstrosus,* or the fasciated forms of certain other plants.

Montbretia (mont-bre-she-a)

Named after A. F. Conquebert de Montbret, a botanist of the French

expedition to Egypt in the eighteenth century *(Iridaceae).* The familiar common montbretias are now listed under *Crocosmia crocosmiiflora* and allied to this genus is *Tritonia,* leaving only *M. laxifolia* of those species grown in the British Isles under *Montbretia.* This cormous perennial is a native of South Africa but does not require the protection of a cool greenhouse in the

northern US. The leaves are very narrow and grass-like and the funnel-shaped flowers are carried on 18-inch stems and are creamy-pink, appearing in September.

Cultivation Although the protection of a cool greenhouse is suitable, this plant may also be grown out of doors like gladiolus in a well-drained sandy loam. In all but the most favoured

perfoliata (US) species, along with its four sub-species, the others having been returned to the genus *Claytonia*. The plants are very fleshy and usually grow to about 1 foot tall. They have narrow, spoon-shaped leaves and inconspicuous white flowers followed by black, often shiny seeds. As a weed it can be troublesome in gardens, but more particularly in arable fields. It may be eaten as a salad.

Cultivation Both sorts will grow in an ordinary garden soil, in shady or semi-shady places. Propagation is by seed sown in spring, where the plants are to flower.

Montpelier Broom—see Cytisus monspessulanus

Montrichardia—see Pleurospa

Montrose Pink—see Dianthus

Monvillea (mon-vill-ee-a)
Named in commemoration of M. Monville, a distinguished student of cacti *(Cactaceae)*. A genus of about 12 species of greenhouse succulent plants, natives of South America. They have very long thin stems which clamber or are semi-prostrate, forming dense thickets. Flowers are formed at the lateral areoles and are nocturnal.

Species cultivated *M. cavendishii,* stems about 1 inch thick, nine ribs, areoles greyish-white carrying thin spines, flowers white, Brazil. *M. spegazzinii,* stems bluish-green, mottled white, usually with 4 angles, areoles are carried on protruberances along the angles, spines small, black, flowers cream coloured, Argentina.

Cultivation The medium for these cacti should consist of a rather gravelly potting mixture to which has been added ¼ part of leafmould and ¼ part of coarse sand, grit or broken brick. A semi-shaded position in the greenhouse is required. Normal greenhouse temperatures in summer are adequate, but maintain in winter a minimum of 50°F (10°C). Give the plants plenty of water from March to October and do not allow the medium to dry out completely during winter. Growth is rapid and the stems are best trained over a trellis. Propagation is usually from cuttings which can be taken at any time during summer. Allow the cut surface to callous over before rooting the cuttings in a mixture of coarse sand and peat. Otherwise plants may be grown from seed which should be sown in a well-drained seed mix and kept moist and shaded at 70°F (21°C) until germination takes place, then allow more light. However, it is quicker and easier to obtain flowering size plants from cuttings.

Moon Daisy—see Chrysanthemum leucanthemum

4

1 The flower of Monstera deliciosa has honeycomb markings within the spathe. Native to Mexico and Central America.
2 Lophocereus schottii monstrosus is an example of a monstrose plant where growth is abnormal in form.
3 and 4 Two of the plants popularly known as Montbretia. Although this is now a genus of a single species which is seldom seen, it is very similar in flower to the plants shown. Named to commemorate Conquebert de Montbret, a French botanist of the eighteenth century, the family is now listed under Crocosmia.
5 Montia perfoliata, a dainty plant from British Columbia to Mexico.

places the corms should be lifted and placed in boxes of soil and stored in a cool room or ordinary basement during the winter months. In very sheltered gardens they can be left in the ground and protected during the winter but they may not survive if the winter is particularly wet and cold. Propagation is by separating the corms at planting time in late spring.

Monterey Pine—see Pinus radiata

Monthly Rose—see Rosa chinensis

Montia (mon-te-a)
Named after Professor Guiseppe Monti, a botanist at Bologna in the eighteenth
5 century *(Portulacaceae)*. *M. fontana* and

Moonflower—see Calonyction

Moonlight Broom—see Cytisus sulphureus

Moonwort—see Lunaria

Moraea (mor-ee-a)

This genus was named after a Swedish physician, J. Moraeus, father-in-law of Linnaeus *(Iridaceae)*. Butterfly iris. Closely related to the iris, these plants mostly have corms rather than bulbs; some species have rhizomes. There are about 40 species, all natives of South Africa with the exception of one from Australia. They have sweetly-scented flowers and are good plants for a cool greenhouse or conservatory; few of them are hardy enough for outdoor planting and then only in a warm, sunny border as found in Florida and California. The flowers appear to have only three 'petals' as the perianth has three broad outer, and three very narrow inner, segments. In most species there is a dark central blotch to the flower.

Species cultivated *M. bicolor*, 1½ feet, yellow flowers with a dark brown blotch, summer. *M. iridioides*, 1½ feet, white flowers with yellow or brown spots, July. *M. pavonia*, to 2 feet, red flowers with a blue-black centre, May. *M. spathacea*, 2 feet, purple-blotched yellow flowers, March.

Cultivation If the plants are to be grown out of doors choose a sunny, warm border that is well-drained and plant the corms about 4 inches deep, and about 2 inches apart. The soil should be light and sandy and contain some well-rotted manure or leafmould. Topdress in the spring with rotted manure or leafmould. For greenhouse cultivation place three to five bulbs in a 5-inch pot filled with a rich, sandy mixture that contains some manure or leafmould and good fibrous loam. Place the pots under the bench of a cool greenhouse or in a cold frame and cover them with peat until growth begins. The temperature should be about 55°F (13°C) during the growing season, with a winter minimum of 40–50°F (4–10°C). Water moderately while the plants are growing, but after flowering, allow the soil in the pots to dry off gradually, keeping the bulbs dry until January. Propagation is by offsets removed when the bulbs are planted, from September to January.

Moraine

This is the term given to the collection of weathered rocks, stones, gravel, sand and soil brought down by a glacier and deposited where the ice has finally melted. This material is the direct result of the action of the ice on the rocks in the path of the glacier and some moraine may be deposited along the edges of the glacier. This moraine provides the right conditions for many alpine plants: snow-covered in the winter, the plants

1 The pure white flowers of Moraea robinsonia, an Australian plant which reaches 5 or 6 feet in height.
2 A moraine or scree garden can be constructed to provide very sharp drainage conditions for some alpines.

are protected, and in the spring and early summer the melting snow supplies ample moisture for the growing plants, which survive with the minimum amount of nourishment, often forming tight hard cushions or rosettes with long tap roots.

These conditions can be simulated in the rock garden by constructing a special bed filled with suitable material. The bed should be about 2 feet deep, the sides sloping slightly towards the centre. Make the lower part of the trench watertight by puddling it with clay or use cement. Near the bottom of the trench make an outlet so that the very bottom few inches only hold the water when the outlet is open. A 6-inch layer of stones and coarse gravel is then placed at the bottom, and on top of this another 6 inches or so of smaller stones

and gravel that will prevent the mixture from the top being washed down into the bottom drainage material. Finally, fill the bed with a mixture of stone chippings, coarse sand, peat and loam; the stone chippings should form about two thirds, by bulk, of the mixture. Next add some ordinary rock garden stones to provide some protection for the alpine plants. This type of artificial moraine can be watered by a pipe, placed at the top of the slope, and controlled by a tap, or with a watering can.

Another method is to construct a bed on a gentle slope, and about 2 feet deep, and fill it as before with stones, gravel and finally the top mixture and then place a pipe about 1 foot below the surface at the top of the slope. This pipe should be controlled by a tap and should allow only a trickle of water to flow through the moraine so as not to dislodge the stones and compost.

If lime-hating plants are to be grown in the moraine be careful to avoid lime-stone chippings.